THE

GREAT HARMONIA,

CONCERNING

THE SEVEN MENTAL STATES.

BY

ANDREW JACKSON DAVIS,

AUTHOR OF "THE PRINCIPLES OF NATURE, HER DIVINE REVELATIONS, AND A VOICE TO MANKIND."

Spontaneous and profound Questions are living representatives of internal Desires; but to obtain and enjoy those pure and beautiful responses, which are intrinsically elevating and eternal, the Inquirer should consult not superficial and popular Authorities, but the everlasting and unchangeable teachings of Nature, Reason, and Intuition.

VOL III.

BOSTON:
BENJAMIN B. MUSSEY & CO.
NEW YORK:
J. S. REDFIELD; FOWLERS & WELLS.
1852.

Reprinted 1974
By
Health Research
P.O.Box 850
Pomeroy, WA 99347

www.healthresearchbooks.com

STEREOTYPED BY
RICHARD H. HOBBS,
HARTFORD, CONN.

THE

GREAT HARMONIA.

VOL. III.

THE SEER.

AUTHOR'S PREFACE.

In accordance with an announcement made in the Preface to Vol. II., "The Teacher," the author has devoted almost all the past year to lecturing and orally teaching the principles of the Harmonial Philosophy. It was supposed that this absorbing occupation would preclude the possibility of writing and issuing the present volume. However, as it still appears, the regular treatment of the subject "Concerning The Deity," which concludes the preceding work, is postponed to another volume of the series.

The subjects treated in the ensuing pages are, in the present state of the public mind, of the utmost interest and practical importance. Several of the discourses are somewhat discussionary in spirit and method, especially those which treat of "Religious Chieftains"—embracing the most prominent personages mentioned in profane and sacred History—the object being to adapt the thoughts to the popular understanding. The difference in style perceptible between the author's works of the past year and the previous volumes, is the difference which must naturally exist between a profound treatise, designed for quiet examinations, and the popular, extemporaneous style adapted to a public audience. "The Approaching Crisis" and "The Seer" are works composed from lectures delivered before a promiscuous assembly.

It is believed that the present work will do much toward giving correct and definite impressions concerning the entire phenomena of Psychology, Clairvoyance, and Inspiration. The whole ground is traversed and examined in detail, and the conclusions obtained are believed to be entirely consistent with the principles of nature, and with the author's personal experience. For a summary view of the subjects treated upon, the reader is referred to the adjoining table of contents. For the position now occupied by the author in relation to the world of Reform, the preface to the "Approaching Crisis" may be consulted; this will give some idea of what the reader may expect during the coming year, should circumstances warrant. Those who have written to the author, concerning the great questions presented in this work, may possibly find satisfactory answers by examining the succeeding pages.

Standing in the vestibule of creation, we are capable of comprehending but a small amount of the truths connected with our present and future existence. But it is truly believed that the volume here presented, will extend the reader's survey of life, and add many rainbow tints to those familiar thoughts which every age has done something toward developing. To the good mind a good result is certain; the inquiring may be placed upon the straight and narrow way leading to joy and peace.

A. J. D.

HARTFORD, *March* 27, 1852.

CONTENTS.

LECTURE I.

THE MISSION OF MIND CONSIDERED AS A MOTIVE POWER.

LECTURE II.

THE MISSION OF MIND CONSIDERED AS A MORAL POWER.

LECTURE III.

ON THE PHILOSOPHY OF CLAIRVOYANCE AND INSPIRATION.

LECTURE IV.

A DEFINITION OF THE SEVEN MENTAL STATES.

LECTURE V.

MAN'S ORDINARY STATE CONSIDERED IN CONNECTION WITH THE EXTERNAL WORLD.

LECTURE VI.

MAN CONSIDERED IN HIS INTERNAL RELATIONS TO THE SPIRITUAL UNIVERSE.

LECTURE VII.

A GENERAL CONSIDERATION OF MAN'S PSYCHOLOGICAL CONDITION AND POWERS.

LECTURE VIII.

ON THE RELATIONS AND DEPENDENCIES EXISTING BETWEEN THE BODY AND THE SOUL.

LECTURE IX.

CONCERNING THE PSYCHOLOGICAL ACTION OF THE MIND UPON THE BODY IN DISEASE.

LECTURE X.

ON THE PHILOSOPHY AND OUTER MANIFESTATIONS OF A UNIVERSAL SYMPATHY.

LECTURE XI.

CONCERNING THE EXTERNAL MANIFESTATIONS OF THE SYMPATHETIC STATE.

LECTURE XII.

ON THE HISTORICAL EVIDENCES OF THE PSYCHO-SYMPATHETIC STATE.

LECTURE XIII.

THE MENTAL CONDITION OF ANCIENT PROPHETS, SEERS, AND RELIGIOUS CHIEFTAINS.

LECTURE XIV.

ON THE MORAL OR RELIGIOUS MANIFESTATIONS OF THE TRANSITION STATE.

LECTURE XV.

THE TRANSITION STATE OF MIND AS DEVELOPED AMONG RELIGIOUS CHIEFTAINS.

LECTURE XVI.

CONTINUATION OF TRANSITIONAL MANIFESTATIONS AMONG RELIGIOUS CHIEFTAINS.

LECTURE XVII.

BEING AN APPLICATION OF PHYSICAL LAWS TO EVERY-DAY LIFE.

LECTURE XVIII.

CONCERNING THE PHILOSOPHY AND PRINCIPLES OF SOMNAMBULISM.

LECTURE XIX.

THE MENTAL FACULTIES CONSIDERED IN RELATION TO CLAIRVOYANCE.

LECTURE XX.

CONCERNING THE PHENOMENA AND HISTORY OF CLAIRVOYANCE.

LECTURE XXI.

CONCERNING THE SPIRITUAL STATE AND ITS EXTERNAL MANIFESTATIONS.

LECTURE XXII.

CONCERNING THE PRINCIPLES AND CAUSES OF TRUE INSPIRATION.

LECTURE XXIII.

THE PHILOSOPHY OF ORDINARY AND EXTRAORDINARY DREAMING.

LECTURE XXIV.

THE SOURCES OF HUMAN HAPPINESS AND MISERY PHILOSOPHICALLY CONSIDERED.

LECTURE XXV.

A BRIEF EXPOSITION OF THE SATAN WHICH TEMPTED JESUS OF NAZARETH.

LECTURE XXVI.

THE AUTHORITY OF THE HARMONIAL PHILOSOPHY.

LECTURE XXVII.

ON THE USES AND THE ABUSES OF THE SABBATH IN THIS COUNTRY.

THE

GREAT HARMONIA.

LECTURE I.

THE MISSION OF MIND, CONSIDERED AS A MOTIVE POWER.

In approaching the examination of a subject so profoundly important, as the *mission of the human mind*, we should not, for one moment, allow our thoughts to wander, or our reason to fail to perform its appropriate office.

In the first place, I desire to remind you that there are many positions from which man can contemplate his fellow-man. Among others, he may be regarded as an object of sympathy and commiseration, and, also, as an object of admiration and profound reverence. I will not now tarry with any unnecessary classifications; but proceed to announce my design, on this particular occasion, to examine and contemplate the human mind as a mechanic would study *a motive power*—as a source of *action*, of *condensed strength*, of *manifold influences.*

I am impressed to begin with this external and material view of the mind, because it is commencing at the foundation principles of *motive power*, so far as man is concerned with the physical world about him. It is generally admitted that "knowledge is power."

Consequently, if we acquire a correct knowledge of man's mental constitution and mission, it is evident that we will be all the more capable of overcoming obstacles and accomplishing exalted designs.

That man is the *masterpiece* of creation—that he is the *imperial lord* of the several kingdoms of *life* and *activity*—that he is *an epitome* of all known forms and structures—that he is *a microcosm* of all nature, in its broadest sense—are no new affirmations to those who have studied the vast generalizations of the Harmonial Philosophy. But why is man thus exalted? Why does he stand upon the towering apex of the visible creation? Is it because his head is more beautiful than the head of the lion? Is it because his face is so diversified with beautiful features, with graceful curves, and harmonious undulations? Is it because his *anatomy* is a finer piece of chiseled sculpture than any form which is known in the spacious academy of nature? Certainly not? But why? Because when from his head, and face, and structure, departs the indwelling principle which has enlivened the whole tenement and given to every feature its beauty and expression, then the power and perfection of man are gone, and the golden flame, which causes him to shine superior to all other things, is extinguished to all outward perception. But what conclusion are we to draw from this fact? I reply, we are constrained to acknowledge that *man* is superior to all other developments in nature, because he possesses a greater motive power, a deeper source of feeling, and a higher mental organization. His *mind* is the foundation of his supremacy; this is the source of his seeming omnipotence.

Without further remark on this head, let me impress your understandings with this principle,—viz., that man is the ultimate and highest development in nature; consequently, that all below man must of necessity enter into the composition of his being. If man is composed of all substances and principles which exist below him in the constitution of Nature, then it follows as a consequence, that he is the focal concentration and sublimated condensation of all the powers and principles which live in the vast organism of the objective world.

Matter and Mind have heretofore been supposed to constitute *two* distinct and independent substances—the latter having no material origin. But it is coming to be seen that TRUTH IS A UNIT, that Nature is every where consistent with herself, and that *mind* is the *flower* of matter, as man is the flower of creation. From the depths of the sea, from the foliage of the valleys, from the fruit of the fields, from the animal kingdoms of the earth, gush forth the elements and essences which enter into and constitute the human mind. That which is *grain* to-day, may to-morrow form a portion of nerve and muscle; on the third day it may become an element of life; on the fourth, a sparkling thought. The evening breeze, ladened with the fragrance of many flowers, may breathe into our nostrils the breath of life; and, by the simple process of inspiration, it thrills our blood, causes our hearts to beat vigorously; then mounts to the brain, and takes up its eternal residence in the domain of mind.

The Sun sends forth its rich, effulgent rays, and the waters dance with new life; the flowers ope their ruby lips; the fields, bathed in the soft radiance, sparkle like seas of diamonds; and every thing receives and enjoys the vivifying emanations, according to its capacity, its requirements, and its degree of life. And after each mineral compound, and vegetable organism, and flower, and vine, and animal, has refined the elements sufficiently, then man receives them and converts their finer qualities into his *thinking* principle. Thus man is the great reservoir into which all powers and substances flow; and it is, therefore, *true* that he is, in his physical and mental constitution, the *source* of great motive power and mental supremacy.

The mission of mind is consequently high and God-like. Standing upon the topmost round of the visible creation, and being a connecting link between the material and the spiritual—a little lower than the angels—the *Mind* is the *master* of all beneath, and the certain prophecy of much above!

Man is destined to put all enemies under his feet. By enemies, I mean, all obstacles and barriers to human progression and happiness.

The motive power of mind is mighty; because its source is knowledge. The strength of nations does not consist in a hereditary monarchical government; in extensive navies and numerous armies; in gigantic castles and impregnable battlements—but in the *liberty*, *unity*, and *enlightenment* of the people. Great physical strength is frequently combined with ignorance; and uniformly it shrinks from the power of knowledge, and cowers down, with the overpowering conviction of innate weakness. David's intelligence slew the physical giant; so, *one* profound student of nature will put to flight ten thousand priests whose only strength consists in their ecclesiastical organizations, and in the superstitious ignorance of their devotees. When the powerful mastiff has given expression to some impulse which displeases the little child by its side, see how, before the uplifted hand of that commanding child, the dog bows, with its eyes full of genuine contrition, and entreats for mercy. But why is it so? Is it because the dog is less powerful than the child? Nay; for the dog possesses twenty times more physical power. What, then, subdues the stronger body? It is the stronger MIND! The child possesses that irresistible *motive power* of intelligence which the dog can not withstand. Did the horse, or lion, or tiger, or elephant *know* the superiority of their physical strength, over that in man's possession, how quickly would they rebel against the enslaving purposes to which they are applied. But man can capture, train, and manage these powerful animals; because his superior knowledge gives him superior strength, therefore, he conquers.

The mission of the human mind, as a motive power, is to subdue the soil, exterminate all unwholesome developments of the vegetable and animal world, and change extensive plains into gardens of health and comfort. By the magic of MIND, the rough places will be made smooth, the crooked straight, the wilderness to blossom as the rose, and the cold, damp, pestilential winds, that now sweep over the earth, and spread consumption and famine in every direction, will be ultimately changed into a healing influence—calm as the evening zephyr, breathing over the gardenized fields and vineyards of the land, fraught with sweet perfumes.

See what MIND has already accomplished! There was a period in the remote history of mankind, when lakes and oceans flowed without a single indication of human life upon their bosoms—when the deep Mediterranean,

> "That tideless sea,
> Which changeless rolls eternally,"

gave no evidence of man's immortal skill in the science of navigation. But now behold upon the waters how proudly sails the ponderous vessel, at whose helm stands the strong and fearless *mind* of man, which conquers all opposition among the elements, and guides the ship to its proper destination. And those lakes and rivers that once rolled in idleness and reflected only the foliage and outlines of craggy cliffs, or the clouds that move above, and the sun, the moon, and stars, are *now* the common highways of nations, conveying from place to place the perfections of art on their laughing tides, and lending their elements to augment the speed of transportation. Yea, the MIND of man has not only spread its power over the sea, and converted the watery element into the vapory air which moves the mighty engine; but it has also caused the musical lakes to pour their refreshing streams into the sick chamber—there to act in the *twofold* capacity of a physician and a medical reformer!

The earth's inhabitants have known the time, when the *electric fire* played frantically, and wholly uncontrolled, through the heavens, now and then leaping from some lofty peak to the peasant's door, strewing its eccentric pathway with dying birds, and beasts, and men; but the human MIND has chained the lightning, now keeps it imprisoned in canisters, and when occasion requires, permits it to perform the duties of an errand boy, in a three-minutes' trip across the continent! When I contemplate what the human MIND has already accomplished with the wood, stone, and physical elements of nature,—when I think of *Italy* with its clustering palaces and terraced gardens, with its stately convents and insurmountable fortresses—when I think of *Egypt* with its pyramids—of the architectural magnificence of *Rome*—of the cities that are springing up in our midst, with their innumerable possessions of art and evidences of human skill,—I can not but be surprised that the conservative and popular theologian has the courage (or *ignorance*, perhaps) to insist upon man's innate inability to transcend all obstacles which lie between him and the attainment of future happiness and universal liberty!

The world of *science* is replete with the evidence of the superiority of the human *mind* over the gross materials of nature. Man exercises an unlimited control and proprietorship over all below his exalted position; and he is the governor, director, and lord of all subordinate creations; because he is the highest and most perfect combination of all elements and essences which exist in the lower departments and kingdoms of nature. In this sense, man pervades all beneath him. He psychologically impresses the beasts of the field and the birds of the air, that he is their lord and superior. Every thing learns instinctively to concede this supremacy to man;

because the invisible *mind* is the source of his sublime powers and abilities, and every thing seems impressed with the consciousness that he is thus exalted and thus endowed.

But need I inform you that man is himself yet ignorant of his latent motive powers—that he does not know how far his mission and powers extend over nature? When I contemplate the mighty works which man is certain to accomplish in the future, on this earth, I start back with the overpowering conviction that he will appear more God-like than human.

The hot deserts of Arabia, now merely seas of sand and desolation, will yet appear, under the well-directed mechanical treatment and skill of man, like the undulating valleys of Italy. Man will yet learn how to *create* and *preserve* an equilibrium between the soil and the atmosphere. He will be enabled to instigate, control, and direct the fall of *rain* over such portions of the land as need moisture; and thus he will elevate much parsimonious soil to the height of richness and abundance and to the bringing forth of pure productions. He will spread civilization over the dominion of the heathen; he will convert the darkest forests into gardens of beauty; and the disagreeable vegetable and animal forms, that now disfigure the face of nature, will be banished; and the lion and lamb will lie down together. The lightning, that now performs the duties of a courier, and which sometimes ventures to declare itself independent of man's power, *will yet be the chief agent of mechanical locomotion*—it will drive the engine more rapidly than ever, and bring states into the most intimate relations; because it will almost destroy the *time* and *space* which now divide the interests of the people that inhabit the different portions of the land. And *electricity* will yet be the means (under man's direction) of conducting away from unhealthy localities, the pestilential miasm which generates disease among men; and meanwhile, in its concentric gyrations through the broad tracery of conductors in the air, the lightning will emit the most sweet æolian music which the mind can possibly imagine.

And then the Winds will no longer retard the flight of the *aerial steamer* across the hemisphere, because man shall have mastered the tempest; shall direct the tides of the atmosphere; and shall have arisen far above the meager *obstructions* which now impede his progress. Man has the power to ascend higher and higher in the scale of knowledge; he possesses the concentrated *qualities* and *properties* of *motion*, *life*, *sensation*, and *intelligence* within himself; consequently, he can and will put all enemies (to his happiness and progression) beneath his feet, and yet he will *never transcend*, *reverse*, or *arrest* the immutable laws of nature, which are the will of Deity.

All mankind, when mental cultivation and intellectual philosophy become universal, will participate alike in the rich blessings and advantages of improved machinery, and other applications of physical knowledge. And then it will be discovered that there is a very intimate and sympathetic connection between the sciences of the mind and its moral altitudes. Indeed, I feel impressed to affirm, that man's *external condition* is so closely and inseparably connected with his *internal condition*, that, by improving the one, he improves the other. Intellectual progress has uniformly kept pace with all improvements in the *art* of education. That *knowledge* which gives man almost unlimited control over the elements of nature, will yet inform him of his more interior and moral powers, and this will lead him directly to true theology and to true religion.

LECTURE II.

THE MISSION OF MIND, CONSIDERED AS A MORAL POWER.

MATTER, in all its strange, grotesque, and harmonious arrangements, discourses profoundly upon the attributes of mind. Here I employ the word *mind* in its most extensive application; comprehending the soul, spirit, love, passions, reason, and understanding which characterize human beings—all of which terms I use synonymously with *mind*. You will, therefore, remember that I am not speaking of any *one* particular faculty or attribute of the soul; but of that entire *combination* of faculties and principles in the spirit of man, which combination I am impressed to term MIND.

It has been shown that *mind* is the *master* of the physical creation—the conqueror and disposer of the imponderable elements, and the great harmonizing *plenipotentiary* of the earth and atmosphere. That innate power which enables man to comprehend the laws, and control, harmonially, the phenomena of the world of matter, has a higher claim upon our consideration than any other terrestrial possession. When the *mind* is exercised upon the superior planes of thought, then all material forms are invested with an unusual significance—every thing has a deep and sacred meaning—the external world is full of divinity. Whilst that mind which is buried in the world of sensuality and materialism, can see nothing of those harmonious breathings of the Divine Principle, which adorns nature with its diversified manifestations and attributes. He alone who feels within *himself* the workings of an immortal spirit, can perfectly sympathize with, and in some measure comprehend, the kindred intelligence and love that emanate from the material forms which people the external world of effects. Such a mind is typical of a class of minds whose mission, in the moral department of life, I am about to consider.

It is a clearly-written fact in human history, that all scientific discoveries and the primary application of all scientific principles have been accomplished and made by a FEW minds. But the masses, having familiarized themselves with the philosophy of those principles, soon widen the sphere of their application. So in the world of thought. A LORD BACON comes forth from his retreat, and shows the world how to succeed in the acquisition of knowledge—how the *observation* and *comparison* of facts and phenomena constitute the only certain means of obtaining demonstrative information. So a NEWTON goes from his seat under the *apple-tree* into his chamber, abandons his strong sympathies and intellectual powers to the teachings of nature, and soon holds up before the world a stupendous conception of planetary harmony. And when the cultivated classes read and digest his explanation, forthwith the principles are incorporated in all the affairs of life. Days and nights, weeks and years, are thereby determined; the Yankee makes his clock, the astrologer arranges his almanac, and the mariner leaves the port, all in harmony with the profound and demonstrative teachings of astronomy.

The midnight dream of the mechanic suggested the steam-engine, and a few additional *dreams* made it the potential agent it is of transporting millions of human beings from place to place over the earth. Thus the ideal begets the actual—the principles of mind incarnate themselves in physical structures. But before *mind* can display its creative and disposing powers in the higher regions of thought, it must have a broad substratum of scientific knowledge as a basis of more exalted and useful superstructures.

Hence, the mission of mind, *as a motive power*, should be comprehended before we proceed to consider its mission *as a moral power*. Science is naturally the primary stratification—the granite foundation—of all philosophical knowledge and moral growth. That is to say, all theology, religion, and morality, to be of any service to mankind, must have a scientific and philosophical basis. The child is more interested in a ball than in a planet; and some men digest food many years before they digest thoughts. The yard stick has much to do with principle; and the pound weight and the *balance* are the established symbols of justice.

The principles of chemical analysis are applicable to an analysis of the mind; and he who can not do the one is equally disqualified to do the other. For the physiology of the animal economy is an incipient development of the physiological principles of the intellectual and moral economy. And a healthy body is closely identified with a healthy mind.

It is undeniable, when viewed in the light of the Harmonial Philosophy, that all true moral growth and wisdom are the higher departments of a divine Temple whose foundations rest upon the broad granite basis of science, and whose turrets extend far above into the tranquil realms of celestial life.

Physical science leads to intellectual science; the latter to the science of morals. Chemical analysis has led to mental analysis; thence we derive a sublime philosophy of the essential qualities and powers of man's immortal soul. We have a better perception and comprehension of the innate capabilities of the human mind. And what does this higher knowledge lead us to? It leads us to universal love and benevolence—to a scientific charity and a philosophical compassion for every member of the human family, which former generations could neither feel nor practice. It leads us to feel that our fellow-men have claims upon our sympathy and efforts; and that we have a similar claim upon them—so that we are, in fact, inspired with the principles of a universal confederation of interests and a community of occupations.

Again, I repeat, that physical science lies at the very foundation of all true theology and religion. Mind must triumph over, and control the elements and phenomena of, the physical world before it can achieve many victories in the world of morals. A philosophy of matter supports a philosophy of mind, as naturally as a house stands upon its foundation. But when we have a true philosophy of the human mind, how are we benefited by it? Does it exert a salutary influence upon the undeveloped multitudes? I answer, it does. But how? I reply, that it benefits the undeveloped and unfortunately situated classes, by enlarging the sympathies and expanding the understandings of those by whom such classes are principally controlled. A true philosophy of the mind is beneficial, because, (in the language of a worthy author,) "it teaches us that the elements of the greatest thoughts of the man of genius exist in his humbler brethren; and that the faculties which the scientific exert in the profoundest discoveries, are precisely the same with those which common men employ in the daily labors of life. * * * The true view of great men is, that they are only examples and manifestations of our common nature, showing what belongs to all souls, though unfolded yet in only a few. The light which shines from them is after all but a faint revelation of the *power* which is treasured up in *every* human being. They are not prodigies—not miracles; but natural developments of the human soul."

How shall I describe to you the mission of *mind*, as a moral power? It is utterly impossible to render its sublimity, importance, and grandeur perfectly apparent with language. At best, we can only describe its general mission, and contemplate the developments of mind as a vast panorama of spiritual realities. There are moments when every soul breathes in a realizing appreciation of its own God-like attributes, and perceives something of that *innate* force, beauty, and grandeur of intellect which lie hidden and undeveloped in the empire of mind. It was in such a moment of inspiration that DE WITT CLINTON wrote thus:—"Pleasure is a shadow; wealth is vanity; and power is pageant; but *knowledge* is ecstatic in enjoyment, perennial in fame, unlimited in space, and infinite in duration. In the performance of its sacred office, it fears no danger—spares no expense—omits no exertion. It scales the mountain—looks into the volcano—dives into the ocean—perforates the earth—wings its flight into the skies—encircles the globe—explores sea and land—contemplates the distant—examines the minute—comprehends the great—ascends to the sublime. No place is too remote for its grasp—no heavens too exalted for its touch."

The boundaries of mortality can not limit the sublime flight of mind. It knows no confinement—no restriction. It ascends high in the firmaments—contemplates the causes, laws, and operations of the universe—and every where displays that transcendent power which renders man a little lower than the angels. This power of mind I design to elucidate on future occasions.

The profound discoveries and keen analogies of scientific men, are interesting prophecies of what will yet be unfolded by moral and spiritual philosophers. I am impressed to regard the beautiful *germs* of moral and spiritual truth, which were deposited by Jesus, centuries ago, as forming a grand *love principle*, to which a body, or a *wisdom principle*, is much required. And the human mind will develop this *external* organism as it did the principle which enlivens it. The mission of mind, therefore, as a moral power, *is to the evils* that pervade terrestrial society. It has made improvements in science, and it will in morals. It is self-evident, that the principle of Reason is the greatest and highest endowment of the human mind; it is *the* indwelling *light* and the *power* of understanding by which man is enabled to read the innumerable sentences and chapters contained in the everlasting volume of nature. It is the divinely inherited treasure of the human soul; it *sees* the indications, *studies* the principles, and progressively *comprehends* the countless and infinitely diversified manifestations, of the Universal God. Nature is the universal exponent of God; and Reason is the eternal exponent of Nature; therefore, Nature and Reason, *combined*, constitute the *only* true and reliable standard of judgment upon *all* subjects—whether social, political, philosophical, or religious—which may come within the scope and investigations of the human mind. It is the nature, and tendency, and divine prerogative of the human soul to explore, to investigate, to classify, and reduce to a practical application, *every* thought, and principle, and science, and philosophy, and religion, which rests upon the everlasting foundations of the universe; and likewise, it is man's nature and prerogative to candidly, freely, and fearlessly—with an eye single to truth—examine *all* sciences, and discoveries, and mythologies, and theologies, and religions, which have been, or which may be, developed among men. It will be found that human happiness, liberty, and virtue are as much within the control of the *combination* of mind, as the locomotive is under the power of the skillful engineer. Hence, when man shall convert bad physical and social *conditions* into good and healthy *influences*, the moral wilderness will blossom as the rose, and the lion and lamb of the interior man will lie down together in peace.

LECTURE III.

ON THE PHILOSOPHY OF CLAIRVOYANCE AND INSPIRATION.

This sublime and important subject elevates itself with great grandeur and majesty before me. I do not perceive it in few of its aspects merely—I do not behold it as a simple phenomenon of the human soul; but, *as a vast and lofty edifice*, replete with spacious compartments, containing much useful furniture, and decorated with the new and almost supernatural trophies of its spiritual inhabitants. It must not be expected, therefore, that I shall treat a subject of such immense magnitude merely as a theme for conversation during a transient hour, but as a new and stupendous development of Truth, applying with equal force to every member of the human family.

But why does this *Truth* rise up so majestically before my mind? Why do I regard it as a great and universally important subject? Simply because I have familiarized my mind with the broad and immovable foundation upon which it rests, and contemplated, with an honest heart, the immutable principles which support the edifice. But why do you not view this matter in the same light? Because you have never entered, and contemplated the beautiful possessions of that *vestibule* which leads to more interior departments of truth and beauty. Why has not the world investigated this subject in a calm and dignified spirit? The answer is too plain. The majority of minds believe, or imagine they see, or are told by their clergymen, that, stationed about the threshhold of this edifice, there are to be found a great many suspicious and dangerous characters; whose names are various,—"Humbug," "Collusion," "Deception," "Ventriloquism," "Legerdemain," and a host of similar characters, whose well-earned reputation renders them very formidable personages for the *weak*, *unthinking*, and *prejudiced* classes to encounter.

Clergymen, I repeat, generally teach their congregations to believe that the *vestibule*, which leads to this great temple of Truth, is literally crowded with these *deceptive* and *fiendish* characters; and thus they succeed, to a great extent, in preventing the proper investigation of a sublime development of mind, which especially characterizes this era of the world's history. But I must not fail to notice a more enlightened class of opponents, or rather, a class who adopt a more intelligent method of opposing this new manifestation of an eternal principle. I allude, especially, to those who refuse to examine this subject on the ground, that there is nothing, they assert, in *the Bible* which sanctions or suggests any manifestations of this peculiar nature; from which untenable argument they very illogically conclude that these new developments constitute the last effort of "Satan" to destroy souls, before he is chained up and cast into prison for a period not exceeding "one thousand years."

I will not now stop to consider the unsoundness of this position, but will simply affirm, as a basis of future thought, that it is entirely false to say that "the Bible" is silent on the subject before us. On the contrary, I not only find the "Sacred Volume" of Christians replete with demonstrative illustrations of *spiritual insight*, *good clairvoyance*, and *practical inspiration*; but I also find multitudinous examples and demonstrations of analogous phenomena in the *Koran* of Mohammed; in the *Zeuda Vesta* of Zoroaster; in the *Shaster* of Brama; in the *Talmud* of the Jewish rabbi; and in the more recent *Roll* of the Shakers—yea, in each of these "sacred volumes" I find incontrovertible evidences and indications of the mental manifestations under present consideration. These statements I will make good on future occasions.

But suppose the Hindoo, the Mohammedan, and the Christian Bible did not contain a single allusion to, or palpable illustration of, the *magnetic* developments of this century. What then? Are we therefore to conclude that they deserve no *mercy* and *calm examination* at our hands? Are we to pronounce every thing which the Bible does not *intimate* or *sanction*, as *false*, *dangerous*, or *devilish?* If we take the ground that the "sacred volume" of any nation contains the *sum total of all knowledge and Inspiration*, then we not only set bounds to reason and human progress, but to the unchangeable and progressive manifestations of Deity.

If we are resolved to reject every thing which is not *intimated* and *sanctioned* by the Bible, then let us be *perfectly consistent*, and forthwith proceed to discard *all* the recent discoveries in mechanism and *all* the wonderful disclosures of modern science! Let us never permit the *sun* to paint our form and features on the burnished plate; let us demolish our railroads—our magnetic telegraphs—our various methods of printing; because the Bible is surely silent concerning these marvelous perfections of this century Indeed, it rather deplores the fact, that man is prone to "seek out many inventions," and especially to be "wise above what is written," and yet we are admonished, among other gettings, to "get wisdom" and to "increase in knowledge" forever! Is all this reconcileable?

It may be proper to apologize for prefacing my examination of the philosophy of clairvoyance and inspiration, thus at length. He who has not thought upon, or investigated this subject to its foundations, is not prepared to enter at once into its vestibule; because, I repeat, his mind is impressed with a species of superstitious apprehensiveness—a kind of educational or religious epidemic, the characteristic symptom of nervous and timid minds—that the *devil* is the "door-keeper," and that correspondingly evil characters lurk within the edifice—devils transformed into angels of light.

The good husbandman, if he be also a wise man, will cleanse his "new ground" of all its stones and stumps—its dead and deathly rubbish and noxious weeds—ere he sows the germs of a future harvest. So I come before you, on this occasion, to lead your minds into a *new field* of thought and inquiry. But ere we can enter upon this broad territory, which commences at our very feet and extends far and wide throughout the realms of immensity, I am impressed to remove the clogs which a false education has fastened upon you, and also, with your assistance, to clear away from the bosom of this new ground, the noxious accumulations which the ages past have cast upon it to the retardation of human progress. But some of you may suffer much mental torture by attempting to burst from *slavery* into the glorious *liberty* of the children of God. Indeed, freedom is seemingly too great a luxury for many minds. There are talented men in this community, who dare not reason, who dare not accord to themselves the mental and moral freedom which they internally feel, because they are sensible of a want of that self-reliance and self-government which render some minds a law unto themselves.

America, as you all know, is based upon a broader and more liberal foundation than any nation or congregation of states in the wide world. But what made our forefathers so free and independent in their views of humanity? It was their intellectual and moral liberty. They were a law unto themselves. The Declaration of Independence resided in their souls before it was given to the world. And when they felt an internal conviction that "all men" should "be free," they immediately proceeded, with great determination and magnanimity, to secure, to themselves and to us, the enjoyment of that *liberty* which no other nation knows on earth. I do not say that American freedom is the acme of Independence—I believe it is not—but that it is superior to that enjoyed by any other government.

But when our bold and resolute forefathers declared themselves free and independent, what was the uniform expression of all the conservatives and bigots among other nations? Why it was, in substance, precisely what the bigoted and prudential conservatives of modern churches and systems of theology are constantly saying of us—namely, that man was never designed to enjoy liberty—that he can not bear it—that it is identical with, or the parent of, anarchy—and that *destruction* is the inevitable *effect* of any attempts to break from established systems of religion and government. But nearly two centuries' experience of the American people has effectually shown all such prophecies chimerical; for our nation is as firm as the consolidations of adamant; and the startling voice of "dissolution," which now arouses statesmen to the elaboration of plans of safety and schemes of reconciliation, is a sound developed, not in consequence of too much intellectual and moral liberty among the people, but in consequence of physical, intellectual, and moral slavery. Some of you, I repeat, may suffer much mental torture in your struggles to be morally and theologically free; but the serene voice of pure reason and conscience tells you to go on, and secure the heavenly state of being, a law unto yourselves. You may suffer, because all births are usually preceded and accompanied with severe pain and anguish; but the issue is certain to be happiness and peace.

Some minds think that it is sinful to strive to be "wise above what is written" in their Bibles. But I have shown you, that Solomon exhorts all to "get wisdom" and "increase in knowledge," and he evidently desired all future kings and generations to become wiser than he; because his actual *wisdom* did not extend further than the science of architectural embellishments, as indicated in the building of his temple; for all his *Proverbs* are simply the constrained admonitions of one who had become fatigued with sensual gratification and weary of life. Therefore, we find hundreds and thousands vastly wiser than Solomon; because he simply wrote several moral maxims for *others* to observe and obey. And he who can *live a truth* is far wiser and more noble than he who merely writes it under a heavy *pressure* of physical pains and self-condemnation; which was manifestly the case with the wise man of the Hebrew Scriptures.

But there is yet another class of opposers to the modern developments of clairvoyance. I allude to those who reject them on the ground of their seemingly contradictory character and manifest mysteriousness. This class is composed of two descriptions of minds—those who reject all new manifestations on the supposition, that what contradicts human experience, and, especially, their peculiar prepossessions and prejudices of mind, must necessarily be deception; and also of those who oppose all new mental phenomena and inspiration, on the ground that the Deity would not permit any revelations and developments of a character so trivial and manifestly absurd.

But first let us proceed to consider the soundness of the proposition, that, what contradicts *all* human experience must be deception. I think there never was uttered a sounder proposition. There is something in our common nature which forms the basis of a universal analogy; and each new development in science, philosophy, and morals, is soon discovered to sustain a relation, more or less remote, to past human experience, and to the common phenomena of every-day life. For instance, when GALVANI discovered the *positive* and *negative* manifestations of electricity, he simply unfolded the germs of a system of truth with which every human body is constantly enlivened. Every organ, in the physical and mental economy, is constructed upon positive and negative principles. So, when JESUS changed water into wine, he simply exercised a magnetic power which was practiced centuries before, and which is now the commonest manifestation of human magnetism. I have seen a class, composed of twenty sane and healthy men and women, solemnly declare that they were drinking wine, while, in fact, the magnetic autocrat (so to speak) himself alone indulged in the process of drinking, and nothing but a few spoonsful of water. So it is with every thing else in the vast empire of human experience. The soul has either developed something which effectually forestalls all miracles, thus rendering the most wonderful revelations perfectly natural, or it has naturalized all startling developments, centuries in advance of their appearance, by intuitively prophesying of the probability of such occurrences. Thus, astrology prepared the way for astronomy; alchemy was the herald of chemistry; soothsaying foreshadowed prophecy; miracles indicated the achievements of human magnetism; and the strange stories of Egyptian priests body forth the ordinary accomplishments of modern science.

Let me be rightly apprehended. I do not affirm that human experience is a sound basis upon which to rest an argument against any new development that seems like a miracle; but I am impressed to say, that there can not possibly be any miracle, in the supernatural or theological definition of such an occurrence: that is to say, in the sense in which theologians understand that Bible miracles were performed—upon principles contrary or superior to, or more divine and especial than, the universally immutable and incessantly acting laws of nature. I make this assertion on the already acknowledged ground, that Deity is both omniscient and omnipotent—"without variableness neither shadow of turning"—and that *unity* and *system* must pervade the entire universe which revolves upon the pivotal attributes of his Divine Constitution. And *human experience* must of necessity run parallel with the incessant operation of immutable principles. Hence, *experience* is not the true foundation of an argument against miracle, but rather the source of strong inferential reasons, and of much justification, for the rejection of any new disclosures or statements which can be shown to be without relation to some correspondential law in nature, and thus utterly without a previous indication or a parallel. Therefore, I turn to Nature's laws for the foundation of an argument. Yet human experience is so faithful to, and so perfectly consistent and inseparably connected with, these unchangeable laws, that I here promise, that if any talented individual will demonstrate *clairvoyance*, *inspiration*, and *spiritual manifestations* to be utterly and entirely contradictory to all past human experience, I will at once reject the whole category as the most splendid development of mental hallucination ever known to man.

The positive testimonies of history on this head are very generally admitted by those who have interrogated past human experience respecting these phenomena. Even the devout Christian, who has hired his thinking done for him ever since his first lesson at Sunday-school, is ready to admit that these mental and spiritual developments have some resemblance to strange occurrences recorded in the Bible. But perhaps he will not believe their source higher than demonism; he thinks they proceed direct from the arch enemy of mankind.

Now, let it be duly remembered, in reply to this fabulous hypothesis, that these high and spiritual manifestations have almost invariably been connected with individuals occupying the most responsible positions of life—persons of fine literary accomplishments and eminent piety, in all ages of the world, among all nations, and indissolubly connected with all known systems of religion. These statements I also will verify on future occasions. But here, in accordance with the preceding considerations concerning the validity of human experience, I am impressed to openly avow my readiness to fraternize with that class of opposers who signify their willingness to test the truthfulness and purity of these developments according to the testimonies of mankind's past experience and history.

But the second class of skeptics can not be so easily disposed of. I allude to those who think the Deity would not be engaged in any revelations or manifestations of a character so trivial, and, as they assert, manifestly absurd. This class occupies a position which is well nigh invulnerable; because it embraces numerous minds who *will not*, *dare not*, or *can not*, think and reason for themselves. They will not believe that the Deity permits such apparently insignificant manifestations; and yet they do believe that he allowed a serpent to talk to Eve; allowed Eve to injure mankind—the highest work of Nature; allowed Moses' rod to turn into a snake; and so, to the end of the entire category of marvelous occurrences and miraculous deeds, these minds are deeply assured and convinced. Still, when we bring before them the altogether natural and more, far more, sublime manifestations of this century, they shrink back into the dark retreats of skepticism, with the lip profession that modern miracles are entirely too mysterious and too trivial to merit their attention.

How shall we obtain the consideration of this numerous class of minds in the community? How shall we obtain from them a calm and impartial investigation of the philosophy of clairvoyance and inspiration? To say that their present opinions are valueless—to say that we can make progress without the honest investigation from them, which we seek—is all very true; but we desire to impart to them somewhat of the enlightenment and happiness which we feel to be in our possession—not for our sakes, but for their sake, and for the sake of the rising and unborn generations. For it is manifestly certain, that correct acting depends upon correct thinking. A reeling brain produces a reeling body; the savage mind will generate savage manifestations; and so, in accordance with the same law of cause and effect, a low theology is the parent of numberless evils and unwholesome consequences. Now, we know that the world is replete with crude and mythological theologies; and, considered in the aggregate, we believe the Christian system of theology to be somewhat superior to corresponding systems among the distant nations; nevertheless, since man, in the more recent stages of his enlightenment and civilization, has discovered himself to be endowed with higher attributes than he has hitherto been taught to believe—attributes which naturally overleap the narrow confinements of any creed or system,—we hesitate not to burst from the shackles of all sectarianism, and thus go free into the temple of God, ourselves to seek for truth and harmony.

But how shall we induce timid and unthinking minds to accompany us thither? They say that the manifestations and phenomena, which we desire them to investigate, are altogether too trivial and mysterious,—not sufficiently exalted in their nature to impress the mind with a conviction of their heavenly origin! But we bring the same argument to bear upon all the supernatural occurrences, in the heavenly or divine origin of which, they profess to devoutly believe. We say that the Deity, in order to govern mankind and to enlighten the nations concerning the scope and nature of his will, would never have intrusted the serenest thoughts of his heart to a few prophets and apostles. Because he would be embarking in a very unsafe and exceedingly frail enterprise. His sacred will, in such a case, would be left at the mercy and disposal of millions of human contingencies—left to honest and dishonest priests; to unsound and sectarian commentators; to both religious and crafty tradesmen, who could print the paragraphs and pages as they pleased, and charge as many dollars for the "Word of God" as best comported with their sectarian and mercenary purposes!

And the same argument which our skeptical friends bring against the phenomena of clairvoyance and spiritual manifestations, we also bring against the *pivotal event* recorded in sacred history, upon which the entire scheme of salvation unquestionably turns, —I allude to the alleged miraculous birth of Jesus. Many minds say that *spirits* would take some other more exalted method of communicating to man—that the Deity would not permit the spiritual powers of the human mind to penetrate the unfathomable abysses of his being. And so we affirm, with regard to the birth of Jesus, that, if the divine Mind had intended to produce a conviction in the world that this great moral Reformer was the particular child of his own Spirit, then some more grand and noble manifestations would have occurred—such as would have been convincing from their very nature—such as would have been lofty, sublime, and magnificent—more becoming the character of the heavenly and omnipotent Parent! And here let it be distinctly understood, that we are perfectly willing to allow this argument its full weight against the subjects under consideration; because we do not regard the stupendous revealments of clairvoyance, or the recent manifestations of spiritual power, any more a particular demonstration of Divine Will than the formation of the Bible or the miraculous birth of Jesus. We esteem them all—the latter as well as the former—as interesting developments of the human mind, pre-eminently deserving a candid investigation by all who seek the truth.

But it is said—we can not rely upon the testimony of those who believe in clairvoyance and modern inspiration, because they are mostly skeptics with regard to the incombustibility of the Sacred Canon. And yet, this same cautious class of minds believe *all* that is recorded in the Primitive History upon the most uncertain authority. They believe that Jesus was born in a supernatural manner; they believe that a violation of physiological law must have occurred—that the immutable principles of reproduction, as established by an invariable Deity in nature, were entirely set aside; that the natural conception was wholly the effect of a supernatural prolification. But why do they believe all this, and much more equally unheavenly? Simply *because* it is related in the Bible—in the first books of the New Testament; but, more especially, because it was believed by their forefathers, confirmed by commentators, and is weekly expounded by talented clergymen.

Now, I am impressed to affirm, that, if men are to accept human testimony as the basis or foundation of faith, then I am ready to array the concurrent testimonies of past human history concerning the alleged realities of supernaturalism, and the "cloud of witnesses" that testify of clairvoyance and spiritual manifestation; and then proceed, with all candor, to analyze their respective merits and to decide as to which class of wonders the preponderance and most respectable portion of the evidence properly incline. But I would here say that, in consequence of a combination of pure reasons,—which I will not now explain,—I am impressed to put no confidence whatever in human testimony as a proper foundation of faith. On the contrary, I esteem it as the most inferior and exterior kind of information; as the most deceptive and unreliable; and yet, by all honest minds, it should be regarded as a source of much inference and suggestion, which may possibly conduct the mind to important truths and principles. I would be pleased to inspire timid and unthinking minds with the glorious dignity of principle; that every thing is to be tested by the rigid laws—not of legal evidence, but—of universal nature; laws which are the only manifestations that emanate direct from Deity.

Philosophical researchers and intelligent investigators do not believe in any *law* as governing Nature, the planetary system, or the universe, merely because it may be recorded in a book, believed by their forefathers, or advocated by enlightened men,—nay, not so; but because their judgments—their interior understandings—are convinced, and because, also, Nature incessantly exhibits demonstration of the truthfulness of the conviction. If this dignified course were pursued by theological investigators and religionists, then hereditary affection, for peculiar modes and systems of faith, would be duly eradicated; and the Reason-Principle—which God has bestowed upon man, not to prove his curse, but a blessing—would receive and cherish only that of which all internal and external things, around and above, perpetually contribute evidence. A good, practical astronomer can prophesy a century a-head exactly at what hour there will be an eclipse of the sun, visible from the City Hall in New York. His faith is based wholly upon principle; and, so far as this disclosure of his exalted science is concerned, he lives absolutely a century in advance of those who know nothing about the source of his enlightenment. And now, if the timid class of minds still refuse to take the dignified position of impartial investigators, and prefer the exceedingly uncertain testimony of individuals, who lived two or more thousand years ago, to the concurring demonstrations of modern scientific discoveries, then we must leave them, for the present, in the Egyptian darkness behind us, while we proceed to explore the magnificent regions, whose rays of truth shed light upon our future pathway. This is the only way in which we can be advanced in harmonious truth; for, to expend our mental energies in a superficial controversy concerning mere human speculations and differences of opinion, is simply to enliven and perpetuate feelings of combativeness among men, quite beneath the higher and nobler objects in which the soul should forever be engaged. The intense light which comes down to man from the bending skies, and the general principles which flow up from the broad foundations of creation, combine to elevate our thoughts superior to the popular spirit of discussion. When high minds combine and form a positive power, the negative and dependent classes will feel the attractive influence, and follow it; and yet, the perpetuity and universality of such a mental potency will be determined, not by any affinity which it may sustain to existing political or religious systems, but wholly by its accordance with, and fidelity to, the general system and laws of nature.

It will be observed, that I have not, as yet, said any thing directly concerning the philosophy of the diversified phenomena of clairvoyance; as it was deemed expedient to remove all possible rubbish from the "new ground" before we proceeded to explore its vast extent and rich possessions, or to sow seed for a future harvest. I am not insensible to the fact that some minds will, "e'en though beaten, argue still;" nor to the numerous objections which can be made to militate, and quite conspicuously and somewhat powerfully too, against the positions which I shall take with regard to the philosophy of spiritual illumination. But as I proceed with the consideration of this high theme, these various objections shall be allowed their legitimate weight, and be disposed of in a manner which will not, I feel impressed, be prejudicial to the progress of any candid and truth-loving mind.

LECTURE IV.

A DEFINITION OF THE SEVEN MENTAL STATES.

MANY minds are doubtless well aware, that, on other occasions, I have uttered my *interior* impressions concerning the philosophy of the phenomena under present investigation. However, as time marches forward more and various manifestations are developed; and the new unfoldings seem to demand, not only a repetition of many explanatory principles which have been previously uttered, but also far more minute and particular amplification of the principal causes engaged in the development of every mental manifestation known in this pregnant century. It is to extend my elucidations of this grand and far-reaching subject, and also to remove the mystery of many recent psychological disclosures, that I present to you this philosophy of clairvoyance and inspiration.

On the very threshhold of the investigation, it is proper to direct your attention to the lamentable fact, that but few minds have learned to reason correctly upon any subject. The human understanding—or the immortal principle of reason within the soul—can be as fully and perfectly educated as any other faculty of the mind. We can learn to think or reason almost as easily as we can learn to walk. In the power and perfectibility of human reason I have unbounded confidence; but I deplore the mis-appreciation and mis-application of this imperishable principle of the human mind as much as I can possibly lament the wrong use of any other power or attribute with which Deity has endowed mankind. Inasmuch as man, in the capacity of a motive power, is destined to discover the principles of material nature, to properly apply them, and thereby subdue the entire physical world to his exalted purposes; so likewise, by the exercise of the same native potency on a higher plane, man is destined to ascertain the principles of his moral nature, to apply the attribute of reason properly, and thus accomplish, in the spiritual and religious world about him, as many harmonious effects and consequences as will ever distinguish the empire of science.

There are two prominent indications by which wrong, incorrect, or unsound reasoning may invariably be detected. First, by an altogether external and superficial method of investigating any subject, phenomena, or principle which may be presented. Second, by the conspicuous absence of consistency between the manner of treating a scientific subject and a question of morals. For example, the superficial and unsound reasoner, if he undertakes the criticism of any literary production, will particularly dwell upon the language—the words, structure of sentences, paragraphs, &c.—with as much tenacity as a profounder mind would examine the *ideas* which those words were designed to convey. Such minds are very externally and unfortunately developed. They prònounce upon men and things, invariably, in accordance with their external aspect or seeming manifestation. Such minds make unsound and unsympathetic parents; improper guardians and legislators; the most unsafe and unrighteous jurors. Motives are, by such reasoners, generally estimated according to action; which is too frequently the fallacious basis of much cruel and unbrotherly judgment. Those who have read the amusing history of "Handy Andy," by Charles Lover, are in full possession of the best illustration of *good motives* beneath *bad actions* that was probably ever published. Handy, with as pure motives as a son of Erin could possibly feel in his bosom, not only vexed and aggravated his master twenty times each day, but actually produced quarrels, alienations, and duels among friends and dignitaries in the adjoining communities. And I venture to affirm that every person, at least once in his life, has found his best and purest motives very unhappily misapprehended by the class of minds of which I speak.

The unsound and superficial reasoners, who do not exhibit consistency in the examination of any thing, are distinguished by their unwillingness or inability to perceive perfect unity and system in the works of Deity. For example, such intellects can not see any distinct connection between the mineral, vegetable, and animal kingdoms; can not understand the unity and unchangeability of God; they can not apply a scientific principle to the successful analyzation of a moral subject; can not see that the generation and evolution of electricity from the mineral bed are identical with the evolution of thought in the human encephalon; can not see that, that principle which digests food in the stomach is the same which digests thought in the brain, on a higher plane of action; and thus, in every thing, these superficial reasoners divorce fact from fact, principle from principle, and nature from Deity, whenever they make any subject a theme of special thought. Among this class I am constrained to include the vast majority of parents, teachers, alumni, commentators, clergymen and congregations of our beautiful country. It is almost a perfect proverb—that the majority is, in the present state of the world, more likely to be wrong than right. If we seek truth only, it were far better for us to embark on a fishing excursion with Jesus and his twelve apostles than to join any popular system of theology in the world. The French have concluded, after a succession of national experiments, that the Lord is generally on the side of those who have the most cannon and the largest army; because *this party* invariably succeeds in any lengthened contest.

Strange and uncertain as it may seem to the superficial observer, it is nevertheless a self-evident truth, that, in the present undeveloped stage of civilization, the majority is most likely to be in the wrong. And I desire to have it very distinctly understood, that the vast majority of minds now existing on the earth, though an evident improvement upon every previous generation, are, notwithstanding their superior enlightenment, a very superficial and inconsistent class of investigators. And clairvoyance and modern inspiration have principally this large majority for their opposers. But why do these minds oppose and repudiate spiritual phenomena? Because they are *external* and *unsound* reasoners. For it will yet be seen, that the causes of every visible manifestation lie, very frequently, much deeper in the bosom of Nature, than the external senses of the corporeal organism can possibly penetrate. How then, without the power of exercising the interior perceptions, which belong to the mind especially, shall we ascertain the internal causes of outer phenomena? The answer is exceedingly plain. Exercise properly your reason-principle. The well-educated astronomer does not wait to see the eclipse in order to foretell correctly the precise occurrence and cause of that phenomenon. Nay, not so. He goes into his most secret chamber, lights his taper, takes the slate and pencil, and seats himself with the immortal principle of reason glowing effulgently from his spacious brow; and there, alone and unseen, he traces the mighty revolutions of the planets, notes their various orbits—their inclinations, their aphelions and perihelions; and ere the sun tints the golden clouds of the distant horizon with its electric rays, the astronomer's soul shouts, "Eureka, Eureka, Eureka!"—for he has caught the sublime mystery of the eclipse, and realized the startling grandeur and overwhelming magnitude of that exalted region with which his Reason has formed an undying acquaintance. So likewise, you who would learn the truth, should go into the most secret chamber of your own souls. The spirit of God lives there. There you should go to pray, to sing, to commune with your guardian spirits. And you will there find that interior principle of discernment by which the hidden laws of every external phenomenon may be easily comprehended. Those who reason correctly never confine their investigations to the sphere of the seeming and the transient. They go deeper, and seek the permanent. They are never captivated with whited sepulchres; never with the platter whose exterior is apparently clean; never with a show of talent, a display of rhetorical flights and figures; but they seek the inward condition of the manifestation, whatever it be, in order to know the fountain causes of that which is visible. And then, too, such investigators are very consistent and harmonious in their application of truth. They do not believe that there are any actual inconsistencies or paradoxes in truth; they do not believe that the Deity can be self-contradictory, or that he can make a truth, uttered by a human being, to conflict with a principle in Nature; but, to such a mental constitution, all truth is simple, harmonious, infinite, and eternal. Now, inasmuch as this method of exercising the reason-principle is adopted by only the exceedingly small minority of minds that inhabit this globe, and inasmuch as no other structure of intellect can fully appreciate the philosophy of clairvoyance and inspiration soon to be disclosed, it is therefore positively certain that the vast majority, who are almost always in the wrong, will continue to think and reason upon, and to speak against, these phenomena of mind as they have for the last twenty or more years. While we, who have entered upon this investigation with honest hearts and with a disposition to employ our reason aright, will proceed happily on our way.

Having, as I feel impressed, removed a considerable quantity of misapprehension and error from the field before us, I will now state the various and progressive conditions into which the human soul is, from a combination of causes, not unfrequently thrown. As an amplification of much that I have already said on this subject, the following is considered the most natural and legitimate classification of human mental conditions,—ranging, progressively and spontaneously, from the moment of birth into this world, to the moment of the mind's introduction into the world of spirits:—

I. The Rudimental State.
II. The Psychological State.
III. The Sympathetic State.
IV. The Transition State.
V. The Somnambulic State.
VI. The Clairvoyant State.
VII. The Spiritual State.

These states, I repeat, are indicative of the progressive conditions into which the human mind, naturally or artificially, and permanently or temporarily, passes in its ascension from the event of birth to the higher circumstance of merging into the empire of spirits. Nevertheless, it is deemed proper to say here, in advance of a more particular definition of these conditions, that the psychological, sympathetic, and transition phases of mind are not to be regarded as absolute improvements; whilst the somnambulic, clairvoyant, and spiritual states are actual advancements upon the rudimental condition.

The *first* condition—or the Rudimental State—I will now proceed to philosophically consider.

LECTURE V.

MAN'S ORDINARY STATE, CONSIDERED IN CONNECTION WITH THE EXTERNAL WORLD.

Man is the coronation of Nature; the highest and noblest work of God. All forms and personalities, in the vegetable and animal worlds, are manifestly inferior to man in every possible respect. And every thing about and within him unequivocally testifies to his physical, intellectual, and moral supremacy. By affirming man to be the highest and noblest "work of God," I do not mean to teach the oriental doctrine of special creation: that the Omnipotent Mind, by the employment of his hands, selected and arranged the physical substances of the earth, and molded them into the most exquisite anatomical and physiological structures, of which he made a single human being; and then, seeing that it was not good for *man* to be alone, caused him to fall into a deep sleep, selected a rib from his side, and, by the assistance of this isolated structure, made a female companion for the first male development of the human species. This hypothesis of the origin of man is very oriental and mainly chimerical. It indicates, however, in a truly interesting and instructive manner, how naturally the human soul goes into the investigation of first causes and first principles.

In the primary stages of human experience and civilization, it should be duly borne in mind, the prominent manifestations of the soul are—Fear, Hate, Superstition, Imagination, Mythology; and chimerical speculations upon cosmogony and anthropological subjects. You are, doubtless, all aware that *civilization* was preceded by savagism and barbarism; that *superstition* existed before religion; that *Mythology* preceded theology; that *Imagination* pre ceded science and philosophy. This principle of the *inferior* existing long in advance of the *superior* is every where manifested as an eternal law of the universe. This is the principle of progression, which God has immutably established in the expanded earth and unfolded heavens.

And yet, notwithstanding the fact that this invariable and eternal principle of progression has been in full operation from all eternity, and always conspicuously before and within the human soul; nevertheless the mind has but just arrived at a point in its development where this law can be recognized and to some extent practically comprehended. The past experience of man shows, conclusively, that his mind has not been sufficiently educated in facts and things, in truths and principles, to read, with an understanding heart, the magnificent volume of Nature which has laid unclasped for centuries, open to human inspection.

Some minds think that *antiquity* is high authority. Our best scholars are invariably in quest of oriental literature. The hidden lore and erudition of the ages past attract the student and the professor; and the spirit of antiquity, though gray and infirm, with a mountain of mythology, superstition, and error on his back, is the *master* of many thousands among us who think themselves, in their intellectual and moral growth, even with the colossal stature of this fresh and youthful, yet manly century. Such minds are centuries behind those who have exchanged their oriental faiths for the scientific and philosophical truths which now walk abroad in the noon-tide light, invulnerable alike to public derision and the high-sounding anathemas of the spirit of sectarianism which hangs, as an incubus, upon the body of the barbarian and civilized nations.

In the midst of such darkness and superstition, which have obscured the religious firmament for ages, there have appeared, now and then, a few seers of truths—like stars which suddenly shine out from among many clouds in the midnight hour. Occasionally, a soul could read the volume of nature sufficiently well, to teach the world, that, the principles of progression and development, which are God's immutable modes of being and doing, would not permit the *best* to exist first; the babe can not succeed the man; the inferior is not to be unfolded from the superior; the least from the greatest. Such clear-sighted minds can not but acknowledge that, "that was not *first* which is spiritual, but natural, and *afterward* the spiritual." In other words—that was not *first* which is superior, but inferior, and *afterward* the superior. Now, if it be admitted that the *Divine Mind* is "*without variableness, neither shadow of turning*," then it is absolutely certain, that *what is true* in one part of his physical creation and moral government must of necessity be *equally true* in every other portion of his immeasurable dominion. Hence, I affirm that man was not created, at first, pure and immaculate; because "that was not first which is spiritual, but natural, and afterward the spiritual." The lowest is always first, but yet contains the highest undeveloped. We do not obtain the "full corn in the ear," until we prepare the ground and deposit the germ. The common is always the precedent of the uncommon; the ordinary of the extraordinary. This is invariably true, because the germ contains all the subsequent unfoldings of the plant; the *lowest* contains the properties, and qualities, and essences of the *highest* within its little bosom,—as the babe contains the future man; the man the immortal spirit.

But how shall we explain the origin of the belief, that God created man at first perfect, in his image and likeness? And we may also ask, how shall we explain the origin of the long-established conviction, that the earth was flat, resting upon the backs of elephants and turtles? The explanation is extremely simple. Superstition is the first indication of religion; mythology is the first of theology; imaginative speculations precede true science and philosophy; and it is altogether undeniable, that, the further we penetrate the dark and eccentric wilderness of mankind's past experience, the cruder do we find all human conceptions of God, of the origin of man, and of the unseen powers by which the visible creation is governed. And we likewise discover the instinctive tendency of mind to speculate upon causes and analyze first principles. If true explanations of existing phenomena can not be readily acquired, then the mind goes as far as its state of intellectual development will permit; and expositions or explanations must come, though they be as super ficial and unsteady as the breeze that moves over the distant vallies. I say, it is natural for man to seek out the causes of visible effects; and, if he can not get real causes, he is certain to fix upon some imaginary explanations or suppositions, which, for centuries, may perfectly satisfy the low and undeveloped philosophy of sensuous and superficial reasoners! Thus, how easy a matter it is to comprehend the reason why, among the many and various stratifications and consolidations of theological and other speculations in the world, every description of mind finds a resting place for its affections and intellect. However, as intelligence advances, superstition retires.

Now, let it be remembered, that the early inhabitants of the eastern hemisphere were as incapable, in the undeveloped stage of their intellects, of obtaining a true explanation or philosophy of the origin of man and of the visible world, as the aboriginal inhabitants of this country were incapable of furnishing, to their own minds, a rational explanation of the origin and design of the myriads of stars that nightly gleamed out in the heavens. And yet the Indians had a sacred hypothesis of what the stars were, and for what purpose they were permitted to shine upon the wigwam and war-path of the red sons of the forest; and this hypothesis or superstitious religion among the Indians, be it also remembered, was just as much a high and sacred theme of faith as the Mosaic mythology of the creation of man is to the thousands of minds who think themselves vastly more enlightened than the poor Indian—

> "Whose untutored mind
> Sees God in clouds, and hears him in the wind."

But I will not discuss these interesting points in this place; but will simply recommend the free inquirer to think for himself on the causes and philosophy of human belief; this can inform him, better than any other thing, how naturally the human mind generates, in the incipient stages of its development, many mythological theories and speculations in the natural exercise of that inward power which bids it seek the parent causes of all external effects. This is an age of free investigation. The reason-principle must be exercised in a proper and dignified manner. And there is nothing too sacred or too exalted for the investigations of that soul, whose religious emotions and moral dignity are inspired with a love of truth. The wonderful panorama of human faith—of past speculations and hypotheses—must be arraigned before the imperial tribunal of reason, whose jurors shall be the *facts* of all theories, indorsed by the unchangeable principles of universal nature. We can not arrest the march of intelligence. Can not successfully impede the progressive tendencies of this age. The mind, having become, by the legitimate operation of eternal principles, emancipated from the shackles of a cruel servitude and a relentless sectarianism, in which for centuries it slumbered, spell-bound to dogmatic creeds and unmeaning formularies, has just merged into light and liberty. Nobly discarding all conventional rules, and proudly elevating itself above the long-established customs and usages of antiquity, the free soul now roams abroad in the boundless spirit of Deity, basking in the enjoyment of its own native energies and immortal attributes.

It should be distinctly understood, that, I am now considering man in his rudimental state. That is to say, in his ordinary condition. It is essential to become perfectly acquainted with him in this natural state of development, to the end that we may still continue to know him, when, by the workings of the principles of progress, he may ascend into the subsequent and higher conditions, already specified. For, it will be found, that the law of an eternal individuality of character will, to an extent more or less perceptible, always distinguish one individual from another in all the spheres and conditions of existence. I again affirm that man, in his natural state and considered relatively, is superior to all other forms and personalities known in the subordinate kingdoms of nature. This is true in every possible respect—physically, socially, habitually, intellectually, morally, and spiritually. And man is not the result of any special creation of Deity, but an *issue* of the stupendous system of nature, whose myriad forms, substances, essences, and principles have, step by step, ascended the spiral path of universal progression! On the summit of this boundless empire of life, stands *man* in his ordinary or rudimental state—a *reservoir* of every thing beneath him, and the splendid *representative* of all the perfections and energies of the grosser worlds of life which move in nature's broad dominion. Now, if it be conceded that man is the grand receptacle of all beneath him in the subordinate kingdoms, then it is very legitimate and logical to conclude, that, in the various departments of his constitution, we shall discover traces or indications of the anatomical, physiological, or phrenological peculiarities of the various plants and animals in nature. Those who are somewhat familiar with the teachings of comparative anatomy, know how distinctly the distinguishing characteristics of the various animal developments of nature are visible in the physical and mental conformations of the human organism. It is clear to a demonstration, that *man* is constituted of all known forms, substances, essences, and principles in a high state of refinement and embodiment; a god upon the very apex of creation.

But here let me direct your attention to the fact, that man, in his rudimental state, is very likely to exhibit one or two of the many living elements which have flowed through the ten thousand channels of the vegetable and animal kingdoms, into his spiritual or mental constitution. Being more closely allied to the *animal*, than to the vegetable, kingdom, he is naturally inclined to exhibit in his character,—especially when undeveloped,—one or more traits of disposition common to some specific animal. I am impressed to regard this fact as very satisfactory external evidence of man's derivation from the subordinate creations of nature. But as he progresses toward harmony and perfection—as he leaves the things which are behind and presses to obtain the things which lie before—man ascends far above the traces of the lower kingdoms, passes rapidly by the ordinary characteristics of the human, and unfolds himself more like unto the divine.

It can not be well denied that every animal appears to be the embodiment of some particular principle of mind; whilst man is the unitary organization of all principles, and, hence, is superior to those partial organizations which contain only a few of the immortal elements which compose the human mental constitution. The *Viper*, for example, seems to embody, without any other element to act as a modification, the principle, or rather (to speak more philosophically,) the propensity of a smooth, insinuating *malice*. The *Spider* seems like a commercial Peter Funk—a maker of *nets* in which to entrap the verdant and unwary traveler. The *Sloth* seems like an indolent man—the consumer of the productions of the industrious and frugal. The *Cat* seems like an organization of the propensity of *secretiveness*—a pouncer upon the interests of other and lesser personalities. The *Dog* is an embodiment of friendship; the Lamb of innocence; the *Cow* of submission; the *Horse* of nobility; the *Gazel* of gracefulness; the *Elephant* of memory; the *Fox* of cunning; the *Ass* of firmness; the *Peacock* of pride; the *Reindeer* of speed; the *Bird* of affection; the *Lion* of majesty; the *Swine* of grossness; the *Beaver* of constructiveness; and the *Monkey* of trickery.

An observer of the mental characteristics of animals has drawn the following synopsis of the analogies existing between the manifestations of the animal and the human mind:—"Bees are geometricians. The cells are so constructed as, with the least quantity of material, to have the largest sized spaces, and least possible loss of interstice. The mole is a meteorologist. The bird called the nine killer is an arithmetician; as also the crow, the wild turkey, and some other birds. The torpedo, the ray, and the electric eel, are electricians. The nautilus is a navigator; he raises and lowers his sails, casts and weighs anchor, and performs other nautical acts. Whole tribes of birds are musicians. The beaver is an architect, builder, and woodcutter; he cuts down trees, and erects houses and dams. The marmont is a civil engineer; he does not only build houses, but constructs aqueducts and drains to keep them dry. The white ants maintain a regular army of soldiers. Wasps are paper manufacturers. Caterpillars are silk-spinners. The squirrel is a ferryman; with a chip, or piece of bark for a boat, and his tail for a sail, he crosses the stream. Dogs, wolves, jackals, and many others, are hunters. The black bear and the heron are fishermen. The ants are regular day laborers. The monkey is a rope-dancer."

Every well informed individual knows that in nature are to be found a vast variety of modifications of the propensities here described. As, for instance, in the different breeds of horses, cows, cats, dogs, birds, &c.; but, in man, the endless variety of these modifications are lost principally in the more compact and harmonious combination of all animal phrenological characteristics or elements in his own mental structure. Nevertheless, when from hereditary bias or other influential causes, the spiritual constitution of man is warped and structurally disturbed in its harmonious development, then it is a very common thing to see such individuals indicate, in their daily walk and conversation, the element or propensity which has thus unfortunately been permitted to obtain the ascendency over the higher principles of the mind. And when some persons feel disturbed, they are too apt to remind, in an unkind manner, such inharmoniously unfolded souls of what animal they most illustrate. It were far better to inform them of the philosophy of these isolated manifestations of character, and tell them how to achieve their emancipation from the peculiarities of the animal kingdom. The important bearing of the foregoing considerations upon the philosophy of clairvoyance and inspiration, will be developed as we proceed with the investigation. But here let our understandings be duly impressed with the conviction, that man is, in every conceivable respect, superior to all physical and mental organizations in the animal world. It is, therefore, not proper to say that man is, in any sense, an animal; but rather a *combination* of all inferior organizations. He frequently illustrates some particular animal in his physiognomical peculiarities, in his inferior moods and habits; but, considered as a man, and compared with the subordinate productions in the world, he appears nobly as the lord of creation, and ascends the throne of human government of all lower nature the self-constituted monarch of a boundless kingdom! Nevertheless, it is to be borne in mind, that every man, who is not perfectly emancipated from the inferior characteristics of the animal world, will illustrate and act more or less *like* some particular animal, bird, or reptile, which exist in nature as so many embodiments of specific principles or propensities tending toward man's mental structure, or, to speak with still more accuracy, as so many chemical laboratories designed to receive, prepare, and impart the proper physical and vitalizing elements for the constant creation and perpetuity of man's individuality.

We have now obtained *one* very important conclusion in the consideration of man in his rudimental state, namely: his absolute supremacy over all the forms, personalities, and principles of the lower departments of nature. But there is yet another very essential point in this investigation, which I feel impressed to urge upon you as worthy of your strict consideration—that is, THE DUALITY OF MAN. By his duality, I mean man's *twofold* organization.

It is a conspicuous fact, in the system of creation, that the lower we penetrate the science of organic development the more certain are we of finding partial and imperfect growths. The lowest indications of vegetable and animal forms are destitute of what might be denominated the twofold surfaces, or positive and negative membranes. Whilst in the higher branches of creation we invariably find all organisms constructed upon the reciprocal principles of a harmonious duality.

And when we examine the anatomical and physiological peculiarities of man's constitution, we discover this system of dual development carried out into the most indescribable minutiæ. Now, I am impressed to confine your attention to this point, in order to lay a firm foundation for future conclusions to safely rest upon. The duality of man, then, is simply extending and perfecting a system of justice, or of reciprocal relations, which are discoverable, partially and incompletely developed, in all the inferior departments of the visible creation. It is a self-evident proposition, that all external effects must spring from invisible causes. Every rivulet has a source; and every song is evidence of an indwelling principle of music. A house is first erected in the mind, and then *outwardly* upon the solid earth. In every thing, the ideal begets the actual; the invisible, the visible; the principle, the outward manifestation.

In accordance with the universality and invariability of this truth, the dual arrangements of the animal and human organism are indicative of an indwelling principle of justice or equilibrium in the constitution of nature. In man we find the perfect and highest manifestation of this eternal principle, because he is the grand receptacle of all beneath him in the various animated kingdoms. The questions may be asked,—Why has man two eyes, two ears, two legs, two arms, two lungs, two kidneys, two stomachs, two livers, two systems of circulation, and two brains? Why could he not have been made more beautifully and economically—more strongly and symmetrically—with half of these structures? What is the use of two eyes, when he can see with one? He can hear with one ear; why then have two? But ere we have put these questions fully, there comes, gushing forth from the many thousand avenues of nature, the sweet reply—that the principle of justice—or the divine attribute of reciprocation, which the Omnipotent Mind breathes through all the universe—incarnates itself in these beautiful and symmetrical organisms, and without them man would be incomplete, and Deity a mere nonentity.

The principles of justice, as above defined, are the causes of all *male* and *female*, *lower* and *higher*, *material* and *spiritual*, *positive* and *negative*, relations in the wide expanse of life and existence. They penetrate and develop, and sustain, every thing. They commence with Deity, and roll, like the waves of the sea, far away to the inconceivable circumferences of the numberless infinitudes. Eternities succeed eternities; universes succeed universes; and one mighty wave of omnipotence rolls over another, all upon the same identical principles which impart to man's organism its minute twofold structures and diversified dualities.

The works and ways of God are perfectly consistent and harmonious. He is *positive;* the universe is *negative.* And this is a rule by which to measure and determine every thing else in existence. The *Sun* is positive; and all the orbs, which roll beneath its power, are negative. What power is it which holds immovably the sun in the firmament? What sustains the planets in open space? There are no foundation walls, no colossal pillars, no ropes and pullies, no mighty levers and iron chains, to sustain the sun and the planets in the boundless ocean of the invisible atmosphere. What, then, preserves them from utter destruction? When the blazing comet—that lawless body of the skies—comes rushing through the viewless main, like an affrighted steed, threatening the world with immediate annihilation: what prevents the awful catastrophe? Timid and apprehensive minds believe that the world is to be destroyed in this way; and I may add, that, many such individuals are very much like the Jonah of Primitive History,—they would rather have their prophecy prove true than have it said that they were mistaken!—as Jonah remonstrated with the Lord for telling him to prophesy to the inhabitants of Nineveh that all should be destroyed in forty days, and then, by changing his mind, the Lord did not annihilate the people, and thus proved Jonah a false prophet. And so, many of our friends who now believe that the Lord intends to purge the earth with fire, and who prophesy accordingly, will certainly discover, by the commencement of the twentieth century, that the Lord has changed his mind, and they will, doubtless, like Jonah, feel a little provoked at the utter falseness of their startling proclamations. Yea; the Sun has shone effulgently for millions of years; the planets have revolved upon their eccentric paths for centuries beyond all human power of computation; and the impetuous *comets* have roamed through space as long, and yet no accident has occurred. What, then, has saved these living worlds from destruction? It certainly will not be presumed that this is done by a direct exercise of the will of Omnipotence. It would be as reasonable to assert that man controls the process of respiration, of circulation, of digestion, &c., by the exclusive exercise of his voluntary powers. While, in fact, all these phenomena occur with as much precision when the mind is engaged in foreign matters, and during sleep. It would, indeed, be a thankless and laborious work of Omnipotence to keep his will perpetually on the rack, in order to preserve the revolution and harmony of the planets. Although Sir Isaac Newton, and Thomas Dick, and Dr. Chalmers, and various other popular authorities, have advocated this view of the planetary harmonies; nevertheless, I am impressed to regard it as a very crude and unhealthy doctrine of astronomical science.

The truth is this: the Deity is himself controlled by the same identical law which controls the revolution of the planets. If it be asked, what preserves the sun, the orbs, the comets, in their respective positions, and what saves the whole temple of nature from destruction, I should say—the Principle of Justice which lives in, proceeds from, and flows to, the Divine Mind. That law which causes a particle of matter to flow, without dependence upon the voluntary exercise of his will, through the entire organism of man—from the crown of his head to the sole of his foot—is perfectly identical with that law which causes the planets to roll harmoniously in the heavens. In other words, the material universe is the physical body of God. The innumerable suns, planets, satellites, are the vital ORGANS of his body—the stomachs, livers, hearts, lungs, brains, &c., of his organization. The diurnal and annual revolutions—the mineral, vegetable, animal, and human productions—of these orbs or vital organs, are perfectly and entirely analogous to the ordinary functions performed by corresponding organs in the physical structure of man. And the Eternal Mind does not any more control the harmonious performance of these legitimate functions of the countless organs in his body, than does man control the circulation of blood, or the quiet secretions of the absorbing systems, which momentarily occur in his corporeal organism.

All these phenomena, I repeat, depend upon the principles of reciprocation which are eternally established in nature. The principles of negative and positive—of female and male—of lower and higher—of matter and spirit—of nature and Deity—are very beautifully indicated and concentrated in man; he is a faithful representation of the WHOLE. Hence I will confine my investigations to this highest development of matter and mind.

The analytical and deductive mind goes naturally from *effect* to *cause*, and from *cause* to *effect*, in its examination and contemplation of Nature. To such a mind, every effect must have a parent cause—every external manifestation must have a corresponding source. For instance, through the medium of our physical senses we discover that the face of nature is diversified with symmetrical *forms* and anatomical structures; hence we infer, that, in the invisible sphere of causes, there must necessarily exist an immutable principle of form and structure—an architectural or anatomical law of action. So, when we behold every thing invested with the power of function—with the requisite qualifications to perform some distinct and definite *use* in the order of being,—then we conclude that there must exist a physiological principle in the constitution of things: a law by which *functions* and *uses* are developed and governed with mathematical precision. This is a philosophy to which the human mind involuntarily turns as a child to its parent for instruction. Is it not self-evident ?. Else why do you turn to the *acorn* to account for the stately *oak?*—to the *germ* to account for the existence of the *rose?* It is because you can not resist the legitimate workings of immutable law! The little child, just learning to lisp the name of its fond parents, turns its sparkling eyes toward the sidereal heavens, and attempts to ask, who made the sun ?—who made the stars ?—who made the soft, deep immensity that envelops Nature? Thus, the first, the deepest, the highest, the eternal effort of mind is unto causes!—and, the utter impossibility on the part of the soul to ever perceive and comprehend the whole system of causation at one time, constitutes the main-spring to an eternal life and to endless progression in wisdom and knowledge.

It is clear, then, that the human mind must explain *effects* by reference to corresponding *causes*. If we see light, we conclude that the source is light; or such elements as will, when properly combined and subjected to the law of combustion and elimination, produce the *effect* which we behold. Thus, I repeat, we turn involuntarily from effects to causes, and from causes to effects, in our observation and comparison of those facts and phenomena which constitute the material world in which we at present live.

The duality of man's physical constitution can be perceived by all sensuous observers; but the *causes* of this duality can not be so easily discovered, and yet the reason-principle, recognizing the law of indispensable connection between cause and effect, is very capable of understanding the truthfulness of the proposition, that all general external effects are the outer manifestations of invisible principles. Taking *this* ground as true and incontrovertible, I proceed to apply the principle directly to man in his ordinary or rudimental state.

Positive and negative powers are uniformly manifested in the construction of the various organs in the physical economy. These principles faithfully express themselves in the outer form and function of the different members of man's body. There are two livers; one is positive, the other is negative. There are two stomachs; one is positive, the other negative. There is a circle of positive and negative relations and processes, commencing with the spleen; going to the kidneys; thence to the liver; thence to the stomach; thence to the heart; thence to the lungs; thence to the brain; and thence to all possible ramifications of the nerves, veins, vessels, arteries, organs, muscles, and bones, which characterize the physical mechanism. There are two eyes; but one is positive, and the other is negative. You can not see as perfectly with one eye as the other, nor with either one separately, as with the two combined. This is true also of the hands and the feet. There are two ears; but one is positive, and the other is negative.

There are also two brains; one is positive, the other is negative. And here it may be well to say, that the two brains determine the distribution, and graduate the quantity, of these positive and negative forces to the dependent system. On the ground, that all general external effects are the legitimate out-births of internal principles, we can not but admit the succeeding proposition, that all external organizations are the spontaneous developments of *invisible* organizations; or, that an organization of principles is the parent of all material organisms of a corresponding form and nature. Hence the common duality of man's physical constitution is alone traceable to the existence of a spiritual constitution, analogous to the outer form in every possible particular. Here, then, is the issue to which all our foregoing reasonings have been conducting us—viz.: that man's physical body is a demonstration of his spiritual body,—the one succeeds the other as naturally as the oak unfolds from the acorn. It is all cause and effect,—a high result of positive and negative principles. And now, having shown you man's *constitutional* SUPREMACY *and* DUALITY, I will proceed to consider the highest phase of this subject,—MAN'S SPIRITUALITY!

Of the perfect spirituality of man there are comparatively but a very few minds entirely convinced. Physicians believe in "a something," which they term "the vital principle." Materialists believe in "mind" as perfectly and inseparably connected with the brain—that mind is developed by the material sensorium as electricity is generated by zinc and copper batteries; and that the manifestation of mind depends upon the proper constitution, health, and actual presence of the brain, as much as electricity is dependent upon the zinc and copper plates for its manifestation. And I am speaking within the bounds of truth, when I affirm that, five-eighths of this world's thinking, civilized population, are more or less skeptical concerning the future existence of the soul, in a state of consciousness and individualization, subsequent to the event of outer physical dissolution. And hence it is highly necessary to consider this question in connection with the rudimental state of man.

In considering this theme of the soul's existence independent of the physical organism, I think it is very essential to understand, that the element of electricity is not *created* by the zinc and copper plates, but is simply developed and accumulated by them, from surrounding substances. It therefore follows, as a consequence, that electricity does not depend upon these plates for its existence, but simply for its more palpable manifestation. And the same reasoning will apply to the elements of man's spiritual principle. The brain is primarily essential—yea, it is absolutely indispensable—to the accumulation and individualization of the living elements of life into a healthy and harmonious mind. Yet the brain is not essential to the *prior* existence of those elements, nor yet to the continuation of the individuality of the mind, after the physical structure has subserved the purposes of its primary organization. After the tree has produced and matured its fruit, the latter is independent. An apple developed by a tree in one field or country can be taken to any other locality, independent of its parent tree, and can bring forth its kind. Now it is clear that the physical organism is the cradle of the mind,—the house in which the spirit is born. There it is nursed and fostered; and gradually,—year by year and hour by hour,—it is introduced to the beauties and influences of the external world. Progressively, it becomes acquainted with the facts and fancies, with the principles and pandemonium of mundane existence; and soon puts forth its feelers to grasp something higher, better, spiritual, and more like its *own* particular nature. But here the skeptic stands armed with a multitude of sensuous reasons, and says to the immortal mind,—"You were born in a physical cradle; consequently you can not walk without it: you were born in this material tenement; therefore you can not move independently; if you go, you must take your physical establishment with you." Is this sound philosophy? Nay! When the soul is sufficiently advanced in strength, it discards its cradle—it steps boldly from the threshhold of the tabernacle in which it was born—and treads the interminable paths of infinitude like an angel of God!

The enlightened and deep thinking members of all professions begin to acknowledge the supremacy and duality of man; they begin to assert, as a fact absolutely undeniable, that man is a spiritual being. Thus the much celebrated Dr. Reid says: "No man can show it to be impossible to the Supreme Being to have given us the power of perceiving external objects without the common organs of sense. We have reason to believe that when we put off these bodies, and all the organs belonging to them, our perceptive powers shall rather be improved than destroyed or impaired. We have reason to believe that the Supreme Being perceives every thing in a much more perfect manner than we do, without bodily organs. We have reason to believe that there are other created beings endowed with powers of perception more perfect and more extensive than ours, without any such organs as we find necessary. However astonishing, it is now proved beyond all rational doubt, that in certain abnormal states of the nervous organism, perceptions are possible through other than the ordinary channels of the sense." Such an acknowledgment is valuable, as it emanates from a member of the skeptical profession.

The spirituality of man is not questioned; but the continuation of his internal principle, after the death of the physical organism, in a state of identification, is the question yet unsettled in many minds. This problem I think will be duly solved as we proceed with these investigations. It will be seen that *the invisible spirit is the real man*, and is not necessarily dependent upon the material organization for its existence or individuality. And the duality of the corporeal body extends, in a more perfect manner, to the spiritual body; the outer is an imperfect representation of the interior. "That was not first which is spiritual, but natural, and afterward the spiritual." In other language,—that was not first which is mind, but the body, and afterward the mind. The body is the cradle of the soul—the former is the mold into which the elements of nature were caused to flow; the body is thus the primary framer of the mind. At first the body is the master, but soon it bows to the inward power; the spirit subdues and subjugates the physical temple to its exclusive control. As the little babe is dependent upon its parents for subsistence and growth, but in a few years walks alone in the fields, tills the ground, and proves itself free of its primary dependencies; so is the spirit. It comes forth clothed in a physical, terrestrial vesture, is dependent upon the outer sense for its first experiences and education, is fixed in a house more or less imperfect, and can not move beyond its narrow courts; but soon the soul marshals its latent forces, assumes the responsible position of master, and thus learns something of its glorious independence and destiny.

And the *soul* knows no retrogression, neither maturity. It is destined for eternal progression, and for the unbroken enjoyment of an immortal youth! I have seen the aged man, as the sun shone brilliantly o'er the earth, draw his old arm chair close to the cottage door, and try to view the distant landscape, with its waving foliage, its undulating surface, and glittering granite. But viewing him externally, Shakspeare says mournfully—"the last stage of all is old age, second childishness, and mere oblivion; sans teeth, sans taste, sans eyes, sans—every thing." But is it so? "Second childishness, and mere oblivion"? Nay; it is not so! This is the error of the world—this is reasoning from the external. True, the physical garment is worn out in consequence of a long contact and struggle with the gross world of matter. It is threadbare. The superficial gloss is gone. It is tattered and covered with patches. It can not conceal the *form* beneath. The *spiritual eye* can no longer freely use the *material eye;* the *spiritual ear* can no longer easily use the *material ear;* the spiritual powers of *locomotion* can not readily use the old worn-out limbs; and the brain can no longer render the spirit assistance in preserving external memories. What then? Why, the spirit of that decrepit, old man is *young* as a bird. It soars gracefully o'er the fields, hears the waters murmur their plaintive music, sees the variegated landscape, and enjoys all the scenes of life anew! For many years, the tattered garment confines the youthful soul. But at a time when ye think not, when all is tranquil in the midnight hour, or when you would summon the old man to his accustomed meal, and go to his room to arouse him from slumber, you will perceive the glossless garment is left motionless on the bed, whilst the immortal youth of the interior is gliding joyfully away to the Spirit Land!

LECTURE VI.

MAN CONSIDERED IN HIS INTERNAL RELATIONS TO THE SPIRITUAL UNIVERSE.

MAN, in his ordinary or rudimental state, still demands our highest consideration. It has been shown that he is the most wonderful and perfect development of the visible creation; that all entities and personalities cluster around him; that he is, conquently, the center of much beauty and many powers.

Let us now fix our attention upon man as a spiritual being. There is a perfect adaptation of every form and principle to their appropriate sphere. The reptile moves on the surface of the earth; the beast is found among the hills and in the dismal solitudes of the forest; the bird sails gracefully through the upper medium; and the fish sports in the watery element. Each of these creatures, and every living thing, is perfectly adapted to the sphere in which it lives, and to all the influences and circumstances of its being. And the same principle is operative, and on a much sublimer scale, in the organization of man. His physical structure is admirably adapted to the conditions and influences of the physical world; and his spiritual constitution is still more harmoniously adapted to the world of spirits. The material eye is suited to the outer world of visible objects, and to the physical element of light which emanates from the sun; but the spiritual eye is more perfectly adapted to the soft, golden light which illuminates the ten thousand crystal spheres that roll noiselessly in the serene depths of infinitude!

The material ear is wisely adapted to the multifarious sounds of the external world; and the spiritual ear is exquisitely attuned to the unutterable musical sounds which pervade the celestial world around us! It is proper, however, to remember that man's physical organism is simply an encasement of the more interior and substantial principle. His spiritual ear in this world is addressed through the material ear; so with all the other organs of his constitution. His duality of organization we must constantly remember,—it is the basis of many conclusions of a holy and sublime nature. The spirit—the soul—is primarily educated through the corporeal senses. The external world is the primary school of all spirits—of all angels and seraphs. In a material body—and in a material world—the interior nature of man becomes incipiently acquainted with the rudiments of thoughts, truths, emotions, and music! Every thing is begun on the natural plane and perfected on the spiritual plane. The external is typical of the interior—the present of the future. That was not first which is spiritual, but natural, and afterward the spiritual.

On earth, the human spirit, through the physical organs of sense, begins to learn something of music! Here, and in this manner, we hear the sighing of the summer breeze—the howling of the blast—the purling of the rivulet—the contralto of the torrent—and the sweet melody of birds. We hear the deep voice of the rolling ocean—the low murmurings of the waterfall—and the music of the lofty pines as, when touched by the flying fingers of the tempest, they breathe forth a strange and grotesque song. These are the rudiments of music. But we do not *acquire* a love for music; because its sublime principles are interwoven in our deepest natures,—yet on earth we learn incipiently how to walk the "crystal billows of sweet sounds," as they roll before the soul, in the immeasurable expanse of the spirit land, beyond the sphere of sense.

Let us bear in mind that man has a spiritual nature; which is exquisitely adapted to a higher sphere. Man is a connecting link between earth and heaven. The terrestial and the spiritual natures are beautifully blended and harmonized in him. Thus the visible and the invisible are brought into close relationship; and man is the flower of the physical creation, and the germ of the world of spirits. The temporal and the eternal—the inferior and superior—the material and spiritual—meet and center in him; and there is one unbroken chain of being, from man down to the smallest animalcule, and extending far, far, upward—through an endless concatenation of high and glorious beings, to the very soul of DEITY. The physical structure of man, I repeat, is perfectly adapted to the forms and circumstances of the earth; and his spiritual constitution is as perfectly adapted to the superior possessions and influences of a higher world. The invisible spirit that animates the visible temple, is the immortal principle. And such is man—the being of a moment, yet the inheritor of an eternal life; in the lower departments of his nature, a mere animal—in his higher character, a bright and immortal spirit!

Let us now proceed to consider the causes of the vast variety of human beings, which people the earth.

In the first place I am impressed to regard it as an incontrovertible proposition, that every mind is constructed upon identical principles, contains the same elements, and is capable of analogous manifestations. No man is gifted intrinsically above another. The Deity does not manifest partiality or favoritism in the fields of his creation. The physiological and anatomical developments of man's body show, unequivocally, that the same identical principles are every where engaged in their production. But how shall we harmonize this statement with the conspicuous fact, that there is an infinite variety of men—possessing, apparently, different qualifications and gifts? In one family is frequently seen a vast dissimilarity of mental endowments. One is a musician; another a sculptor; another a husbandman; another a poet; another an idiot; another a philosopher; another a prodigal; another a miser; and all from the same parents. Now, admitting all to be in the possession of identical principles of mind, how shall we explain the causes of these remarkable differences? How shall we explain the diversities of gifts? Why is one man a warrior; another a Paul; one man a worshiper of Truth, another of Mammon? These are important questions. I am impressed to reply, that these anomalies of character are not to be explained on the fabulous ground that Deity has endowed intrinsically one man above another, but rather on the broad and expansive philosophy of mental organization. All faculties and elements are deposited in the mind, but the infinite variety consists wholly in the various and many combinations of these faculties. Therefore, we should study the philosophy of combination. If we come to believe that we are all equally endowed with the elements of mind,—that we internally possess what Isaiah, or John, or Jesus, or what celebrated mathematicians possess,—then we will experience a universal love for man, irrespective of his birth or social position; and the thought is, moreover, a strong incentive to mental culture and universal progression. I feel impressed to say, that what is possible and natural to one individual is possible and natural to all men. All can be happy as easily as one. Harmony of organization is the principal essential; for no man is destitute of the elements of mind, or the principles of immortality. It is only the *unfortunate combination and education* of the mental faculties which produce unhappiness and generate discord. Now, the reason why so many contradictory characters or mental incongruities and conformations issue from one source, is to be found in the dissimilar circumstances by which the parents are surrounded—especially, those which act upon and control the feelings and emotions of the mother! Physicians acknowledge the extent of hereditary influence upon the mental organization of the offspring. But I think there is a more important philosophy in the extensive action of progenitory magnetism than is generally perceived by those most skilled in a knowledge of human character. Of this I will hereafter speak.

It is good to feel that every soul contains the same elements of energy and intellect. Such a conviction will inspire us with a philosophical compassion for every individual, whose mind is unfortunately developed. It is time to regard a "change" of the *combination* of the mental faculties, as far more essential to personal righteousness and social harmony, than the so-called "change of heart" which is caused merely by the psychological influence of talented clergymen and excited congregations.

I say that that power or gift, which distinguishes one individual from another, is a universal attribute and is therefore perfectly natural to *all* the human family. Every mind is constitutionally and essentially enriched with those splendid powers which characterized Shakspeare, Sir Isaac Newton, and Kepler; yet the different *combination* of identical powers produces entirely different individuals. For example,—take the gigantic oak, which is a specific organization of the same essences, fluids, and substances, which, when differently combined, might produce a chestnut tree—a pine—a walnut—or a sycamore. If you take that solid oak, and subject it to the proper processes in mechanism, you will find that chairs, tables, doors, window-frames, &c., may be made from the dissimilar combination of the same identical substance. So with man. One *particular combination* of essentially good elements and faculties will make a poet; another, a pirate; another, a Moses; another, a Milton; and so, throughout the entire catalogue of dissimilar beings that people the earth, it will be found that the *same* principles, in different states and degrees of refinement and combination, are capable of developing an infinite variety of men. Let us study, therefore, into the science of combination; first, what particular arrangement of the mental faculties will develop a *deceiver*,—what, a *murderer*,—what, a *righteous* man; second, let us then study the external circumstances which act upon the individual,—what *combination* of circumstances will brutalize, and what will spiritualize, the human character. From the modern teachings of phrenological science, the investigator may obtain various confirmations of the science of combination. Evil and good are traced to this source. A defective machine produces deformities; so an unbalanced mental organization develops corresponding results. Without a requisite education, the human mind may manifest or unfold a life replete with crude and unwholesome deeds. Destitute of organic harmony, it may generate a congress of blunders—a large congregation of inconsistences and deplorable angularities. But in the great multitude of common men, you may see, (if you will but examine their interiors,) many a "mute, inglorious Milton," or many magnanimous apostles of the soul;—heroes, legislators, poets, physicians, theologians, philosophers. Such is man in his ordinary or rudimental state.

LECTURE VII.

A GENERAL CONSIDERATION OF MAN'S PSYCHOLOGICAL CONDITION AND POWERS.

WE will now examine the human mind in the next stage of its manifestation.—I mean, in the Psychological State.

There has been a large amount of chicanery and unmeaning pretension connected with this branch of mental science, which has unquestionably done much toward confounding the ignorant, amusing the careless, and disgusting the man of science. All this I have frequently deplored.—Because it detracted much from the natural dignity of Truth, and has repelled many an honest investigator from the sublime realms of psychological philosophy, leading to the highest themes of contemplation. Having seen only the mountebank side of psychology, and not imagining that there could possibly be a higher and better phase to the subject, many minds have seized, with eagerness, upon a preconceived conviction—which the unenlightened portion of the scientific world generally entertain—that the wonderful phenomena of magnetism are mere delusions or mental hallucination.

Perhaps it is necessary to remind you, that, naturally succeeding the ordinary or rudimental condition, is the psychological state, which I am about to consider. According to my interior impressions, the true psychological condition can be attained in two ways—one is natural, the other is artificial. This is true of all the subsequent states into which the human soul is constitutionally capable of ascending. The little plant can, naturally, attain unto its maximum growth by being left to struggle with the surrounding obstructions, and thus, perhaps, acquire a greater power; or it may be assisted, by artificial and quickening means, to attain its highest development many weeks in advance of its natural period of maturity. So with the human mind. Some men naturally obtain an intellectual power and brilliancy of understanding at the proper period of life; but others, if duly influenced by a spiritual magnetism or encouraged by surrounding circumstances, may attain all the strength and illumination of mind, which characterize the naturally developed intellect, years too in advance of the ordinary season of such maturity. Now here, let it be duly understood, is the first legitimate indication of psychological principles. I affirm that an early or extraordinary development of mind may be accomplished by the influence of a spiritual magnetism, or by the encouragement which may be extended toward it by surrounding circumstances. That is to say, a human soul may be matured and unfolded, in some particular sphere, or in many departments of science and thought, years before the ordinary growth of intellect, by the psychological influence of spiritual powers and contiguous circumstances. And I may here add, that the psychological action of the mother's spirit upon the body and mind of her child, during the season of its utero-gestation and development, is the primary source of much pre-disposition to discord or harmony, to lowness or elevation of mind, which will, inevitably, more or less characterize the future physical and mental manifestations of the offspring.

But it is deemed expedient to consider the principles of psychological science, as they exist in the constitution of nature, before we apply them to the various conditions of the human mind.

The philosophy of *positive* and *negative* relationships has been already partially explained. But it is now time to make an application of these reciprocal principles. When the mind once grasps the doctrine of an *infinite gradation* of forms, series, degrees, essences, and elements—beginning with the lowest form of matter and reaching upward to the most interior soul of Deity—then it becomes comparatively an easy thing to comprehend the philosophy of positive and negative relations in the construction of the universe. But those who have been taught to regard nature as so many specific creations, without any reference to a regular system of harmonious and progressive developments, will find it somewhat difficult to recognize the psychological principles which universally pervade the territories of nature, and which bind all of her productions into one stupendous system of sympathetic cause and effect.

Now to my interior perceptions, it is clear to a demonstration, that all the animated kingdoms of creation are intimately related—like the human family—with near and dear friends, noble ancestors, and happy descendants. The *earth* may be regarded as the parental foundation of all these psychological sympathies. Here commences that progressive line of inferior and superior forces, which hath no termination. Thus the *mineral* kingdom is *positive* to the earth; the vegetable kingdom is *positive* to the mineral kingdom; the animal world is *positive* to the vegetable world; the human world is *positive* to the animal world; the spiritual world is *positive* to the human world; the angelic is *positive* to the spiritual; the seraphic to the angelic; and the Divine Mind is *positive* to the immeasurable universe. Between all these kingdoms and the Divine Being there are constantly existing the most intimate psychological sympathies. The series, degrees, and gradations of these *positive* and *negative* relations are altogether beautiful and innumerable. Now, it is solely in consequence of man's physical and mental supremacy to the animal and other creations of nature, that he is the center of a power which is *positive* to every thing beneath him. He is the highest source of psychological influence on earth.

The viper will crawl out from its dark retreat, elevate its head, and fix its sharp, penetrating gaze upon the affectionate little songster that sits on the bough of the waving tree. The glittering eye, flashing bewitchingly in the sunlight, arrests the little bird's attention. Their eyes meet. The positive viper, by the careful use of its psychological power, fixes the gaze of the negative bird, which does not fly away, because magnetically held by a strange infatuation—which might be considered a cross between *admiration* and *astonishment*. There is nothing that can do this to man, if he wills to the contrary. But the bird grows nervous. It feels drawn to the viper by a fascination, and repelled by fear. Its will-power is captured. It can not fly away into the open fields, and feel at liberty; but nervously jumps from bough to bough, spreads its tiny wings, and encircles the seducer's head. And finally—exhausted with fear, excitement, and infatuation—it draws close to the glittering eyes and falls prostrate before the extended mouth of its relentless destroyer. The winged insect is, in the same manner, and according to the same psychological principles, *infatuated* by the flame of a candle. It will encircle the blaze for hours, and then willingly subjects itself to the disposal of the dissolving element.

But man possesses a motive and a moral power, superior to that in the possession of any other creature. His positive influence is felt to an extent which is always proportionate to his own interior consciousness of supremacy. His intrinsic growth of soul is the measure of the real and permanent influence which he can exert upon the world. A man may have placed an unjust estimation upon the character and volume of his mental power, and may feel greater and more high-minded than he really should; nevertheless it matters not what opinion a man may entertain of himself, so long as he does his best honestly and energetically, for it will soon be discovered to what mental height he has in reality grown. His influence will invariably be extended to the full measure of his interior development, and no further. And as he mentally or spiritually unfolds, so the circle of his power is proportionably widened. So that one strong mind may yet psychologize a world! His influence may be slightly felt at the outermost circle of humanity; but more upon the body of a nation, still more upon society, and most powerfully upon the innermost vitality of the family combination.

Hence, in accordance with the last named fact, the psychological power of one mind is more available in the compact assembly; but its legitimate action is manifested very conspicuously upon the isolated individual. How common a thing it is to see affectionate companions grow to look, and talk, and walk, and think in a corresponding manner! Husbands and wives are thus often regarded, by strangers, as brothers and sisters. In accordance with this principle of positive and negative action, the mother or the father imparts her or his likeness to the unborn child. This is an important fact of psychological science. It points us to the proper generation and improvement of our species. The strong *mother* of Napoleon marched in the battle array, before her child was born. Consequently, being herself powerfully magnetized by the spirit of war, she let flow the excitement of her soul, and the heated blood of her throbbing heart, through the unfolding constitution of her unborn child, and thus made an intrepid warrior!

I have said that there are two ways to produce the psychological state,—one is natural, the other artificial. But I am now impressed to fix upon your understandings this simple classification of the two causes of all the states into which the human soul enters. It is proper to divide all these mental conditions into states—

SPONTANEOUS

and

SUPERINDUCED.

Spontaneous psychology is identical with natural mental power; but *superinduced* psychology means mental power as *specifically* and prematurely developed by the *direct action* of individuals or circumstances. The natural relationships, established in nature by these *positive* and *negative* principles, give rise to all natural psychological phenomena. Some things and personalities—and some individuals and some circumstances—are, naturally and constitutionally, *negative* to all corresponding creations and influences which occupy a higher plane in the order of being.

Now, it is undeniable that some peculiarly constituted individuals are constantly psychologically influenced by a class of minds or circumstances, to which other individuals might be almost wholly insensible. This is properly denominated *natural* psychology, which is always contra-distinguishable from the *superinduced* condition, because the latter is accomplished by the voluntary volition of mind. But here let me urge upon you the necessity of not confounding the psychological state with the high magnetic, or clairvoyant, or spiritual states, which will be hereafter examined. I am impressed to regard the psychological condition as the *first remove* of the human mind from its ordinary or rudimental state; therefore, to be estimated as the second degree of mental manifestation, on a numerical scale of seven,—the *last* being, in the harmonial philosophy, always esteemed as the *highest* and most superior development of the system under consideration. Nor must the psychological condition be confounded with the sympathetic state. For the latter condition is distinguished from the former by the elimination of an atmosphere from the mind, which does not occur in the true psychological state. This latter condition is simply the manifestation of the mind, in the exercise of its *positive* and *negative* relationships, without the transmission of any vital or mental fluid to the parts or personalities thus affected.

Every man is psychologically influenced by something. Some minds are constitutionally *positive* to one set of circumstances; and *negative* to another. The *absolute* freedom of the human *will* is, therefore, an impossibility and absurdity. The very fact, that there are some things which man can not subdue and transcend, disproves the doctrine of the absolute freedom of the will, while it unquestionably demonstrates the philosophy of psychological principles. All liberty is comparative—all freedom is unqualifiedly relative and partial. It is necessary to understand, that all manifestations of *positive* and *negative* principles, when considered psychologically, occur according to the law of equilibriums. Any influence, which will disturb the equilibrium of the circulation of man's spiritual or mental principle, is capable of psychologizing the individual, and for just so long a time as the voluntary powers of the mind are unable to assert their supremacy. Thus, for example, in moments of danger, some minds lose what is generally termed "their self-possession" and become frantic with fear. Now, the truth is, they are simply psychologized by fright; and will continue thus affected until the controlling power of the soul resumes its high prerogative, and restores to the mind its proper equilibrium.

This philosophy will urge you to the daily cultivation of the will-power of the mind,—to give you the mastery over the influence of inharmonious individuals and circumstances, which surround you in the world. By the proper and perfect application of this power, the soul *can* and *will* put all enemies under its feet. The startling omnipotence of mind is not yet visible!

Any thing which *can* disturb permanently the harmonious equilibrium of the mind, has the power to take the soul into captivity. On this principle, the mother of Napoleon instilled into his soul, while it was yet unmatured, the spirit of war; consequently, he was powerfully psychologized all his life by the *desire* to combat and conquer. This is what physicians term, in pathology, "hereditary predisposition;" but, in mental science, it should be called "psychological misdirection."

You will doubtless be surprised when I tell you, that mankind have the power to improve the race infinitely; and *all*, by the judicious application of the principles of psychological science to the physical and mental organization of the unborn child. The *catholic* does well in regarding, deferentially and with much reverence, the *mother* of Jesus; though I do not feel impressed to sanction their unnecessary and customary idolatrous adoration of certain departed spirits. But Mary was a gentle woman;—simple-hearted, a good neighbor, and very affectionate. Her husband was a plain, pure, unscientific mechanic. The country was occasionally excited, with anxious anticipations, concerning the coming of a "King of the Jews;" but of the time and parentage no one ventured to speculate. But Mary's soul was very religious in its aspirations. And one night, when nature was wrapped in the folds of silence, and when tranquillity reigned universal, she dreamed, that the Lord of the Hebrew scriptures came to her and said—"A virgin shall conceive and bear a son; his name shall be great in the land of his birth; and thou shalt call him "*Emmanuel*;" for his divine power shall spread from generation to generation, from the east to the west, from sea to sea, and thou wilt be blessed among women."

On the succeeding morning, Mary related her impressive *dream* to Joseph. But as she had long been excited upon religious matters, he did not then give much heed to her impressions. However, the same dream was dreamed three nights in succession by Mary; and now she earnestly, but very privately, BELIEVED IT ALL. Now I am impressed to regard all this as a spiritual impression, imparted to Mary's spirit when she was internally quiet and very impressible. She was a "virgin" in the same sense that all pure and high-minded married men and women are spiritually virtuous; but in no other respect, as claimed by sacred historians.

Now, what conclusions are we to derive from these truthful premises? Why, we are to logically conclude, that Jesus was made a *great moral reformer* strictly in accordance with pure psychological principles. He was born with the constitutional impression of his mother's mental and religious disposition,—and, more especially, with the pre-possession of mind that his "name should be great in the land of his birth," that he was a "king of the Jews," and that "his power should spread from generation to generation," over the earth. *His whole subsequent life was tinted, and, more or less, characterized by the psychological influence which his mother exerted upon him* during the entire period of his utero-gestation and the incipient formation of his individuality.

In this way, we are all, to a greater or lesser extent, constantly psychologically affected. On one occasion, I was visited by a very respectable clergyman of New York, who said the devil tempted him at least once every week to commit suicide. This was proof to his mind that there was in reality a living demon, who exerted himself energetically to destroy both soul and body in hell. I inquired if he was not diseased? He answered, that his "health was perfectly good." But he desired me to make an interior inspection of his condition. I did so. And instantly discovered that his *suicidal temptation* originated from the psychological influence of his mother's spirit, upon his mind, before birth. Of this I immediately informed him. "O yes," said he, "my mother has often told me that 'the devil' tempted her in the same manner." But I was soon enabled to inform him, that his mother's mind was agitated by *a disease of the liver and diaphragm*, which invariably produces mental depression and sadness, under certain conditions; and a tendency to suicide was a common feeling to minds thus affected, especially when associated with small hope and feeble resolution. This explanation was rather *too rational* and unsupernatural for the clergyman, and it overthrew a strong evidence of the devil's existence; and so—"he did n't believe a word of it!"

Many individuals are constantly psychologized by some passion or propensity. Some are actuated and tempted by the *spider-propensity*, which may possibly predominate in their mental structure. Others by the horse, the cat, the dog, the fox, the wolf, the lion, the mule, the swine, &c., &c.,—just as these different propensities happen to preponderate in the mind. Any passion, or propensity, or faculty, which has been, either *before birth or afterward*, allowed to gain the ascendency in the soul, will most certainly disturb the true equilibrium of the mind, and thus make the latter subserve the purposes of its angular and displeasurable manifestation. In this manner, all men are more or less affected. The remedy consists wholly in a true application of the will-power to the harmonization of body and soul,—a psychological subjugation of the discordant elements of the mind—a true pacification of the lion and lamb of the interior man—by the proper exercise of the supreme power of the wisdom principle. It is very essential to understand the invariable *nature* and immutable *value* of positive and negative principles. For the highest welfare of our unborn generations depends very much upon our fidelity to this class of nature's laws. Those religious and psychological influences which acted upon the mother of Jesus, and made him a moral reformer from birth, are identical, in principle, with those conditions which make natural poets, mathematicians, physicians, and philosophers. All this is significant of the power of mind over matter.

Many years ago, in France, a criminal was to be publicly executed upon the wheel. And a mother, whose child was yet unborn, desired to be present. Notwithstanding the strong entreaties of her husband and physicians to the contrary, she yielded to her impulse to witness the execution. The terrible scene completely psychologized her. She stood transfixed. She heard the bones of the poor criminal snap and break on the wheel, like dry sticks in a strong man's hand. It was too horrid; and she sank exhausted, and swooned upon the ground. Ninety days from that time, her child was born, *with every bone of its little body broken and separated in a corresponding manner!*

Ecclesiastical teachers in every country have embraced and inculcated convictions often totally at variance with the Living Revelation of the Divine Will contained in the constitution of the material world, and more particularly as expressed in the organization of man. The facts and laws of science can not be other than the developments of the Great Controlling Soul. Any *faith* antagonistic to such developments and progressive unfoldings, is, according to my impressions, to be rejected as pernicious, and unworthy the attention of intelligent minds. The principles, capabilities, and superior merits of human nature have been too long obscured and unknown. Teachers, who know little of psychological science, will erect the most unwholesome forms of faith, and urge them upon the human mind, forsooth, because they think the natural powers of man are, and always will be, to every individual,—*causâ non cognitâ*,—buried in impregnable mystery. But the laws of psychological science, or at least the *external effects* of their operation upon the unborn, but incipiently developing, child, have been perceived and acknowledged by many eminent physicians. That law which causes national *features* to be transmitted, almost wholly unchanged, for successive centuries, from parents to offspring, is the psychological principle for which I am now contending. In regard to hereditary or psychological transmission, Dr. Caldwell observes: —"Every constitutional quality, whether good or bad, may descend, by inheritance, from parent to child. And a long-continued habit of drunkenness becomes as essentially constitutional, as a predisposition to gout or pulmonary consumption. This increases, in a manifold degree, the responsibility of parents in relation to temperance. By habits of intemperance, they not only degrade and ruin *themselves*, but transmit the elements of like degradation and ruin to their posterity. This is no visionary conjecture, the fruit of a favorite and long-cherished theory. It is a settled belief resulting from observation—an inference derived from innumerable facts. In hundreds and thousands of instances, parents, having had children born to them while their habits were temperate, have become afterward intemperate, and had other children subsequently born. In such cases, it is a matter of notoriety, that the younger children have become addicted to the practice of intoxication much more frequently than the elder—in the proportion of five to one. Let me not be told that this is owing to the younger children being eglected, and having corrupt and seducing examples constantly before them. The same neglects and profligate examples have been extended to all; yet all have not been equally injured by them. The children of the earlier births have escaped, while those of the subsequent ones have suffered. The reason is plain. The latter children had a deeper psychological taint than the former." It was remarked by the celebrated Esquirol, "that the children, whose existence dated from the horrors of the first French Revolution, turned out to be weak, nervous, and irritable in mind, extremely susceptible of impressions, and liable to be thrown by the least extraordinary excitement into absolute insanity."

Now it is distinctly clear to my mind, that the proper application of psychological principles, especially to the unfolding character and constitution of the child, will develop almost any description of soul or intellect which is most desired by the parents. When we shall have harmonized our souls, and thrown open the avenues of our interior natures to the high *positive* and *psychological* influences which descend upon us from higher spheres, then we will realize the holier sympathies of a more exalted race, and feel ourselves more intimately related to that high and pure Divinity which pervades the illimitable universe!

LECTURE VIII.

ON THE RELATIONS AND DEPENDENCIES EXISTING BETWEEN THE BODY AND THE SOUL.

THE human mind has been practically treated by metaphysicians in all ages as a mere abstraction ; as the most impalpable and unreal of things. For long and dark centuries, the leaders of the scientific and religious worlds of thought, have, both in theory and practice, denied the intimate connection which actually exists between physiological and psychological sciences. And yet systems of mental philosophy have abounded,—systems, founded in imagination, not in nature. Theory has succeeded theory like waves of the sea. But the relation between mind and matter is not yet scarcely comprehended.

Forty years ago, a prominent physician was absolutely ridiculed out of practice by his professional brethren, for promulgating the doctrine that insanity is always accompanied with cerebral derangement. And the idea of demoniacal possession is not yet extinguished. We are occasionally challenged from modern pulpits to prove that maniacs are not subjected to satanic influences. The most enlightened sectarians of these times,—the New Jerusalem Churchmen,—boldly state and defend the opinion that delirium tremens conjures up tormenting fiends and chimeras dire from the bottomless pit of burning marl. In some instances, we are soberly warned not to practice the principles of human magnetism, on the ground, that it is identical with the heaven-daring crime for which the guilty, under the old Mosaic law, " died without mercy." But all these obstructions can not impede the rising tide of intelligence. The opposition of priest or physician is as a vapory cloud before the blazing sun. It can no more arrest the progress of psychological science, than a pebble can stay the mighty flowings of the gulf stream. For the world has received a momentum—has an impetus forward—which no conservative or sectarian plans can counteract. No bold and honest mind is now in danger of personal destruction. Liberal thought is generally indulged and tolerated; and the *influence* of medical and psychological reformers, is spreading far and wide through European society.

The very intimate connection between the body and mind is now very generally acknowledged by the enlightened of all professions. But the full extent of this connection, and the highly important results to which it conducts us, is not yet comprehended by scarcely a single individual who is willing to acknowledge "some truth" in the science. The phenomena of human magnetism are mainly admitted by all American minds; but yet they can not believe in the actuality of independent clairvoyance. This is, they think, going a little too far into the mysteries of divinity. They are very apprehensive of its tendencies. They think it encroaches too much upon sacred ground,—ventures too far into the celestial courts,—and searches too deep into the sublimities of Godliness. But this is all very inconsistent. To believe in human magnetism, and to disbelieve clairvoyance, seems to me like believing in the existence of herbs and plants, but that *large trees* are impossible and absurd. For *clairvoyance* succeeds the phenomena of human magnetism as naturally as the blooming harvests succeed the deposition of the little germs. So likewise, the application of psychological principles, to the molding and harmonious elaboration of the human type, is as natural and inevitable as the fine results which flow from a judicious application of agricultural science.

Again, I must urge the idea, that Man is a production of nature; that he is a result of the stupendous mechanism of all the forms, motions, and forces which *adorn* the visible world. He comes forth as the crowning result of immutable principles! These principles are the *methods* in accordance with which the Deity lives and acts. They express His nature, His actions, His omnipotence, and His immutability. God is, therefore, a being of absolute unchangeableness. And his divine essence penetrates every thing, and imparts to every thing *light* and *life*, which are the expressions of *love;* and *order* and *form*, which are the expressions of *wisdom*. And *man* is the grand consummation of these divine attributes. He can not be depraved; for he came forth from the fertile womb of nature, a child of God! He can not be interiorly contaminated, because God is over all and *in all* things—He is all in all! And man must search and explore forever! To his progress and development there is no limitation—no conceivable boundaries. And the Infinite Father is not jealous lest his earth-born children should approach too close to the majesty of His own unutterable omniscience and omnipotence. In no part of the boundless domain of the universe, upon which man enters, is he treated as an intruder on Jehovah's secret possessions. Nay: for the multifarious elements of physical and mental nature,—extending far down into the bottomless abysses of the material universe, and reaching upward through a galaxy of angelic spheres to the soul of Deity,—are all thrown open to man's inspection and eternal progress! There is nothing too sacred for human investigation. An angel's clairvoyance sees more of truth than we can imagine. Yet there is nothing too holy for the immortal soul to investigate.

While, to thousands of minds, the *thunder* was God's voice speaking in sublime accents to rebellious mortals—while the *lightnings* gleamed in vengeance from his invisible hand—and while earth and heaven were filled with portentous signs and startling wonders—earthquakes, meteoric showers, and blazing comets—I say, while thousands were thus overwhelmed by these manifestations, and dared not even erect a lightning-rod to conduct away the frantic elements, the venturous Franklin calmly investigated these terrestial phenomena, and extracted from the clouds the high knowledge that the electric fire can be rendered subservient to the *will*, purposes, and improvements of man! God desires his children to become enlightened and happy; for what pleasure even can a good earthly parent experience in the ignorance and unhappiness of his child? If the prying investigations of men required a rebuke, why was the world not taught a lesson, once for all, on the head of that rash experimenter, who, while heaven's artillery blazed and roared above him, first snatched the fiery *bolt*, all sparkling from its lofty forge? Instead of being blasted for thus obtaining his fearful prize, the author of this *promethean feat* is honored with immortal renown! Thus progression is encouraged.

Man may fearlessly examine all things; and the more he grows in wisdom, the happier will he become. Physically and spiritually, he issues from the magnificent organism of nature, and thus stands as the *crowning* development of immutable principles. But matter is the servant of mind,—the latter can *mold* the former as easily as the potter *shapes* and *fashions* the moistened clay! But this can be accomplished only by a requisite amount of knowledge; this is power. By this knowledge and power, the soul can apply the teachings of psychological principles to the harmonious development of the unborn organism, and the earth might be peopled with well-proportioned and happy beings. Let me urge you to ponder these truths; for the reformation of the world depends, to a very great extent, upon the physical and mental *capital* which an individual inherits from his immediate progenitors. This is true: because the infant organism is in existence before the young mind begins to think and act for itself. Hence the *defects of birth* are difficult to set aside *by subsequent education.* This fact we should well consider, *because* it lies at the very foundation of individual and social reformation. With this knowledge in our possession, it is very unjust to sanction improper alliances between the sexes; exceedingly wrong to bring into existence unsound and unwholesome children! How many regret the hereditary defects of their natures! How many feel discomforted by irregular features, or deranged organizations! All this, and much more, can be prevented by the proper employment of psychological science. Men are *innately* inspired with *a love of the beautiful* and harmonious. And I am impressed to consider it altogether the result of *ignorance* and injustice, that all men and women are not endowed from birth with the physical harmony and spiritual beauty of angels. The spirit of *Venus* and *Apollo* might be impressed upon every child; and all unseeming *defects* of the physical organism be easily eradicated. The human mind, when considered in its twofold capacity, is very powerful. As a motive-power, it can *shape* the physical world, and all the external circumstances thereof, to favor the proper development of the human character. As a moral-power, it can ascertain the moral laws; and man's highest moral beauty can be transferred to unborn generations.

I do not believe *that God makes every human being*, any more than he makes every particular vegetable that adorns our gardens. Nay; but I am most emphatically impressed to tell you, that man absolutely *manufactures* his type, according to the immutable principles of reproduction; but always *perfect* or *imperfect* as he maintains himself in harmony with nature's laws, which are the will of Deity. And thousands are *defrauded* out of a large proportion of mundane enjoyment by the imperfections of their organisms! Hereditary defects have made poets and pirates; fools and philosophers; moral men and maniacs; and hundreds are all their lifetimes subject to bondage and sadness; because the *mirror*, or the *sun*, reveals to them the horrors of their organic deformity. Their love of beauty is momentarily offended; and they grow to dislike themselves, and soon their fellow-men.

How philosophically William Shakspeare gave this lamentable truth an utterance through the mouth of Richard the Third:—

> "But I,—that am not shaped for sportive tricks,
> Nor made to court an amorous looking-glass;
> I, that am rudely stamp'd, and want love's majesty,
> To strut before a wanton ambling nymph;
> I, that am curtail'd of this fair proportion,
> *Cheated* of feature by dissembling nature,
> Deform'd, unfinish'd, sent before my time
> Into this breathing world, half made up,
> And that so lamely and unfashionable,
> That dogs bark at me, as I halt by them."

Here Richard sarcastically complains that he has no—

> "Delight to pass away the time,
> Unless to spy my shadow in the sun,
> And descant on mine own deformity."

Then he makes up his mind that he *did not merit* all this personal ugliness, and hence takes the position, which many individuals assume in their ignorance, that sin is productive of pleasure; and says:—

> "Therefore,—since I can not prove a lover,
> I am determin'd to prove a villain,
> And hate the idle pleasures of these days."

Now, this is all wrong! It is a *result* of no Adamic curse; it is an *issue* of no innate depravity; but it comes forth as a living demonstration of the startling fact, that the psychological principles of nature, are wofully misapplied to the production and development of our species. "A very intelligent and respectable mother," says a well-known author, "upon hearing these principles expounded, remarked that there was a very wide difference in the intellectual and moral development between one of her children and the others; and accounted for this difference by the fact, that, during pregnancy, she received intelligence that the crew of the ship on board of which was her son, had mutinied,—that when the ship arrived in the West Indies, some of the mutineers, and also her son, had been put in irons,—and that they were all to be sent home for trial. This intelligence acted so strongly upon her, that she suffered a temporary alienation of judgment. The report turned out to be erroneous, but this did not avert the consequences of the agitated state of the mother's feelings upon the daughter she afterward gave birth to. That daughter is now a woman, but she is and will continue to be a being of impulses, incapable of reflection, and in other respects greatly inferior to her sisters."

It is surely very unjust to bring personalities "half made up" into this breathing world; and, then, teach them that they are perfectly free moral agents! What an unphilosophical thought: to teach the world that God is the creator of every man that lives; while, at the same time, many are sent—unconsulted, unasked, without having the privilege to decide upon such an adventure in advance—sent into this *conflicting*, *uncertain*, *probationary existence*—"deformed, unfinished," and curtailed of that "fair proportion" which constitutes a beautiful exterior, adapted to the production and entertainment of a sound and healthy mind! Most emphatically, I am impressed to affirm all this to be the doctrine of Ignorance and Error.

That the body and mind are closely allied in structure and essence can not truthfully be denied. And it is equally undeniable, that the *internal principle* is, in a certain sense, perfectly material; and is susceptible to as much material *action* and impression as any other organism in nature. But this is all accomplished according to the positive and negative relations or operation of psychological principles. Before I leave this branch of mental science, let me present a few more illustrations of this proposition. I have said that the human mind was essentially material, and susceptible to the chemical or psychological action of material substances ; that is to say, the *spirit* of a medicine acts upon the spirit of man in accordance with positive and negative principles. For example: iodine induces sadness; gold generates or excites hope; arsenic causes melancholy; carbonic acid gas begets mental tranquillity; empyreumatic oils generate peevishness and morbid sensibility; belladonna stultifies the intellectual faculties; canabis produces quietness; opium and tobacco stimulate the sexual propensities, excite the intellectual powers, and generate unhealthy imaginations; cicuta deadens the intellect; and hyoscyamus causes violence, moroseness, and jealousy.

These chemical agents *will not always* produce the effects here described; because the *mind may be positive to them*,—in which case their *action* will be very slight, and, perhaps, altogether imperceptible. But the simple fact, that the equilibrium of the spiritual principle *can be* thus disturbed, and the mind thus taken into captivity by *narcotics and stimulants*, is sufficient to demonstrate the materiality of the spirit, and also its unconditional dependence upon the many agents which move the vast panorama of the external world. In truth, I may say that we have an *ocular demonstration* of the materiality of the mind, and also of its natural psychological principles of action and power of daguerreotyping, in the "marks" upon children; indicating the fact, that the mind receives and transfers shapes and colors with the utmost accuracy,—as the *form* and *color* of any fruit, animal, or thing, which made an impression on the mind of the mother, in accordance with psychological principles.

This is an immutable law of nature ; and is conspicuously operative in her every department. It is the same harmonious law in the kingdoms beneath, as it is in the spheres above, our present existence. For instance, it is related in the New York Sun, April 14, 1843, that a *hen*, belonging to Benjamin Gallaway, of Weakley

County, Tennessee, was severely bitten by a rattlesnake, but, by proper attention, the wound was perfectly cured. Nevertheless, strange to tell, *every* egg laid after that time by this hen, had a complete picture of a rattlesnake represented upon the shell! Now in harmony with this principle, every human being, that comes into this world, is impressed with certain peculiarities and constitutional tendencies. An instance is related, by Dr. Howship, of a woman who was crossing a frozen river, in a state of pregnancy. But the ice *cracked* and *burst open*, and she was terribly frightened. When the child was born, its skin was *opened* and *cracked* considerably in several places, and in a corresponding manner.

Let your understandings be thoroughly impressed, therefore, with this conviction—that, that principle of psychological action, which will, when inverted and misapplied, produce a human fiend or a human monster, is equally capable, when rightly understood and philosophically directed, of developing heroes, poets, saviors, metaphysicians, philosophers, and reformers. Physicians and agriculturists have been gradually coming to the discovery and application of this principle in the lower departments of Nature. Combe, that clear-minded author, has brought out many details on this head. "In cases of varieties of the same species," says Dr. Edwards, "we see one common principle, namely, that the mother often produces a being of a type different from her own—less so, however, in the latter case. This principle is seen even in the same variety; for here also the mother, in producing a male, gives birth to a being whose type differs, and in some cases differs very much, from her own. Now, says Dr. E., the same is observed in man. The varieties which differ most strongly, such as the negro and white, when crossed, produce mulattoes; and when varieties more nearly resembling each other are crossed, the descendants sometimes resemble one parent, sometimes the other, sometimes both. This, Dr. Edwards looks upon as the cause of the great variety observable in modern nations; among which, however, he thinks we can always observe specimens of the pure types which have entered into their composition. Every one knows that the hen of any bird will lay eggs, although no male be permitted to come near her; and that those eggs are only wanting in the vital principle which the impregnation of the male conveys to them. Here, then, we see the female able to make an egg, with yelk and white, shell and every part, just as it ought to be, so that we might, at the first glance, suppose that here, at all events, the female has the greatest influence."

I am impressed to assure you, most deeply and religiously, that the proper application of psychological principles, to the generation and improvement of the human species, will accomplish more good for the great mass of mankind than *all* the preaching and praying that ever fell from the human tongue! Let all this fable about the "original sin," the "first curse," the "efforts of satan," the "total depravity" of the human heart, *be forever buried* in the tombs of ignorance and error; and let there be a *universal resurrection* and *development of reason and philosophy*, which shall, most harmoniously and inevitably, improve the individual and elevate the human race generally to health, harmony, and to fair proportions!

LECTURE IX.

CONCERNING THE PSYCHOLOGICAL ACTION OF THE MIND UPON THE BODY IN DISEASE.

On this occasion, I will proceed to consider and explain how natural psychology operates and is exhibited in disease.

Every well-informed individual is familiar with the influence of the mind upon the body. When the Asiatic Cholera prevails in a community, how common a thing it is to see impressible persons psychologized by the epidemic. I am keeping within the bounds of truth, when I say, that one half of the victims of that paroxysmal disorder, die solely in consequence of being psychologically captured by fear and fright. The *fear*, of getting the complaint, disturbs the proper equilibrium of the mind; and thus an avenue is thrown wide open to the admission and possession of the enemy. When this epidemic prevailed in New York, I had a patient who expected every next hour to have the "agonies of the disease" upon him. I admonished him not to read the coroner's daily reports of the number of victims. He said: "it was next to impossible for him to resist the temptation to notice the various publications concerning the complaint," and yet he confessed that, "every time he read the reports he felt that he had actually swallowed the disorder," so *piristalitic* were the motions which the *fear* communicated to his dependent viscera. This man was ultimately obliged to leave the city in order to preserve his mental equilibrium and escape the disease.

A good illustration of this psychological action of mind upon the body, was originally published in the Zoonomia, and was subsequently attested by the poet Wordsworth: A young farmer in Warwickshire, England, finding his hedges broken, and the sticks carried away during a frosty season, determined to watch for the thief. He lay many cold hours under a hay-stack, and, at length, an old woman, like the witch in a play, approached, and began to pull up the hedge. He waited till she had tied her bundle of sticks, and was carrying them off, that he might convict her of theft; and then springing from his concealment, he seized his prey with violent threats. After some altercation, in which her load was left upon the ground, she *kneeled* upon the bundle of sticks, and raising her hands to heaven, beneath the bright moon, then at full, spoke to the young farmer, already shivering with cold,—"*Heaven grant that thou mayst never know again the blessing to be warm.*" The psychological effect produced upon his mind *was so distinct and powerful*, that he complained of cold all the next day, and wore an overcoat, and, in a few days, another; and, in a fortnight, he took to his bed, always saying *nothing made him warm;* he covered himself with many blankets, and had a *sieve* over his face as he lay. From the effect of this one *insane idea*, or psychological impression, this man kept his bed above twenty years, for *fear* of the cold air, till at length he died.

All psychological phenomena, be it remembered, are naturally confined to the common plane of *positive* and *negative* manifestations; for when higher results are produced, they are invariably developed on the higher planes of mental science, which I will consider on future occasions.

In psychology, any thing, I repeat,—every element, person, or substance,—which disturbs the equilibrium of the mental constitution, is capable, for the time being, of capturing the mind, and controlling its thoughts and impressions. Thus,—when disease has obtained a preponderance of power in the system, the *mind* is disturbed by the deranged psychological impressions which are conducted to the sensorium. According to this philosophy, *dreaming*, as a precursor and accompaniment of diseases, deserves continued investigation. Not because (says Dr. Winslow) it is to be considered as a spiritual divination, but because the unconscious language often very clearly shows, to those who can comprehend its meaning, the physical state of the patient. *Lively dreams* are, according to psychological science, in general *a sign* of the attenuated excitement of the nervous action. *Soft dreams* are a sign of slight cerebral irritation; these vaporish dreams also often denote a favorable *crisis* in nervous fevers. *Frightful dreams*,—wars and combats,—are *a sign* of a determination of arterial blood to the head. *Dreams* about blood and red objects,—houses and ships on fire,—imps, demons, &c.,—are signs of *an inflammatory* condition of the semi-intellectual and perceptive faculties of the cerebrum. *Dreams* about rain and water,—floods, deluges, &c.,—are often signs of diseased mucous membranes and dropsy. *Dreams*, in which the person sees any portion of his own body, especially in a suffering state, indicate disease and disturbance in that portion. As, for instance, when the mind *dreams* of seeing food,—rich viands, a feast, &c.,—the *cause* of the dreaming is generally traceable to the *digestive functions* of the physical system, which are evidently impaired.

It is deemed expedient to remind you, that I am not, by this explanation of a certain class of dreams, giving a solution of all mental phenomena of this nature. On the contrary, there are *two classes* of dreams originating in a very different manner; which will be duly examined and explained in subsequent lectures. But here, let it be understood, I am treating of the natural psychological science of man, which differs from the science of sympathy, somnambulism, clairvoyance, mental illumination, in this particular respect:—that psychology treats exclusively of the native positive and negative relationships of things, and explains how naturally equilibriums may be and are disturbed without the impartation of any sphere, fluid, or cerebral element, which occurs in the superior phases of this high theme as will be hereafter shown.

From what has been said on the subject, you will readily perceive, that the *mind* is frequently taken into psychological *captivity* by the physical organism. This is especially the case in delirium tremens. The convolving clouds of the inflamed blood which loads the entire encephalon, fill the room with dissolving masses of fire; interwoven with which are the imps, serpents, and demons of the inflamed memory, which has entertained these fabulous beings from the *first* impressions of youth; the nursery tales written by Christian poets and oriental romancers.

When the mind is agitated by *fear* of receiving any disease, that moment the body is susceptible to the invasion of the enemy. Some minds get panic-struck—that is, psychologized—by the apprehension of having an attack of *cholera*, *plague*, *small pox*, *yellow fever*, &c., and the consequence is, that, in *five* cases out of ten, the individual is eventually captured with the disorder *most* dreaded, or by some disease very analogous. The constant fear of heart-disease, of consumption, or of cancer, is very likely to induce the very complaint which is feared. I have seen this truth verified in several instances. The *body*, therefore, is first permitted to *take the mind* into psychological bondage or captivity; then, the *mind* induces upon the corporeal organism *any disease* with which the controlling principle is most deeply impressed. This points us to an important truth. For we have seen that the same principle of psychology which will, when *misapplied* to the generation of the human species, give rise to human monsters and horrid deformities, is also capable, when *properly* applied to the same purpose, of producing the very Magnus Apollo of human grace and beauty! Even so, after the individual is introduced into being, the same psychological principles which can, when *wrongly* exercised, cause disease, are perfectly adequate, when *rightly* employed, to *cure* the same disease and to effectually *prevent* it. Let us now examine this point. Let us inquire—What is disease?

Disease is a want of *equilibrium in the circulation* of the spiritual principle; hence, also, *a derangement in the motions* of the dependent fluids and forces.

What keeps the body alive?

The spiritual principle.

What is the *governing power* of this principle?

WISDOM.

What agent does wisdom employ in maintaining and executing its government?

WILL.

What does the will act upon?

Upon LOVE.

What is Love?

Love is *the life* of the body and mind.

Is love the actuating and enlivening element of the whole individualism?

It is.

Is love the finest and purest ingredient of the mental organism?

Yes, love is the very essence of the life of the mind.

What, then, is wisdom?

Wisdom is, to use a figurative expression, the *form or flower* of Love,—the *head* of the spiritual constitution.

Can love come in immediate contact with the elements of the blood?

Nay.

Why not?

Because the Love essence is many millions of millions of degrees finer than the constituents of the blood.

How, then, can the material and the spiritual bodies be so closely inwrought—one, in and through the other?

By the fine cement of interposing or mediatorial agents.

Can the wisdom-power act upon the blood and the bone?

Yes; with great force.

Does wisdom act thus through intermediate elements?

Yes.

Suppose the wisdom-principle desires to operate upon the bone, how could the operation be accomplished?

The wisdom-power would act upon *will;* this upon *love;* this upon the *vital magnetism;* this upon the *vital electricity;* this upon the *nerve;* this upon the *muscle;* and this upon the *bone!*

If all these processes occurred at every instigation of the wisdom-principle, would there not be a perceptible difference or lapse of time between the effort and the result?

Nay; because even common electricity can encircle the globe in an instant.

How can the principle of wisdom prevent all diseases?

In the first place, by arranging all *foods, habits, occupations, situations,* and *sentiments* into such harmony as will not improperly tax the strength and energies of the physical and mental constitution. In the second place, by feeling *superior* to the invasions of disease—by feeling the entire individualism to be *impregnable* to any such unnecessary molestations; for, generally speaking, "as a man thinketh so is he."

I come now to consider the relation of natural psychology to the mind, irrespective of its connection with the body.

This phase of psychological science is manifested in wars, panics, insanities, and sympathetic contagions. This is not accomplished by the elimination of an atmosphere from one mind, which is inhaled by another; but by the configurations of the countenance, by the flashing and sparkling eye, by the up-turned head, and lofty gesticulations,—all of which excite to intense corresponding action every impressible mind which is either *negative* or *passive* to the disturbing causes. Every religious *faith* known in the world has begun and spread, like an epidemic, as far as the ignorance and superstition of the people, by rendering them *negative* to it, would permit it to capture their minds. Let it be remembered, that knowledge is power; that ignorance is weakness; and that we are mentally *positive* or *negative* to prevailing faiths and excitements, just in proportion to the actual growth of the soul in wisdom and knowledge.

One mind will be frantically conducted by a methodistical panic to the altar; another will be totally unmoved by the sympathetic contagion. All this is mainly produced in accordance with the *ignorance* or *knowledge* of the two individuals. The exceptions to this rule occur, whenever the mind is *captured*, and taken *into psychological bondage*, during moments or periods of *the passivity* of the wisdom or governing principle. Thus, we are sometimes astonished, that our very intelligent neighbor should be "carried away" with some popular excitement.

How common a thing it is, to see a large party convulsed with ungovernable laughter, when only one or two of the whole company can tell "what there is to laugh at." But should there be a person in that assembly, the equilibrium of whose mind is not disturbed by the mirthful sounds and sights before him, he will remain sober and solemnly unmoved. In a word, whatever will *epidemically* spread from mind to mind, according to psychological principles, may *philosophically* explain the prevalence of many *crimes*, and certain forms of mental hallucinations, which have, from time to time disturbed and distressed the human family. Sometimes a terrible crime is committed; and then, by a psychological contagion, its flagrancy excites a kindred predisposition in another mind, and in another, and so on, until *many crimes* of the same magnitude follow each other in rapid succession.

Natural psychology is frequently manifested upon large assemblies. A word or a gesture from one individual disturbs the equilibrium of the whole. In this way, mobs are excited and aggravated to ungovernable fury; and soldiers, in the day of battle, rush on in the face of death; or, panic-struck, the *fear* spreads from one to thousands; and those who but a few moments before, were ready to "seek the bubbled reputation even at the cannon's mouth," are now trembling with fright, and find it impossible to summon either courage or self-possession. At other times, a *word* or a *look* from *some master-spirit*, instantly *psychologizes* the mass around him, and from one to another the *impulse* communicates a feeling of *heroism* and intrepidity, which increases as it spreads, till the entire mass are impatient to throw their lives away in the whirlwind of their vaulting ambition.

One of the greatest psychological excitements ever developed in Christendom, was that produced by the Crusades; and this entire epidemic originated with *one individual*. Peter the Hermit, during the pontificate of Pope Urban II., traveled all over Europe, describing the *indignities* practiced by the Turks, in Palestine, on believers, and calling on *Christians* every where to *rally* around the standard he had raised for the rescue of the *Holy Land* from the infidels. So humble was Peter's demeanor—so saintly his appearance, and so vehement his eloquence—that he gathered, in accordance with the principles of psychological instigation, an army of sixty thousand men, with whom he marched to Jerusalem; in this manner he kindled throughout Europe that ardent spirit of war and conquest, which, for ages, found busy employment in the crusades against the infidels.

In his ignorance of science, man refers many religious excitements and conversions to the power of God, and many crimes and heinous offenses to the influence of satan, while, in fact, the causes are wholly and unqualifiedly referable to the operation of psychological principles. And here we find a valuable truth—a high and noble power! The myriad suns and planets revolve harmoniously, upon these *positive* and *negative* relations. According to them, the Deity *lives* and *acts* in his magnificent temple. The *knowledge* of the existence of this *law* and *power*, adds very much to our ability to overcome *all physical*, *social*, and *mental* enemies—to banish the causes of terrestrial discords and diseases.

The incoming of this century was signalized by the introduction of a new influence into Christendom; the spirit of reformation. At first, it advanced like the beginning ripples of an ocean storm. But, anon, the billows rose high in their mighty strength, and cast their glittering spray far over the granite sides of monarchial Europe! And avenues, where the purifying element had never flowed before, are now being cleansed by the rising tide of reformation. By the gradual ascension of this onward tide, you will see Lapland's "eternal snows" melt into means of cultivation, and miasmatic climes will give sweet encouragement to the growth of perennial flowers. And it has been shown that what *is possible* in the physical world is equally possible in the world of morals. By the immutable action of his psychological principles of omnipotence, the Deity fills the world with *life*, which is LOVE, and with *order*, which is WISDOM. And with the mighty spirit of reformation, the human heart begins to throb most musically every where. But let us apply rightly the high powers of our mental constitution. It should be constantly remembered, that all "*sin*," and "*error*," and "*unhappiness*" are demonstrative *evidences* that a misdirection or misapplication of good persons or principles exists some where in the world. I am deeply impressed that every individual should learn *rightly* to employ the psychological powers of his own mind. The same power which produced the thirty years' war, is capable of producing as many years of peace. The same law of sympathetic contagion, by which one individual commits a crime and *thereby* psychologically *excites* a corresponding propensity in other minds, is *identical* with that *divine influence* by which many minds may be advanced to *virtue* and inward peacefulness. Every one of you, brethren, are endowed, naturally and constitutionally, with this psychological power; but in different degrees. And to exercise it is the high prerogative of your being.

> "When each fulfills a wise design,
> In his own orbit he will shine."

Like the rushing flame on the burning prairie, the fire of harmonial reformation will spread from village to village, from city to city, from hemisphere to hemisphere; and the ennobling principles which now flash upon us from the effulgent spheres on high, shall be communicated, with *all the sweet contagion* of a psychological sympathy, to every human heart! You should be distinguished from the world's inhabitants,—by your nobility: by your happiness: by your brotherly love: by your superior offspring: by your high intelligence, and eloquence, and *psychological power*,—by ALL, in a word, which distinguishes the kingdom of heaven from the discords of earth.

LECTURE X.

ON THE PHILOSOPHY AND OUTER MANIFESTATIONS OF A UNIVERSAL SYMPATHY.

THE lecture this evening is concerning man in the *sympathetic state;* but I will first, as preliminary, proceed to explain to your minds *the* FOUNDATION *of sympathy in nature*, which will form the most of what I shall say on this occasion.

The human mind is a beautiful combination of substantial and immortal principles; it is the organization of essential realities,—a unitary development of the most interior essences of all external forms and visible substances. Hence the mind is the most practical and actual agent in nature; and every thing in existence sustains to it a relationship, more or less remote, or a sympathy of greater or lesser intensity and power. So real and practical is the mind, in its principles, that it can neither inhale nor emit any absolute falsehood, replete with spurious imaginations; for its every breath is loaded with similes, substances, and correspondences, which bear some distinct friendship for all the living truths in nature. Thus: every romance derives its inward vitality from the hiding-places of humanity; and every so-called fiction is but a novel arrangement of actual occurrences and scenery. The *facts* of our common nature are sometimes *too* roughly hewn for finely strung temperaments; consequently, such minds will frequently decorate them with a youthful and spiritual tapestry. Many splendid thoughts and facts of science, are thus darkly concealed beneath the fable's livery. The mystic garments of mythology infold innumerable forms of truth; and the wildest fancy that ever floated along the broad horizon of human speculation, may safely claim a *relationship*, more or less intimate, with the common developments of modern times. Hence I am impressed to affirm, that every scheme of thought,—every surmise and vaticination of the human mind,—is entitled to a certain amount of deference; for there is, properly speaking, no system without valuable suggestion,—no theories or philosophies without some important essence of vitality.

Men throw fancy or drapery around facts, only because the wisdom-principle of the mind is unbalanced or undeveloped. To the spiritually minded, all realities are clothed in a glowing divinity; every-day occurrences are miraculous. To the truly wise, there is *no* poetry, *no* fable, *no* romance which is so beautiful and so inspiring as a simple fact in nature. To such a mind, the rose needs no additional hue; the sun no brighter rays; the rainbow no more vivid tints; nor the violet a sweeter fragrance; but the softest luxuriance of an omnipresent divinity radiates from the blade of grass, the stones, and peaceful trees, which dress the landscapes that spread out in endless perspective before the vision.

But he whose mind is not sufficiently unfolded to see, as he walks, the perpetual breathings of the living divinity,—the spirit of God emanating from the forms and objects around him,—is very often tempted to convert the substance of a fact into the structure of a gaudy fable; so that many truths may walk abroad under the strange disguise of romance,—and a fictitious dress may be worn by our most familiar thoughts. Yet there is some substantial vitality in every theory or speculation that ever emanated from the human mind. The constitution of the soul will not *permit* it to generate unmingled or unmixed error. There must be something *actual* and *practical* in its most extravagant imaginations. The Persianic cosmogony,—or world-building philosophy,—to be found in the first chapters of our Bible,—is not without certain tints and relationships to truth. Mythology has some true theology in it; alchemy has a chemical basis; and astrology depends very much upon mathematical and astronomical science. Plato says,—"Poetry comes nearer to vital truth than history." The mythological drapery which man has gradually thrown around truth, in consequence of not recognizing the intrinsic beauty of her realities, he as gradually unwinds as he unfolds himself in wisdom. So that, when men shall have grown to be wise, you will see the deformities, cumbrous shapes, complicated envelopments, mazy ambiguities, and oracular sophistries with which *facts* and realities have been for long centuries invested, all carefully unrolled and removed, and TRUTH will be seen in her native simplicity and beauty, which are the foundation of her mighty power and colossal magnificence! You may prepare yourselves, therefore, to behold your most cherished theologies dismantled; your serious or sacred errors freely and fairly exposed; your traditionary religions and dogmas divested of their *oriental* costume; your supernaturalism and miracles reduced to natural occurrences; and your long fostered and cherished superstitions weighed, analyzed, and cleansed of all their noxious connections.

If all human thoughts and speculations were properly divested of the artificial clothing in which they are enveloped—all, in consequence of man's undeveloped state of mind,—we would each recognize a certain friendship to their inward properties: a *sympathy* for the little germs of truth which those thoughts and speculations embosom. Let the civilization of an analytical and harmonial philosophy be duly spread abroad—rendering *men* and *things* altogether natural, wise, and spiritual—and, I can assure you, the superficial, the partial, the incomplete, and the disagreeable of the outer world will rapidly disappear. Let this spirit be introduced into the soul of the multitudes, and all disagreeable appearances—says a writer—swine, spiders, snakes, pests, madhouses, prisons, enemies—will vanish; they are temporary and shall be seen no more. The sordor and filths of earth, the sun shall dry up and the wind exhale. As, when the summer comes from the south, the snow-banks melt, and the face of the earth becomes green before it; so shall the advancing spirit create its ornaments along its path, and carry with it the beauty it visits, and the song which enchants it; it shall draw beautiful faces, and warm hearts, and wise discourse, and heroic acts, around its way, until evil and deformity are no more seen. In all this, I am consciously impressed that I am drawing a picture of man's future on earth; a period when all men will be seers and discerners of the hidden and the beautiful. Every thing, in that era, will possess interest and truth; and will be interrogated as capable of yielding a clear and useful reply. Deformity in all things—in art, religion, and morals—will disappear in proportion to the progressive refinement and harmony of the human mind. This result is mathematically certain.

The whole empire or temple of creation seems, to the undeveloped mind, to lack congruity, and lies broken into fragments,—its pillars support no weight; its doors open upon nothing; its foundations are buried in the depths of darkness; and its turrets run far up and are lost in immensity—all, because the man, who thus contemplates nature, *is disunited within himself*. To him, creation is one vast battle-field,—the master-spirit being the enemy of man; where sympathies are at war with antipathies; where evil spirits and good spirits are contending for the highest throne; where the flowers, and birds, and trees, and streams of nature are unentertaining and almost inanimate. He sees no universal law of sympathy; no unity in the constructions of nature; he is, as it were, without God and hope in the world. In the church, of such a man it would be said, that he had not experienced the "new birth." But true philosophy would regard him as an undeveloped mind—one, in which *wisdom* had neither put forth its petals, nor ripened, nor bloomed; though he may have a large capital of book-learning and of traditionary knowledge in his possession. But Wisdom is the heart's prime minister—the *flower* of the inward consciousness; and, when it looks abroad, it reads the radiant lessons of harmony, as first they were written on the face of nature, by the living Divinity.

> "There 's not the smallest orb that thou beholdest,
> But in its motion like an angel sings."

The true artist sees harmony and unutterable beauty in the forms and colors of nature; but the superficial man, seeing neither, as they are, throws into his composition an unnatural congruity and tints it with the grotesque colors of his own inharmonious thoughts. So a man's theology is the legitimate offspring of his own mental state. His religion will be *savage*, *barbarian*, *patriarchal*, *semi-patriarchal*, *civilized*, *republican*, or *spiritual*, according to his outer education and intrinsic growth of soul. If the mind is well educated in wisdom, if its deepest affections are attuned to the sweet devotion of a universal religion in nature, then it will feel itself *related* to every thing great and small, terrestrial or celestial —to every *fact* of science, every head and heart, to every mountain stratum, every thought and feeling, every blade of grass, every stone and bird, every law of color, and to all forms of flowers, animals, and shells even, which make up the sum of existence.

It is highly essential to our happiness and development, that we allow our souls to grow into the religion of a universal sympathy. In truth, the proper understanding of any subject depends, to a certain extent, upon the true appreciation of this law of immutable relationships. It would seem that all the sweet thoughts and devotional hymns ever entertained or uttered since the meditations of Zolena, flowed through the affections and understanding of

George Herbert, the poet of the seventeenth century, in his poem on Man. In this place, I am impressed to introduce his view of nature:—

" Man is full of symmetry,
Full of proportions, one limb to another,
And to all the world besides.
Each part may call the fartherest, brother;
For head with foot hath private amity,
And both with moods and tides.

" Nothing hath gone so far
But man hath caught and kept it as his prey;
His eyes dismount the highest star;
He is in little all the sphere.
Herbs gladly cure our flesh, because that they
Find their acquaintance there.

" For us, the winds do blow,
The earth doth rest, heaven move, and fountains flow,
Nothing we see, but means our good,
As our delight, or as our treasure;
The whole is either our cupboard of food,
Or cabinet of pleasure.

" The stars lead us to bed:
Night draws the curtain; which the sun withdraws.
Music and light attend our head.
All things unto our *flesh* are kind,
In their descent and being; to our *mind*,
In their ascent and cause.

" More servants wait on man
Than he 'll take notice of; in every path
He treads down that which doth befriend him
When sickness makes him pale and wan.
O mighty love! Man is one world, and hath
Another to attend him."

The philosophy of sympathy is the tracing out of universal relationships to their sources. The seal of these natural and infinite friendships, is Deity. His celestial essence flows, fresh from the chambers of his innermost heart, through the myriad veins and veinlets which form the illimitable net-work of nature's great nervous system. And every thing receives some assurance of life from that exhaustless fountain. Hence the divine essence is in every thing to a greater or less degree; and the foundation of a universal sympathy is the universal recognition and reciprocation of this supercelestial principle.

When the human soul has unfolded the finer elements of its constitution, and *feels*—as a matter of *intuitional* consciousness—this *great law* of sympathetic impregnation, whereby the Deity enlivens his spacious edifice and renders every *atom* an indispensable ingredient in the one stupendous brotherhood of cause and effect,—then that mind has passed the ordeal of a "new birth," has passed from death unto life, and its religion will inevitably be universal justice and love. But such a growth of soul is the work of steady progression. It must commence with the individual and expand to the whole.

In the first lecture of this course, I was impressed to present the proposition, that all external effects must of necessity be the outbirths of internal principles; that all outer manifestations are the ultimate results of the operations of invisible causes. This simple proposition lies close to the philosophy of sympathy, which I am now investigating. Indeed, a right comprehension of any subject depends very much upon a prior understanding of the foregoing proposition. I have said that the Seal of this universal law of sympathy, IS DEITY. But we should now proceed to examine the foundations of the innumerable particular *sympathies*, *antipathies*, or *relationships*, as these effects are exhibited in the subordinate departments of nature. In the first place it is essential to constantly bear in mind, that all the external phenomena of psychological principles are reproduced in the sympathetic state with the important addition of several higher manifestations, natural to the human mind.

In order to bring this subject properly before your minds, I will detail the impressions which I received on first viewing the surface of the earth with the powers of spiritual perception. The philosophy of this mode of interior observation will be duly explained in future lectures. The following is a brief sketch :

By placing myself in proper relations to the operator by turning my thoughts inwardly, and shutting out of mind, by the exercise of will, the fleeting disturbances and interruptions of the outer world, I passed readily into the high magnetic condition. This occurred on the evening of the first of January, in the year 1843. At that time, and for a period of four years subsequently, I could not recall to my mind, when *out* of this condition, any thing which I had seen or said while *in* it. But, now, the vast scenes break upon my memory in all the *vividness* and *beauty* with which they were originally invested and impressed upon me. And I doubt not, I should more frequently refer to them as illustrations, were it not that I can now view, with far more certainty and with deeper satisfaction, the same fields of contemplation in connection with higher planes of existence and thought.

When I seated myself in a chair, facing the operator, I observed a few individuals in the room ; but had not at the time the least idea of having any thing resembling a successful experiment performed upon me. I knew then but very little of human *magnetism*, having simply heard the term used a few times, but had not learned of the wonderful phenomenon of clairvoyance, or second sight, and hence did not entertain the remotest conception of such a psychological condition. Nevertheless, the magnetic state was completely induced in thirty minutes ; and my mind, for the time being, was incapable of controlling the slightest muscle of the body, or of realizing any definite sensation, except a kind of waving fluctuation between what seemed to me to be either decided *action* or *inertia*. This was a very strange feeling, but not at all unpleasant. In a few minutes, all this mental commotion subsided; and I then passed into the most delightful state of interior tranquillity possible to describe. Not a discordant sensation rolled across my spirit. I was completely "born again," being in the spirit. My thoughts were of the most peaceful character. My whole nature was expanded. I thought of the joys of friendship—of the unutterable pleasures of universal love—of the sweetness and happiness of united souls; and yet, I experienced no unusual emotion—no increased pulsations of life, which one might suppose would be a natural consequence of these pleasurable themes of thought upon the mind.

Now, notwithstanding my mind was meditating in this manner, I perceived as yet not the least ray of light in any direction; and therefore, concluded that I was but lost physically in "a deep sleep," and that my mind was simply engaged in a peaceful reverie. But this conclusion had no sooner settled among my thoughts as a strong probability, than I instantly perceived an intense blackness before me, apparently extending hundreds of miles into space, and enveloping the earth. Gradually, however, this midnight mass of darkness disappeared; and, as gradually, my perception of things was enlarged. Our room, together with the individuals in it, were all illuminated. Each human body was glowing with many colors, more or less brilliant. The figure of each individual was enveloped in a *light* atmosphere, which emanated from it. The same emanation extended up the arms, and over the entire body. The *nails* had one sphere of light surrounding them; the *hair* another; the *ears* another; and the *eyes* still another. The *head* was very luminous; the emanations spreading out into the air from four inches to as many feet.

The utter strangeness or novelty of this view overwhelmed my mind with astonishment and admiration. I could not comprehend it. I could not feel perfectly certain that I was living on earth. It seemed that earth, with all of its inhabitants, had been suddenly translated into something like an elysium. I knew then of no language which could describe my perceptions; hence, I did not attempt the slightest exclamation or utterance, but continued to observe with a feeling of unutterable joy and reverence.

In a few moments more, I not only beheld the *exteriors* of the individuals in that room clothed with light, as they were, but I also as easily saw *their interiors*, and hence the hidden sources of those luminous emanations. In my natural or ordinary state, I had never seen the organs of the human viscera; but now I could see all the gastric functions,—and the liver, the spleen, heart, lungs, brain, with the greatest possible ease. The whole body was transparent as a sheet of glass! It was invested with a strange, spiritual beauty. It looked illuminated as a city. Every separate organ had several *centers* of light, enveloped by a general sphere peculiar to itself. I did not see the physical organ only, but its *form*, *aspect*, and *color*, by observing the peculiar emanations surrounding it. I saw *the heart* as one general combination of living colors, interspersed with *special* points of illumination. The auricles and ventricles, together with their orifices, gave out distinct *flames* of light; and the pericardium was as *a garment of magnetic life*, surrounding and protecting the heart in the performance of its functions. The pulmonary department was illuminated with beautiful flames, but of different magnitude and color. The various air-chambers seemed like so many chemical laboratories. The fire in them wrought instantaneous chemical *changes* in the blood, which flowed through the contiguous membranes; and the great sympathetic nerve, whose roots extend throughout the lower viscera and whose topmost branches are lost in the superior *strata* of the sensorium, appeared like a column of life, interwoven and super-blended with a silvery fire!

The brain was likewise very luminous with prismatic colors. Every organ of the cerebellum and cerebrum emitted a light peculiar to itself. I could easily discern the *form* and *size* of the organ by the *shape* and *intensity* of its emanations. This view, I well remember, excited in me much admiration; but I was so deeply in the magnetic condition, and was likewise so impoverished in language, that I did not openly manifest any delight, nor describe any thing which I then beheld. In some portions of the smaller brain, I saw *gray* emanations, and, in other portions, lower shades of this color in many and various degrees of distinctness, down to a dark and almost black flame. In the higher portions of the larger or superior brain, I saw flames which looked like the breath of diamonds. At first I did not understand the *cause* of these beautiful breathings; but soon I discovered them to be the *thoughts* of the individuals concerning the strange phenomena manifested in my own condition. Still I continued my observations. The superior organs of the cerebrum pulsated with a soft, radiant fire; but it did not look like any fire or flame that I had seen on earth. In truth, the brain seemed like a *crown* of spiritual brightness, decorated with shining crescets and flaming jewels. (Here I will parenthetically remark, that what is thus *natural* to the human brain in this, its first stage of existence, is preserved and indescribably improved in the Spirit Land to which we all are tending.) Each brain seemed different—different in the degrees, modifications, and combinations of the flames and colors; but very beautiful! From the brain I saw the diversified currents of life or fire as they flowed through the system. The bones appeared very dark or brown; the muscles emitted in general a red light; the nerves gave out a soft, golden flame; the venous blood, a dark, purple light; the arterial blood, a bright, livid sheet of fire, which constantly reminded me of the electric phenomena of the clouds. I saw every ligament, tendon, cartilaginous and membranous structure, illuminated with different sheets and magnetic *centers* of living light, which indicated the presence of the spiritual principle.

Thus I not only saw the real physical structures themselves, but also their *indwelling* essences and elements. And I knew the individuals had garments upon them, because I could see an element of vitality, more or less distinct, in every fiber of clothing upon their persons. And yet, as you would look, by an act of volition, from the blisters in a pane of glass, through it, at the objects and scenes beyond; so I could discern, and that without a conscious effort, the whole mystery and beauty of the human economy, and enjoy the illumination which *the ten thousand flames of the golden candles of life* imparted to every avenue, pillar, chamber, window, and dome of the living temple.

But the sphere of my vision now began to widen. I could see the *life of nature*, living in the atoms of the chairs, tables, &c.; and could see them all with far more satisfaction, as regards their *use*, *structure*, *locality*, than I ever remembered to have known in my ordinary state. Then I could perceive the walls of the house. At first they seemed very dark; but soon became brighter and transparent; and presently I could see the walls of the *adjoining* dwelling. These also immediately became light, and vanished, melting like clouds before my advancing vision. I could now see the objects, furniture, and persons in the adjoining house as easily as those in the room where I was situated.

At this moment I heard the voice of the operator. He inquired, "if I could hear him speak plainly." I replied in the affirmative. He then asked concerning my feelings, and "whether I could discern any thing." On replying affirmatively, he desired me to convince some persons that were present, by "*reading* the title of a book, *with the lids closed*, behind four or five other books." After tightly securing my bodily eyes with handkerchiefs, he placed the books on a horizontal line with my forehead, and *I saw and read the title* without the slightest hesitation. This test and many experiments of the kind were tried, and repeated; and the demonstration of vision, independent of the physical organs of sense, was clear and unquestionable.

At length, feeling somewhat exhausted, I resigned myself to a *deeper sleep* that seemed to be stealing over my outer form; and, presently, my *former* perceptions returned with greater power. The village was now instantly subjected to my vision. It was as easy for me to see the people moving about their respective houses as in the open thoroughfares, and it was also as easy to see their most *interior* selves as the lights and shades of their physical bodies.

But my perceptions waved on, and the village with its inhabitants melted away.

By a process of *inter-penetration*, I was placed *en rapport* with nature! The *spirit of nature* and *my spirit* had instantly formed,—what seemed to me to be,—a kind of psychological or sympathetic acquaintance; the foundation of a high and eternal communion. Her spacious cabinet was thrown open to me, and it seemed that I was the sole visitor at nature's fair!

The properties and essences of plants were distinctly visible. Every fiber of the wild flower, or atom of the mountain violet, was radiant with its own peculiar life. The capillary ramifications of the streamlet-mosses,—the fine nerves of the cicuta plant, of the lady's slipper, and flowering vines,—were all laid open to my vision. I saw the living elements and essences flow and play through these simple forms of matter; and, in the same manner, I saw the many and various trees of the forests, fields and hills, all filled with life and vitality of different hues and degrees of refinement. It seemed that I could see *the locality, properties, qualities, uses, and essences of every form*, and species of wild vegetation, that had an existence any where in the earth's constitution. The living, vivid beauty of this vision I can not even now describe; although I have since frequently contemplated scenes far more beautiful and ineffable.

But my perceptions still flowed on! The broad surface of the earth, for many hundred miles before the sweep of my vision,—(describing nearly a semi-circle,)—became transparent as water. The deep alluvial and diluvial depositions of earth were very easily distinguished from the deeper stratifications of stone and earth, by the comparative and superior brilliancy of the ingredients of the former. Earth gave off one particular color; stones another; and minerals another. When I first discerned a bed of minerals,—it was a vein of iron ore,—I remember how I started with a sensation of fright. It seemed that the earth was on fire!—for the *instantaneous elimination* of electricity from the entire mass, gave the appearance of a deep-seated furnace in the earth. And my agitation was not lessened by perceiving that these *rivers of mineral fire* ran under the ocean for hundreds of miles, and yet were not diminished in a single flame!

I soon saw innumerable beds of *zinc*, *copper*, *silver*, *lime-stone*, and *gold;* and each, like the different organs in the human body, gave off diverse kinds of luminous atmospheres or emanations,—more or less bright and beautiful. Every thing had a glory of its own! Crystalline bodies emitted soft, brilliant emanations. The salts in the sea sparkled; sea-plants extended their broad arms, filled with *hydrogenous* life; the deep valleys and ravines, through which old ocean flows, were peopled with countless saurian animals,—all permeated and clothed with the spirit of nature; and the sides of *ocean mountains*—far beneath the high pathway of commerce—seemed literally studded with *emeralds*, *diamonds*, *gold*, *silver*, *pearls*, and sparkling *gems*. O, the ocean is a *magnificent cabinet* of beauty and wealth; and I am impressed to say, that man shall yet possess it!

I now looked abroad upon the fields of dry land; and *saw* the various species of animals which tread the earth. The external anatomy and the internal physiology of the animal kingdom were alike open to my inspection. The idea of *comparative or relative anatomy*, entered my mind in an instant. The philosophy of the vertebrated and avertebrated, the crustaceous and molluscan divisions of the animal world, flowed very pleasantly into my understanding; and I saw the brains, viscera, and the complete *anatomy* of animals that were, at that moment, sleeping, or prowling about, in the forests of the eastern hemisphere, *hundreds and thousands of miles from the room in which I was making these observations!*

It must not be expected that I shall detail, on this occasion, a three-hundredth part of the particulars of my *first* introduction to a spiritual perception of nature. At best I can but give you a rude outline, for words do not answer the purpose; they seem to me like *dark, stone prisons* in which we too often coercively incarcerate our highest thoughts!

In the foregoing vision, I saw every thing just as *you* all will perceive forms and objects, with the penetrating eyes or senses of the spirit, after you have passed away from the body at the event of physical death. It was very beautiful to see every thing clothed with an atmosphere! Every grain of salt or sand; every plant, flower, and herb; every tendril of the loftiest trees—their largest and minutest leaves; the mineral and animal forms, existing in the broad fields before me, were each and all clothed with a dark, or brown, or gray, or red, blue, green, yellow, or white atmosphere,—divided and subdivided into an almost infinite variety of degrees of intensity, brilliancy and refinement. And in each mineral, vegetable, and animal, I saw *something* of man! In truth, the whole system of creation seemed to me like the *fragments* of human beings. In the *beaver* I saw *one* faculty of the human mind; in the *fox* another; in the *wolf* another; in the *horse* another; in the *lion* another; and so, throughout the entire mass of the spirally progressive and concentric circles of mineral, vegetable and animal life, I could discern certain relationships to, and indications of man. Had I then possessed the language, I could have truthfully exclaimed, in the words of the *poet-psalmist*,—

> "Herbs gladly cure our flesh, because that they
> Find their acquaintance there.
>
> * * * * * *
>
> All things unto our flesh are kind."

Understood in this high sense, how instructive and appropriate was *Peter's vision*,—(related in the tenth chapter of Acts,)—in which he saw a great white sheet let down from heaven, containing all manner of four-footed beasts, creeping things, &c., and was told to slay and eat! All this was simply saying thus:—"Peter, thou needest not feel too exclusive, too partial, too aristocratic, too high-minded and above the meanest of thy fellow-men, nor yet above the little worm that crawls beneath thy feet, for behold *thou art related to every four-footed beast and creeping thing that the Lord hath made;* acknowledge, therefore, thine universal relationships and sympathies, and be kind and lenient to every thing that lives." Now, I find *too many* that need Peter's lesson. They, like him, shrink from this new method of tracing out their *genealogy* and ancestral derivations; and say they are not used to eating "unclean things;" but I perceive that the time is fast approaching, when mankind will feel their *oneness* with nature, and with nature's God, to the total annihilation of all narrow-mindedness and empty superficiality.

In my vision, I well remember how I gazed at the little plants in the fields, and saw around each one an atmosphere of life peculiar to itself. This emanation, surrounding some species of vegetation, was apparently from four inches to eight feet in diameter. Some animals gave off a sphere three or four feet thick, and beyond this a very fine, thin air—as many feet more, losing itself in the surrounding space. From all this the great *law of sympathy* was very distinctly visible. I saw that every thing in nature was arranged and situated in accordance with this great general law; and by it, all true sympathetic relationships are established and reciprocally maintained. The relative positions of mineral bodies in the bosom of the earth; the situation of trees, vegetation, animals, and human beings; yea, the relative positions of the sun and stars even, were manifestly conducted by this universal sympathy. I saw the different crystalline bodies, in the earth, act upon each other, and, intermediately, upon the solid substances to which they were attached by a generous commingling of their magnetic emanations. I saw the flowers exhale their odors, with which they clothed themselves, and then formed attachments with neighboring flowers, by breathing upon them, according to a spontaneous blending of spheres, the sweet breath of their life. There was not a dew-drop, chambered in the petals of the rose, that did not glitter with a living essence,—prophetic of coming animation. I saw currents of electricity flowing from a mineral bed in one portion of the earth, to its kindred, but *positive*, neighbor in another department of that hemisphere. And I saw the little flames arising from the essences of plants and trees, leap upward into the flowing currents, which were instantly absorbed, and wafted away to more proper and foreign destinations.

Language can not describe this scene. All nature was radiant with countless lights, with atmospheres, colors, breathings, and emanations—all, throbbing and pulsating with an interior life-essence that seemed just ready to *graduate*, and leap into the human spiritual constitution! Every thing tended to man; apparently, emulated to be man! I could no longer endure the exquisite happiness; I felt incapable of maintaining a quiet feeling; my emotions had become so deep and unutterable! Yet I yearned for association. I then realized that I was viewing all this magnificence, alone! This thought made me feel isolated and incapable of retaining a recollection of all that I had witnessed. I began to think of the village—of the room, in which I had taken a seat for an experiment—of the individuals, whom I had seen in the room, and of the operator. And immediately my vision began to diminish. The distant continents, oceans, fields, hills, forests—all gradually disappeared. The lights were left behind! Now I could see, as before, the interior condition of those in the room, and the operator; who now spake to me and asked, if I had "any thing to say." I made an effort to describe what I have, for the first time, related,—on this occasion. I remember how I struggled for words, and as I was about to relinquish all attempts to pronounce a word, I exclaimed, in a low, tremulous voice:—"How beautiful!" *I heard my own accents*, and never did I realize a stronger sense of the total *inexpressiveness* and impotence of human language. At that time I said and beheld no more. In a few moments, I felt the hand of the operator passing over my head; and by it was soon awakened to my ordinary state, with not a single idea—of what I had seen—alive in my external memory. Therefore, all that I have just related to you is a revival of the first impressions which were made upon my mind.

From what has been said concerning the philosophy of sympathy, I think you can not but be somewhat prepared for all the mental phenomena which result from the *positive* and *negative* or psychological operations of this sympathetic law in nature. I am impressed to present you with sufficient evidence and philosophy, as a foundation for all your future reasonings upon the subjects under investigation. You will be able to see, I think, that the same principle which *in man* is termed *magnetic*, also exists, in certain degrees and states of modification, in the *mineral*, vegetable, and animal kingdoms. It is necessary that every principle *be first* understood in its scientific application, because, (as I have before said) all true *moral and spiritual truth* must have in the mind a broad *sub-stratum* of scientific and philosophic knowledge; else the mind may possess much high truth, but can not successfully *apply it* to the welfare of himself or the human family.

The philosophy of sympathetic influence, when understood, is visible and applicable every where. For instance—"the *apple-tree*,"—says a writer,—"planted in the forest, soon becomes gross and gnarly, as by sympathy with the *wild* vegetation by which it is constantly surrounded; whereas, on the other hand, wild vegetation introduced into the society of that which has been refined by cultivation, soon changes its aspect, in such a manner, as can not be entirely accounted for by the mere difference in the quality of the soil. Again: often, on meeting a person for the first time, one will feel, almost before a word has been exchanged, an *attraction* toward him, which can not be accounted for by any external process; on the contrary, how often in first coming into the presence of a *man*, do we *feel* an indescribable 'something' about him which *we do not like*, at the same time having no doubt of his integrity of character."

How common a thing it is for two congenial associates to find their minds simultaneously impressed with the same thought! In certain impressible states of the mind, how distinctly some persons can feel the approach of an event or individual! The wife of a clergyman in Maine, related that her father, while lying on his death-bed, had a distinct impression of the approach of his son who resided at a distance, though none of the family expected him at the time. When he mentioned that his son was coming, and was then *near* the house, they supposed him to be wandering; but in a few moments afterward the son entered the room! There are numerous instances recorded in medical history, where individuals, long afflicted with fevers, experiencing, as a consequence thereof, great nervous acuteness and preternatural exaltation of the sensibilities, have become capable of telling, merely by their sensations, what any persons near them are doing, or even saying, without the use of bodily vision or hearing. It is worthy of note, how fasting and prayer, combined with a fervent action of the religious faculties of thought, characterized the habits of many of the early prophets. All this lies at the very foundation of many exhibitions of clairvoyance and mental manifestations; which are now engaging the attention of a large proportion of the civilized world. In laying this foundation for a future discourse, and for future facts and experiences to safely rest upon, I trust I have also done something toward expanding your conceptions of nature, and of enlarging your sympathies toward every thing that breathes on earth.

LECTURE XI.

CONCERNING THE EXTERNAL MANIFESTATIONS OF THE SYMPATHETIC STATE.

In the last discourse it was shown, in various terms, that all nature is locked together into one brotherhood of harmonious relationships, by a concentric chain of sympathies or affinities, whose Heart and Head is Deity. And it was also shown, that every thing in the vast domain of terrestrial and celestial existence is pervaded by an *atmosphere* of life and beauty; that every blade of grass, every fiber of wood, every atom of earth and stone, and every organ and particle of the human body, is enveloped in an emanation peculiar to itself. In order to familiarize and simplify this philosophy to your minds, I am impressed to term this universal ethereal essence of sympathy, MAGNETISM.

Every thing hath its own magnetic atmosphere; its own medium of sympathetic relationship. And Man, particularly and pre-eminently, possesses this *sphere of mind*, so to speak, constantly surrounding his body; which sphere is negative or positive, attractive or repulsive, gross or refined, passive or active, and less or great in magnitude, just in proportion to his general refinement and intrinsic development of mind. This atmosphere, surrounding man, can not be detected by the material organs of sense; but, to the spiritual senses of the soul, it is very visible, and its manifestations are familiar to you all. It frequently happens that when one person is approaching another, even at a great distance, that other will think and speak of him long before he has made his appearance.

A clergyman relates "that his mother-in-law, Mrs. P——, residing in Providence, Rhode Island, had a distinct consciousness of the approach of her husband on his return from sea, although she had no other reason to expect his arrival at that time. This impression commenced several hours before he made his appearance, and she accordingly prepared herself for his reception. She *knew* the instant he placed his hand on *the latch* of the door, and had arisen from her seat and advanced to meet him before he entered." It is perfectly impossible to explain such a fact, on any other ground than that occupied by this philosophy of sympathetic emanations. She *felt* the approach of her husband on the same principle that we can detect the odor of plants before we see or touch them, simply by coming within their atmospheres. If you will keep this principle of magnetic sympathies distinctly before your understandings, I can then furnish you with a very simple and truthful explanation of the so-called magnetic state.

When there is a full and uninterrupted exercise of all the organs and powers of the body; when there is a harmony existing between all the vital functions throughout the entire physical system; when all parts are in perfect unison and friendship; then, I should say, the body is properly and thoroughly MAGNETIZED. That is to say, the equilibriums of the positive and negative forces are not disturbed,—the organization is in perfect accord with itself; and the individual is neither physically or mentally under any description of subjugation or captivity. Now, if you desire to induce the *de-magnetic* state,—to put the physical man in subjection to the mind,—then you must, in some manner, disturb and overcome the general equilibrium; extract or transfer the positive power of the physical organism by a power still *more* positive; and then you will produce the unconscious state called the magnetic slumber. This state does not in any way contradict, confuse, or subvert the established laws of nature; on the contrary, this condition should be regarded as a progression and further development of the laws which govern organic beings.

In the true magnetic condition, the subject is the *negative or passive*, and the operator is the *positive or active*, member of one body; thus bringing the positive and negative principles which control *one* system in all its parts into complete *unison* with the corresponding laws in another system; consequently, for the time being, the *subject* and the *operator* constitute, so far as the body is concerned, *one identical individual.*

But let us ask,—How can the unconscious state be produced?

By one person coming in close contact with another, the *positive power* will be overcome in the *negative* organism, which will be either extracted or transferred.

What is the positive power?

It is the magnetic medium of sensation which pervades the nervous system, and envelops the whole body.

What relation does this magnetical atmosphere sustain to the soul or mind?

It is an emanation of the mind—a species of radiation from the most interior essences of the spiritual constitution—like the light and heat which flow from the material constitution of the sun.

When the real magnetic condition is artificially induced, where does this "sphere" exist?

It is partially withdrawn from the subject's organism, and partially transferred to the mucous surfaces of his vital organs, and to his nerves and muscles. The negative forces remain; but the positive power is gone either into the mental faculties of the subject, or into the external magnetic atmosphere surrounding the operator.

What is the consequence which succeeds this result?

The consequence is this: the Subject is no longer susceptible to *external* impressions or foreign disturbances, because *the fluid*, which connected him, when in his ordinary state, to all the outer world, is now transmitted and vanished from all the surfaces of the body. In a word, his system is perfectly *de-magnetized*—leaving sensation and consciousness existing *only* upon the internal or mucous surfaces; which sensational powers continue the vital processes; which functions, however, become torpid and feeble according to the absence of that volume and equilibrium of power which controlled them so vigorously in the ordinary or rudimental condition. The patient is thus placed in an unconscious condition, so far as the immediate objects and influences of the external world are concerned.

What is the proper term by which to designate this state from other mental or magnetic conditions?

I am impressed to consider this phenomenon as the Psycho-Sympathetic State.

Why so?

Because the Subject is temporarily blended into a sympathetic *oneness* with the operator.

How can this phenomenon be explained?

By remembering that the Subject is negative; the Operator is positive. Hence the two form ONE system in sympathy and power. The state is a result of a disturbance and captivity of the equilibrium of two forces, which exist universally in all organic bodies, as the indispensable agents of motion and consciousness.

How can the operator *disturb* this organic equilibrium of forces?

By coming in immediate contact with the atmosphere of the patient. A physical or personal contact is not, however, always necessary. It is through the agency of this invisible *fluid-sphere* that the magnetic state is produced. The operator is *determined*—is resolved—to arrest the attention of his subject and induce the unconscious slumber. All the powers of the mind are, therefore, concentrated upon the accomplishment of this object. His WILL being exercised powerfully to this point, the magnetic element passes from the batteries of his own brain, along the nerves and muscles of his body, to the corresponding parts of the Subject's body, and thus establishes a chain of sympathy. The one is completely under the control of the other, on that principle which is illustrated in *your hand* being altogether controllable by your brain or will.*

The brain is composed of a sensitive and complicated composition of fibers, to which no other part of the body bears any analogy. Being sensitive, it is *attractive* or *positive* to all that is existing on the nervous medium: hence it receives impressions irresistibly. It possesses within itself the positive and negative poles, or greater and lesser parts: the one controlling, the other subject; the one receiving power, the other transmitting and exercising power. The ethereal substance which serves as a medium, may be termed *Magnetism*. The muscular motion of the system is performed through the medium of the substance which may be termed *Electricity*. When there is a full and uninterrupted exercise of all the powers and organs of the body; when there is a harmony existing throughout the whole physical system, there is perfect health and enjoyment; because its forces (which are positive and negative, or magnetic and electric) are regularly performing their functions: and this indicates a perfect condition of the magnetic or nervous medium. Nevertheless, when the body becomes deranged in any of its various parts, it is a *loss* of the positive or negative power which produces its health and harmonious action. But when all parts are in perfect unison and harmony, then the system is thoroughly *magnetized*. In order to *de-magnetize* it, you must in some way overcome the equilibrium, and extract the positive power by a power still more positive; and this will produce the unconscious state called the magnetic. The medium, heretofore explained, exists between all organic beings. Magnetism composes the sphere—rather the atmosphere—by which every person is individually surrounded. And besides this, there is

* See Nat. Div. Rev., p. 32.

a medium existing which extends through all things, placing man over the lower animal creation. For animals are subjected to man's control by the positive or subduing power which he possesses; and they receive this to their minds by the same medium which exists between an organ and the brain. Man being positive, and all else negative, the latter must yield to his control.

Nature is always consistent in her operations; hence one thing entertains a sympathy—a correspondence or an analogy—more or less intimate, for all other things in being. If you should deposit a bar of iron in the earth,—pointing north and south,—the magnetism of the invisible atmosphere would thoroughly take that *bar* into sympathetic captivity, and render it strongly *positive* to some elements and atoms, and equally *negative* to others. If you should make three downward passes with the horse-shoe magnet over a proper piece of steel, the latter would be rendered completely sympathetic with the magnet, and would cleave to it in the strong embrace of an invisible affection; but, by making the *reverse* passes with the *same* magnet over the *same* bar of steel, the latter would instantly lose all its sympathy for the magnet, and there would be no attraction visible between them. This represents, and corresponds entirely with, the manipulations and consequent phenomena, which occur between the operator and his patient.

But the question may be asked—Is not the *psycho-sympathetic* state identical with the clairvoyant or spiritual condition? Nay. This state is frequently confounded with independent clairvoyance; yet it is quite inferior to the superior condition. In the *sympathetic* state, the patient sees, hears, smells, tastes, feels, and describes whatever the operator imagines or experiences; or else, the patient obtains his impressions from the minds of other persons who may be positive, or from the recollections and educational prepossessions of his own mind. Such subjects invariably describe diseases, places, personages, and scenery according to the impressions of the individual, or combination of individuals, with whom they are in sympathetic relation or connection at the time. This has been too often mistaken for perfect clairvoyance. And this is as frequently done by the professed believers and advocates of this sublime science as by any other class of individuals,—resulting always in much confusion among its friends, and in much skepticism among those who know still less of the beauties and realities of its general philosophy.

For the present I leave this branch of the subject, and proceed to consider some of the phenomena which naturally flow from the unalloyed psycho-sympathetic condition.

Numerous well-authenticated examples of what I am impressed to term sympathetic impressions, may be gathered from the experiences of all nations in every age of the human world. These impressions may be made upon the minds of very susceptible persons from either of three general sources: First, from the sympathetic action of mind upon mind; second, from the sympathetic emanations of many and various *things* in the material world operating upon the impressible mind; third, from the sympathetic action of spirits who have departed from the material body, but who draw nigh and impress the spirit of the susceptible individual in this world.

It was said of Elisha the prophet, that he could tell the *king of Israel* the *words* which the *king of Syria*,—with whom he was at war,—spake in his bed-chamber. Now, this could be easily accomplished by Elisha placing himself in sympathetic connection with the mind of the Syrian king. Occurrences of this general kind are to be found in the sacred records of all so-called heathen nations. By interior observation, I discover instances of *psycho-sympathy* indicated on the hieroglyphical tablets of Egypt and Central America. Among all people these interior impressions and powers, whereby some persons could describe distant scenery and prophesy correctly of many future occurrences, have been regarded as direct endowments or privileges especially granted to them by the Lord. Indeed, in the undeveloped ages of the world, it would be very difficult to find any psychological phenomena, of this peculiar nature, free from the clouds and habiliments of superstition. In Roman, Grecian, and Egyptian history, I discover records of these wonderful achievements of the human mind, and always associated with that peculiar religious or *superstitious* reverence which characterizes all similar records among the Jews. In the Hebrew writings—in the received writings of Moses, Joshua, Isaiah, and Paul—you may find many affirmations, of the authors themselves, that they were influenced by spiritual visitors to go *here* and *there*, and to do certain things; all of which they very honestly, and with much reverence, referred to the direct dictations of Jehovah.

But this is not a superstitious age! We can now read of, and behold, these wonderful displays of psychological power, and of spiritual sympathy with angelic beings, without rushing fanatically into the superstitious conclusion, that *all* is accomplished by the specific instigations of the Supreme Being. We can see these things understandingly; hence, what an additional pleasure it is to read those *old sacred records;* and, although we must allow much for the superstition and fanaticism of the writers, yet we gather many fine examples of mental and spiritual manifestations from the histories in question. It can not be successfully denied, that many phenomena, recorded in the Primitive History, are identical with the psychological sympathetic manifestations which have been exhibited in all ages, by all impressible persons who have yielded their minds to the wild-fire of religious excitement. A strange fantasy, commencing in one individual, will almost inevitably and irresistibly spread and communicate itself to hundreds and thousands,—so that five thousand persons might be baptized, (at least in the fires of ungovernable religious enthusiasm,) in a single day. Such minds, although they *think they see* into heaven and hell, and see evil spirits and wondrous signs, yet do not, *in fact*, see any thing. Their state of ecstasis is induced by the action of external things upon them,—induced by the sympathetic contagion arising from the prevailing influence surrounding them,—and hence they *see*, and *hear*, and *describe* in their imaginations, precisely such persons, voices, and scenery, as the majority accept as real. You have probably heard of the religious infection or epidemic which appeared in 1686, in Dauphiny, in France; which spread, like the Asiatic cholera, so rapidly, that five or six hundred Protestant Christians gave themselves out to be prophets of Jehovah, inspired of the Holy Ghost! This epidemic soon extended to several *thousands* of both sexes—all professing, in like manner, to be divinely inspired.

The psychological phenomena which these fanatics exhibited were precisely analogous to the strange manifestations of mental excitement and sympathy which occur among the Catholic Monks and Nuns, among the Jewish fanatics, and among the Mormons, Shakers, and Methodists, of this century. The French prophets—relates a historian—"had strange fits, which came upon them with tremblings and faintings, as a swoon, which made them stretch out their arms and legs, and stagger several times before they dropped down. They remained awhile in *trances*, and, coming out of them with twitchings, uttered all which came in their mouths. They said they saw the *heavens* open—saw angels, and paradise, and hell. Those who were just on the point of receiving the spirit of prophecy, dropped down, not only in the assemblies, but in the fields and their own houses." Now, what I desire you to understand is this: that the foregoing is not at all resembling the quiet and harmonious state of independent clairvoyance, except in the partially cold and lifeless condition of the physical body; and unfortunately for the welfare of those who know comparatively *nothing* of our glorious philosophy, there are, as yet, but very few cases of real and perfect clairvoyance developed.

Some of the Jewish prophets were frequently in the psycho-sympathetic condition, above referred to, in which they received many *visions* and strong impressions. The most prominent examples are recorded in the histories attributed to *Ezekiel* and *Daniel*, the Jewish prophets. The visions related by *Ezekiel* generally commence with such expressions as the following:—"The hand of the Lord was upon me"—"the heavens were opened," &c.; showing, most conclusively, that every somewhat extraordinary mental occurrence was, in that benighted era of mankind, attributed to the supernatural interposition of the Great Jehovah, or to the direct agency of the Lord.

There is *one* very perfect illustration of Ezekiel's sympathetic condition, induced by the powerful action of his own mind assisted, possibly, by the influence of a spiritual being—his own guardian angel—from the world of spirits. I allude to the highly significant imagery which was impressed upon his mind, in his vision of the valley of dry bones. This account is introduced—in the thirty-seventh chapter—with these expressions: "The *hand* of the Lord was upon me, and carried me out in the spirit of the Lord, and set me down in the midst of a valley which was full of bones," &c. Now it is certainly very reasonable to believe, that Ezekiel was, as several persons knowingly are in this age, attended and influenced, during particular moments of mental susceptibility and exaltation, by a spiritual visitant or guardian angel. Observe, for example, the extraordinary relations and visions of DANIEL, particularly in the last portions of his record. He affirms that many of his impressions were received by him while in a "deep sleep," with his body in a state of partial insensibility. In the tenth chapter, he gives a highly excited description of his guardian angel, "whose face was as the appearance of light," and then says,—in the seventh verse,—"And I, Daniel, alone saw the vision; for the men that were with me saw not the vision; but a great quaking fell upon them so that they fled to hide themselves." Now I am impressed, that these men would have seen as much as *Daniel* saw, if they had been as susceptible at that moment to the contagion of psychological sympathy. The "*quaking*" was the agitation awakened in them by the strange motions exhibited by Daniel; who thus continues his relation: "Therefore I was left alone, and saw this great vision, and there remained *no strength* in me; for my comeliness was turned in me into corruption, and I retained no strength. Yet I heard the voice of the words: and when I heard the voice of the words, then I was *in a deep sleep*, on my face, and my face toward the ground." You will readily perceive that this is a very good *ordinary* description of the magnetic state, induced mainly by his own mind, a state which is now a common phenomenon among men.

It has been long supposed, and the same thing is promulgated from modern pulpits, that the power of truthful prophecy, so frequently exhibited in the doings of the Hebrew prophets and Bible authors, is a conclusive evidence that those minds were led by the Lord. Thus JOHN, the alleged author of the APOCALYPSE, affirms, that he was "in the spirit on the Lord's day," and received many visions and instructions concerning things which were to, and did, "shortly come to pass," and also concerning the "new heaven and the new earth," and many things pertaining to its ultimate establishment.

In the Old Testament there are said to be many truthful prophecies of the coming of JESUS, none of which could have been uttered, it is also affirmed, unless the *Lord* had *himself* put the words into the mouths of the holy prophets. But I am distinctly impressed that the Lord had nothing to do with these prophetic utterances; for, in *certain conditions* of the human soul, the power of sympathetic *vaticination* is as *natural and as easy* as the inspiration of air into the lungs. For example: Tacitus, the well-known ancient historian, had this power of pre-vision or of intuitive sagacity, as it has been termed, so well developed, that he clearly *foresaw* the general calamities which were to desolate Europe on the downfall of the Roman empire; all of which he clearly predicted and set forth in a book written five hundred years *before* his prophecies were fulfilled! It is surely just as reasonable to believe in the miraculous inspiration of Tacitus as of Moses, Daniel, or John. Lord Falkland foresaw the character and course of Cromwell:—"This coarse, unpromising man," said his lordship, pointing to Cromwell, "will be the *first man* in the kingdom, if the nation comes to blows." SOLON—the Athenian lawgiver—contemplating on the port and citadel of Munychia, exclaimed thus: "How blind is man to futurity! O, could the Athenians foresee what mischief they will do, they would even eat it with their own teeth to get rid of it." Now, it should be remembered, that more than two hundred years after Solon had gone to the Spirit Land, this simple prediction was verified to the letter!

There are numerous instances of prophetic dreaming, in accordance with the laws of psychological sympathy which I have explained to you from time to time: that is to say, the mind, being *in sympathy with a certain current of events*, will intuitively *perceive*, *feel*, or *prophesy* of some particular occurrence which will result from the revolution and progress of those events—not infallibly, but frequently with a seeming supernatural confidence and accuracy.

This is especially the experience of many females, whose exquisitely fine temperaments render them highly susceptible to sympathetic dreams,—which are perfectly identical with prophetic inspiration. I have already given you several illustrations of this fact; but here is another:—The murder of Mr. Adams, in New York, some years since, by J. C. Colt, was anticipated by the wife of Mr. Adams, before it took place. Two days before her husband's disappearance, she *dreamed*, twice, that he was murdered, and that she saw his body *cut* into pieces and packed in a box! The dreams gave her great concern in consequence of their exceeding vividness; and she went once to relate them to her mother, but did not do so, from the apprehension of being laughed at for her imagination. It will be perceived by the foregoing, that truthful prophecy,—"the gift of prophecy," as Paul expresses it,—is perfectly natural to certain peculiar mental organizations and temperaments. Hence all the evidences of miraculous inspiration, which are based upon these psycho-sympathetic manifestations of the human mind, are utterly valueless; and there is *no other* kind of prophecy than this, except the tracing out of certain future events by a mathematical or deductive process of reasoning, as illustrated in the occasional truthful inferences based on astrology, and in the always accurate prophecy of eclipses of the Sun or Moon as accomplished by good astronomers. Thus, I come to the conclusions, set forth in Nat. Div. Rev., on the principles of prophecy—viz.: To prophesy or foretell truly an event, the person must be in communion with the original design of the Divine Creator, and with the laws which are fulfilling design. The mind, in correctly apprehending these, is enabled to foretell occurrences throughout eternity. There can be no truthful prophecy unless the laws fulfilling design are familiarly comprehended by the person prophesying. It is impossible to foretell an occurrence absolutely by the indications of any external event or circumstance. It is a thing which never has been done, and can not be done by any being in the Universe. All things that are truly foretold, occur as the result of *immutable laws*, and not of any mere fleeting and evanescent circumstances. To definitely foretell war, an accident, or any incidental circumstance, is positively an impossibility; for it is not in the power of any *internal* and general principle to foreshadow to the mind a merely incidental circumstance. It is upon *interior principles* alone that a prophecy can be made with an absolute certainty of its accomplishment; and therefore if it were possible for these to foreshadow external and incidental circumstances, then prophecy concerning such might be relied upon. But as this is not in the nature of general principles, and is beyond the power of individual influence, it is impossible for any being, either in this or higher spheres, to proclaim the particular circumstances of an event, with the *absolute* certainty of their occurrence.

We are just ascending the scale of the philosophy of mind. The subject is man. He is the source of much that confounds and depresses us; yet he commands our attention and gives much vitality to all our investigations. But we should not convey superstition into our analysis. True, we *may not deny* the spirit of prophecy to any man, but *we must discard* every thing which savors of excitement and supernaturalism. There is, properly speaking, nothing supernatural; every thing is governed by immutable laws. The grass grows, the oceans flow, the planets roll, birds sing, and *men* think and *prophesy*, all in accordance with an unchangeable system of cause and effect; there is nothing which can imvair the unutterable majesty of this Eternal Truth!

LECTURE XII.

CONCERNING THE HISTORICAL EVIDENCES OF THE PSYCHO-SYMPATHETIC STATE.

In the preceding discourse, I presented to you the philosophy of the psycho-sympathetic state, and concluded with several illustrations of the natural action of the mind while in that condition.

The invisible transmission of *thought and sensation* from one mind to another, is, in and of itself, a deeply interesting and profound mystery—especially, to those who have never indulged themselves in the contemplation of spiritual or metaphysical subjects. You have heard it said,—"Convince me that one mind can transfer its thoughts, by an act of volition or will, to another mind, and I will confess such a phenomenon to be as wonderful and mysterious as clairvoyance."

Another says—"I can easily believe in what is commonly called 'Animal Magnetism,' but I can not admit clairvoyance." But, friends, what means this statement? Shall we dignify it with the high name of Reason? No; never. But why not? Because it is the offspring of ignorance and prejudice. It is saying, in substance, that we may believe in the creeping of children, but in the *walking* of grown men we can place no confidence. We may believe in arithmetic and similar studies, but in *algebra* and *trigonometry* we can not believe any thing. Now, such a statement as this you all would put down to the ignorance of the person making it. How unreasonable, therefore, must the first opinion appear to me,—seeing, as I do, that clairvoyance *succeeds* the phenomena of

Animal Magnetism as naturally as manhood succeeds youth; walking, creeping; or harvest, the sowing of seed.

Another says—"I am perfectly willing to accept magnetism, and the sympathy of the subject's mind with the mind of the operator, but I can not admit the idea of *independent clairvoyance*, because I do not know where it will lead me." But what does this mean? It means simply that the individual, who could seriously utter such a sentiment, has no actual confidence in his heavenly Father. He feels no reliance upon Truth. He doubts the light of Reason and intuition—"the light which lighteth every man that cometh into the world"—and thinks the Deity may have endowed him with a faculty, his Reason, which, if followed implicitly, might lead his soul to destruction. Do you think, friends, that a perfectly *wise* and *good* Parent would place a power—a knife, perhaps—in his child's possession which *could, in any possible or conceivable way or emergency*, prove that child's complete or even partial destruction? A simple and well-meaning earthly parent might err an hundredfold in the bestowment of gifts upon his offspring; and the receiver might be mortally injured by the *wrong use* of the powers which the parent gave him. But suppose, what is every where conceded, that the Father of Spirits saw *the end* from the beginning—with *perfect wisdom* and *perfect goodness* in his soul—do you believe it possible, or in any conceivable manner *consistent with the attributes* just designated, for that Being to give to one of his dependent creatures a faculty, *power*, or *principle* which *could*, in any case whatever, result in that creature's everlasting curse? Nay, you do not believe a doctrine so repugnant to the common conceptions of the human mind. But you say—"the ways of God are past finding out."

This assertion is erroneous. For we are "finding out" the "ways of God" more and more every day! The ways of God must certainly mean the *laws* of God. These laws are being constantly discovered; hence the *ways* of God. Every new law of colors; every new discovery in geology, or conchology, or zoology; every new development of mind and matter—the discovery of the world's rotation, its formation, and inherent essences and elements—all, stand as a monumental demonstration that the *assertion*, referred to, is unequivocally erroneous, and prove, moreover, that man is the being, above all other personalities, to whom the heavenly Father turns in order to be progressively comprehended.

Hence we should not stop to question the wisdom and goodness of God,—to question his ability to manage his own laws, to control the destiny of his own offspring, to regulate the operations of his own material and spiritual universe,—we should not hesitate, in our investigations, to ask where independent clairvoyance will conduct us, or where any other development of science will lead; but the only questions we should ask ourselves, are—Do we search the ways of God with an honest heart? Do we desire Truth for its own sake? Do we candidly weigh all evidence, separate from educational dogmas or local prejudices? The man who feels confidence in the Ruler of the universe; who has any reliance whatever in the *eternal* action of *immutable* laws; who is honest and faithful to the dictations of conscience; who lets his internal "light" shine in the chambers of his soul, like the sun in the firmament—such a man, will never be heard to say—"I can not admit the doctrine of clairvoyance, because I do not know where it will lead me." Such a low and deformed *thought* would never come into his mind. His thought would invariably be—"What is Truth?" In this, I have given you an unfailing rule by which to measure the growth and condition of every mind with whom you may converse, and the same rule will always apply to yourselves.

Let us now return to the general subject under investigation.

Something of magnetism and psycho-sympathetic clairvoyance has been known in all ages of the world. But I do not regard antiquity as any recommendation. On the contrary, the more aged a doctrine is shown to be—like the mythology of hell, and evil spirits, and a devil—the more we should question its soundness; because all the follies and absurdities which thousands of so-called "talented men" are this day believing, can be traced to the dark climes of the eastern hemisphere, where mythologies originated and many of the cardinal points in popular theology. Nevertheless, it is a pleasant thing to read and hear of what other minds have taught, for in this way we can form a comparison between the darkness of other ages and the enlightenment of this era,—learning, by contrast, the sublime law of progress, and tracing out, at the same time, the common affinities and sympathies natural to the whole family of man.

In this place, however, I must express my surprise at the apparent ignorance of antiquarians and biblical scholars—men, who profess to be called to "expound the word of God," but who, at the same time, raise their voices against the developments of magnetism and clairvoyance, as the works and efforts of Satan. I am surprised, because the Bible, like the sacred book of every other nation, is replete with the most beautiful examples of magnetism and exhibitions of sympathetic clairvoyance.

In the *Janitar* temples of India are many hieroglyphical representations of the process of *laying on* of hands. Upon the walls of an ancient temple of Thebes, there are represented a great many human figures, in various postures, corresponding to the positions taken by practitioners, in our day, when they attempt to induce the different degrees of magnetic phenomena upon their subjects. And it is very evident that MOSES learned something of this science by familiarizing his mind with the Egyptian mysteries, which were confined particularly to the physicians and magicians of Pharaoh. Hence, in the thirty-fourth chapter and ninth verse of Deuteronomy, this power is brought into requisition by Moses, who therein declares that Joshua "was full of the spirit of wisdom, FOR MOSES

HAD LAID HIS HANDS UPON HIM." In modern language, we should say—Joshua was rendered prematurely and permanently *intellectual* in consequence of being properly magnetized by Moses.

Hippocrates says—"there exists a singular property in the human hand to pull and draw away *pains*, *aches*, and diverse *impurities*, from the affected parts, by laying the hand upon the place, and extending the fingers toward it."

Solon says—

> "The smallest hurts sometimes increase and rage,
> More than the art of physic can assuage;
> Sometimes the fury of the worst disease,
> *The hand by gentle stroking can appease.*"

If you will turn to the 1st Kings, i. 1—4 verses, you will discover that the principle of psycho-sympathetic contact was acted upon by the physicians of king David—seemingly, with the express intention to restore the vigor and animal heat to the body of the revered monarch. I could quote numerous paragraphs from the sacred writings of other nations, to show *how familiar* some persons have been, in the most ancient stages of humanity's growth, with the incipient processes of magnetism, and with some of the common exhibitions of clairvoyance. But the subjects of these mental powers were superstitiously supposed to be divinely inspired. Hence they were almost invariably deified and worshiped. All religious chieftains have been thus unnaturally regarded; and truth has thus frequently been obscured beneath the superstitious garments of deification. This was the case with *Moses*, and *Jesus*, and *Mohammed*, and every man, in fact, who ever was sufficiently clairvoyant to *read the thoughts of another*, or to find any thing which was hidden from the superficial gaze of the bodily senses. This description, or degree, of clairvoyance is the common possession of many minds, and is familiarly exhibited in all parts of the inhabited world; and yet, for the exercise of the same *identical* power, Jesus has been deified into a supernatural personage, and is worshiped as the representation of the eternal God,—endowed with prophetic and miraculous powers. But the age of deification is rapidly expiring, and personal excellence will supply its place!

Did you ever, friends, take your Bible and read, and without any unnatural or exaggerated reverence, the simple accounts of clairvoyance, as that *power* was frequently manifested *by Jesus* during his three years' labor for humanity? If you never have read it thus, I trust you will soon be able to do so. Read, for example, the first part of the fifth chapter of Luke; how Jesus told Simon to cast his net, who complained that he and his partners had "toiled all the night" and had "taken nothing." But Jesus, perceiving where the fish were then swimming, said—"Launch out into the deep, and let down your nets for a draught." By following his directions implicitly, "they inclosed a great multitude of fishes;" so large a quantity that their net was broken. Now, this is an example of good ordinary clairvoyance.

But again, turn to the fourth chapter of John; where it is related how Jesus was joined at Jacob's well by the woman of Samaria. And after some very highly correspondential conversation with her which she did not understand, he thought he would convince her that he knew more concerning truth than she believed. Hence he said unto her, "Go, call thy husband, and come hither." But she was skeptical, and said, in order to test his powers, "I have no husband." Thou hast well said, "I have no husband," said he; "for thou hast had five husbands; and he whom thou now hast is not thy husband." This astonished her very much, and she said—"Sir, I perceive thou art a prophet." Now, it does not appear that Jesus gave her any *other* personal evidence of his spontaneous clairvoyance; but it is distinctly clear that her ungovernable enthusiasm, in consequence of being thus unexpectedly convinced, was so strong that she went about telling her exaggerated story—saying, "Come, see a man which TOLD ME ALL THINGS THAT EVER I DID"—from the simple fact, which has frequently occurred in our midst, that one mind perceived, sympathetically, the thoughts of another! It is good to fix this idea in your minds—that the woman did not tell the truth. She said he told her "all things" that she "ever did;" whilst, from John's relation, we learn that he simply told her about the five husbands,—all the remainder of his conversation being expressly of a correspondential and prophetic nature. And yet it seems that "he that believeth shall be saved;" notwithstanding much belief was the direct offspring of the exaggerated testimony of men and women who witnessed the occasional manifestations of magnetism, as a curative agent, and of clairvoyance, as a power of discerning thoughts, future events, and hidden things. Thus, in the thirty-ninth verse of the same chapter, we read, that "many of the Samaritans of that city *believed on him* for the saying of the woman, which testified, He told me all that ever I did."

Another good instance of sympathetic clairvoyance is related of Jesus. In the fifty-second verse, a nobleman was convinced, together with his whole family, that Jesus was "the Saviour of the world," by his simply informing the nobleman that his son was still living, and that the fever had left him the day before, "at the *seventh* hour." It appears, also, from John's record, that Jesus said to those who surrounded him—"One of you shall betray me;" and to convince *Peter* that he perceived correctly, said—"He it is to whom I shall give a sop, when I have dipped it"—this he gave "to Judas Iscariot, the son of Simon," and subsequent events demonstrated the fact that Jesus did read Judas correctly. In the same chapter, Jesus gave evidence that he understood very nearly *when* and *how* he was to die. This power of prophetic sympathetic discernment of future events is possessed by many individuals; and I find interesting demonstrations of its exercise among all nations—especially, among gifted and talented leaders of great political or religious movements. The Swedish philosopher, Baron Swedenborg, discerned the *time* and *manner* of his own death, and expired at the precise time predicted. The celebrated Dr. Walker, of Dublin, foresaw *when* he was to die, and also that he would be certainly buried *alive*, which was subsequently verified by examining his body a few days after interment. Dr. Binns concludes his narration of this case thus—"Here is a man who possessed an *instinctive* knowledge that *he should be buried alive*, and who was so convinced of it, that he wrote a treatise, with a view, if possible, to avert so horrid a calamity; and still further to assure himself, entered into a compact with a second party, for the fulfillment of certain precautions before he should be consigned to earth, yet, disappointed in the end, he was, as it were, compelled to bow to the inscrutable fiat of that law of natural contingencies which the imaginative Greeks erected into supertheism, and consecrated by the tremendous name of *Destiny*."

In reading the Primitive History, why are we not as reasonable and consistent in our deductions as we generally are in the perusal of other writings? When we read of the manifestations of modern clairvoyance; when we hear of the correct reading of thought, or of disease, or witness the constant fulfillment of common prophecies; why do we put it down sometimes as "deception," "imagination," or "unaccountable instinctive knowledge?"—Whilst, when we read the descriptions of the same mental sympathy, and of powers of psychometrical discernment, in the pages of the Old or New Testament, we put it down to the direct influence of the Holy Ghost, or to "the miraculous interposition of God?" If you will analyze your own minds, you will receive the proper answer to these questions. Habits of thought—first impressions—prevailing custom—popular theology—existing methods of education, by which your minds have been unconsciously molded; these are the unequivocal answers.

But it may be urged that modern manifestations of mind can not be depended upon, in all cases, with regard to the fulfillment of prophecies, as the Bible prophecies can be relied on—the latter always being correctly fulfilled. Hence, that we can not make the Bible miracles harmonize with recent disclosures in magnetism and psycho-sympathetic clairvoyance. In reply to this, I will here promise to furnish, from the great storehouse of modern developments in mind and science, to any individual who will undertake to institute a biblical comparison, miracle for miracle, testimony for testimony, prophecy for prophecy, mistake for mistake, fulfillment for fulfillment; and show that *we* have as much, yea more, reason and incontrovertible philosophy for believing modern developments to be "miraculous" and "divinely instituted," than the advocates of supernaturalism have for believing their prophets to have been "divinely inspired" of God.

In order to convince you that the clairvoyance of the Old Testament authors was not *always* good and reliable—being sometimes merely the result of psycho-sympathy, as already explained—I am impressed to remind you of a few facts in illustration. About two thousand four hundred years ago, Ezekiel prophesied (see twenty-ninth chapter, 10—12) for the Lord, as he supposed, in this wise—"I will make the land of Egypt waste and desolate; no foot of man nor beast shall pass through it; neither shall it be inhabited forty years." This prophecy has never been fulfilled. Again (see Ezekiel xxxvii. 22,) "I will make them ONE nation in the land upon the mountains of Israel, and *one* king shall be king to them all." And Joel says, in his third chapter and twentieth verse, "Judah shall dwell forever; and Jerusalem from generation to generation." These passages, and many others might be cited, to demonstrate the conspicuous fact, that hundreds of common prophecies, uttered or written by the Old or New Testament authors, have never been even partially fulfilled. These prophecies will not admit of any figurative or correspondential interpretation:

because, as you will observe, they are the *political opinions* of ancient *Jewish* prophets concerning the restoration and permanent re-establishment of all the tribes of Israel and Judah, *as a nation of Jews*, not Christians, upon the mountains of Israel. But the *ten tribes* never returned to Palestine; and not a vestige of them is known to exist on the face of the earth; hence these prophecies *can not* be fulfilled.

In a peculiar condition of the human mind, *prophetic dreams* are natural as the falling of rain. We modernly or conventionally call these operations of the soul—"presentiments," "premonitions," or intuitive perceptions of the prognostication and foreshadowings of future events. These phenomena, I repeat, are perfectly *natural* to certain mental organizations; and, generally speaking, the same individuals are endowed with sympathetic clairvoyance. All Bible accounts are, more or less, prefaced with, or based upon, what may be termed prophetic dreams. Thus, "the angel of the Lord appeared unto Joseph in a dream," the "angel appeared unto Mary," &c., &c.; showing the general faith which was then based upon this species of mental or intuitive vaticination. Of this description of mental phenomena, I have already given you several illustrations. But I expect to hear soon, emanating from the mouth of some modern devotee to antiquity, the following warning and anathema, quoted from the thirteenth chapter of Deuteronomy: "If there arise among you a prophet, or a dreamer of dreams, and giveth thee *a sign* or *a wonder*; and the sign or the wonder *come to pass*, whereof he spake unto thee;" * * * "thou shalt not hearken unto the words of that prophet, or that dreamer of dreams." * * * "And that prophet, or that dreamer of dreams, shall be put to death." In this connection, I am impressed to ask this question—If the Lord inspired Moses to reveal eternal Truth, and if his writings are to be regarded as fixed Truths, then why was not the foregoing commandment, or positive law, applied to Joshua, to Daniel, to Isaiah, to Joseph, Mary, and Jesus? The latter remarkable personages came a long period after Moses wrote that law; and each exhibited, more or less, of the power of prophecy, and the disposition to *dream out* many things, antagonistic to the Lord or law of Moses. If you reply, that the Old Testament truths were superseded by the commandments of the *New Testament*, then I desire you to bear in mind that you thereby *demonstrate* two-thirds of the so-called "word of God" to be, not fixed and eternal truths, but local laws, historical accounts, and jurisprudential expediencies—altogether temporal and fragmentary in their character and application.

The truth is, the foregoing law was particularly instituted by Moses for the express purpose to prevent any thing like a *change* of views among his followers—to set up a strong and formidable *defense* against any and every description of innovation. This is precisely what Catholics are doing to Protestants; and what Protestants are doing, to the full extent of their influence, in order to avoid the deep analysis and far-reaching investigations which will characterize the present century. Every thing, however, must come to the imperial test of Nature and Reason. The *trial* will go on; and the *verdict* shall be given. The crowned heads of the world will learn the necessary lesson, that *Knowledge is power*, and that *Right* is stronger than might, according to the progressive laws of Nature's unchangeable God. The tides of Truth will continue to rise higher and higher, and will increase in strength and majesty as they roll forward.

In speaking against mental slavery,—which lies at the foundation of all political, conventional, and theological slavery,—I know of no language too strong or pointed. Those customs and dogmas, which forbid our thoughts to "choose the channels where they run;" which arrest the tides of reformatory sentiment; which impede the currents of free thought; and which prevent the expansion of benignant and fertilizing principles; should always be regarded as direful enemies to our happiness and progression of soul. Ignorance is the greatest foe of man; knowledge is his greatest friend. But love is the *soul* of all—the binding principle of every thing. Yet love without wisdom is blind and impetuous. It is, therefore, very necessary that we obtain wisdom. By wisdom, I mean a strong *intuitive* understanding of truth, without the cold and fatiguing process of cogitation, and wearying our mental faculties with useless exercises in ratiocination. This power of truthful discernment will increase in you from the moment you discard all superficial habits of thought and life; become perfectly natural; and all errors and supernaturalisms will pass from your mind, as clouds glide away from the face of the firmament.

As you are now educated, you see things *as* they are not, and *where* they are not; and you have worshiped idols and personages, instead of devoting the strength, means, and energies of your existence to the *perception* and *application* of principles. You are too much mortgaged to the past—too devoted to the deification of personages who lived centuries ago! You have deified men, like yourselves; and have attributed to the patriarchal inhabitants of antiquity, an unnatural greatness and character—simply, because some finely-strung temperaments and well-developed minds, have expressed in high-sounding terms and orphic hymns, what the ignorant and undeveloped frequently *think* in plainer words!

In this way, and according to this propensity of habitual exaggeration in your thoughts, you have erected a supernatural being in your minds and called it Christ. You can reason properly upon *magnetic* and *intuitive* powers—upon the principles of human magnetism and the manifestations of clairvoyance—particularly when these phenomena occur in our midst; but, when the miracles and achievements of any religious chieftain, and the prophetic powers of the Jewish writers, are referred to the same identical attribute of the human soul, with which you are equally endowed, then you shrink from the test—like the pagan devotee from any sacrilegious treatment of his beloved idols. What a relief it is to strip off the garments of supernaturalism from the personages of antiquity and be able to see them *as* and *where* they are! By it, the mind is purified of much error; and there is more mental room for the entertainment and cultivation of high and happy sentiments.

The unnatural greatness of any being of the past, or any that exists, or may hereafter be deified, is very much like that, (says some writer,) which is occasionally observed in mountainous countries—for instance, upon the summit of the Brocken. The enthusiastic admirer looks up, on a misty morning, and in the vapor, on the top of the mountain, he sees the huge *form* of a human being, of colossal dimensions and proportions—one, to whom the fabled giants are but pigmies—a being, in short, who might ride the ponderous mammoth. The observer gazes on this figure with a kind of veneration as something wonderful and supernatural; but, by and by, he discovers that when he moves, it moves also; when he inclines his head, it does the same toward him; when he stretches forth his arm, it extends its arm likewise; when he kneels, it kneels; and, at last, he perceives that this gigantic human figure, *upon which he has been lavishing his admiration and veneration*, is merely the *reflection* in the mist of *his own form*—an unsubstantial magnification of himself!

You doubtless perceive the application. In this manner, on the *broad*, *misty*, *vaporish*, *mythological* canvas of the PAST, you have drawn out personages after the likeness of your own minds; and then, you have *admired*, and *venerated*, and *worshiped*, and thrown *your whole being* at the feet of the supernatural *form* of colossal proportions—the mere magnified expression of your own form and growth of soul. Thus, Baron Swedenborg painted Christ *so large and preternatural*, that he was compelled to *change the name* of his theological production, and call it the DIVINE HUMANITY. But *priests* and *monks* did this before, and for, Swedenborg; so that now, the vast night of antiquity is literally swarming with *plutonian ghosts and gigantic phantoms*, to whom thousands are constantly bowing in silent admiration and avowed reverence, as the stranger before the mountain-image of himself. And they, and you, friends, will continue to admire and revere the gods and idols of your own making, or which your forefathers made for you, until you become sufficiently *intuitive* to perceive that you are *worshiping* and *fostering* the deformed and sickly *offsprings* of religiously excited but inharmonious minds. However, I am impressed to say that your *salvation* from the bondage and mental slavery of superstition, fear, and error is now even at the door of your hearts, and your joy and high pleasures will be inexpressible; whilst the *cold* and *gloomy* conservatives of the land, will, *more than ever*, strive to *tie* people to the worn-out superstitions of the past—to dwell in the sickly shadow of things by-gone; and will endeavor, by preaching and religious excitements, to distort your vision, causing you, if possible, to regard the rising sun, whether of thought or political liberty, as *owls* and *bats esteem* the appearance of that magnificent luminary which sheds joy and brightness over all creation!

LECTURE XIII.

THE MENTAL CONDITION OF ANCIENT PROPHETS, SEERS, AND RELIGIOUS CHIEFTAINS.

The subject of these lectures has already unfolded and expanded under the pen far beyond my own anticipations. True, the sublime theme before us towered up, in the very commencement, like a spacious edifice, with many compartments and lofty turrets. Nevertheless, I supposed that the beautiful grounds, extensive parks, different vestibules, and attractive departments of this particular temple of truth, could all be shown you in a much less period of time. But it is highly gratifying to me to continue the reception of a philosophy so exalting; or the illustration of a science so intimately related to the hidden impulses and powers of our common nature.

As it will be observed, this philosophy of the psychological and psycho-sympathetic manifestations of the human mind, is fatal to all theological assumptions of supernaturalism. It most beautifully harmonizes all developments of mind with the established laws of Nature; shows the psychological condition of the ancient prophets to be substantially identical with the mental illumination or aberration of several persons in this age; and thus, most distinctly and permanently, our philosophy lays bare the stupendous arcana or mysteries of human life; and develops, without any virtual disparagement, the real character and intrinsic excellence and beauty of all Scriptural accounts and other sacred developments of prophetic power

The vast utility of such a spiritual philosophy, is very manifest to the thinking mind. In the first place, it throws a new and beautiful light over the mental constitution of man. The soul is no longer a dreamy, vaporish breath—a bubble in the air—a thin, shapeless combination of ethereal elements—floating, after the event of death, in the vortical depth of infinitude—conscious, yet undestined; meditating, yet unsubstantial as the passing breeze. Nay; not so. Nor yet, a mere undefined nonentity, sleeping in the cold prison-house of death; the mere companion of dust and corruption; until the thundering tones of the fabled trumpet shall arouse the dreaming soul to unite with its cast-off body, and ascend on high, to await its trial and final verdict. But unspeakably superior to all this mythological teaching, are the disclosures of the philosophy under investigation. The soul is made to appear in its true character,—as a high-destined, beautifully endowed, and symmetrically substantial individual,—the inheritor of an eternal life of infinite progression! And all superstition passes away beneath its benignant influence, as tears of sorrow before the joys of the Spirit Land. In this respect, its teachings are inexpressibly important and happifying. If it frees our mind of certain local attachments—of peculiar forms and institutions of theology—of long-fostered household gods and revered personages; it, at the same time, provides us with vaster fields of thought—with the profoundest disclosures concerning the moral and intellectual nature of man—with the most stupendous attainments in every possible sphere of knowledge—and with a new and divine development of the hitherto hidden arcana of a world beyond the tomb! If the supernaturalism of religious superstition be thoroughly stripped from the character of any deified personage,—what then? If the true philosophy or psychology and mental sympathy is logically and intrinsically adequate to remove, from your minds, much unhealthy veneration for certain opinions and doctrines—what then? Are you injured by the Truth? Are you deprived of any means of salvation from error and imperfection? Far from it! Every new disclosure, in science or in religion, is a new power placed in your possession. Every discovery of error adds another gem of wealth to the casket of your intellectual knowledge. When error is removed, truth is seen in its native majesty. Gold is pure and beautiful only when chemically disengaged from its earthly impurities; and believing so, I can not but press forward in the work of separating truth from the noxious superstitions and absurdities of supernaturalism, which have been thrown around its body by perverted and misdirected men. By these means, the world will progressively learn to highly respect all prophets, and seers, and religious chieftains; not with that unnatural and unhealthy veneration whereby men are converted and deified into Gods, but with that sound and healthy deference which is due to all our brothers who stand, or have stood, before the world in the pure character of philanthropists or moral reformers. Such are the motives which actuate me—such the thoughts which perpetually flow into my understanding.

It will be remembered that, in the foregoing lectures on the general philosophy of clairvoyance, I have progressively treated on man in the rudimental state, in the psychological state, and the sympathetic state; but, in accordance with my present inflowing impressions, I will proceed to consider the human mind in the transition state, which is midway, or intermediate, between the sympathetic state and the opening of the interior or spiritual senses.

The transition state, as the term implies, is characterized by neither absolute sympathy nor absolute perception, but by a blending or interfusing of one condition with the other—to the confounding and utter superconfusion of both. The individual, in this state, is, occasionally and transitionally, sympathetic and independent. There is a constant fluctuation between two extremes. The mind indicates a distinct vision at one moment, or during one period of its exercises; but perhaps, on the succeeding occasion, the same mind will utter the thoughts and impressions of its own memory, or will lose its individuality of character in a close and apparently complete sympathy with the minds or circumstances which surround it.

It requires a thorough understanding of the laws of mind to properly comprehend the phenomena consequent upon this condition. In this state the mind is not clairvoyant, neither is it occupying a spiritual position from which the soul can discern the broad territories of the Spirit Land. But the mental state is one of momentary fluctuation—a passing to and fro from one extreme of sympathy with surrounding things to a more interior communion with the inward elements and educational prepossessions of his own mind, which are magnified and multiplied to an extent almost beyond belief.

These operations of the soul are very interesting phenomena to study and analyze; but they have been the cause of much misunderstanding and even superstition among religious sects. And especially, is this form of superstition reviving in this century, supported by a strong array of ecclesiastical erudition, and with a splendid display of apparently logical argumentation. My mind is now upon those who have received the theological writings of Baron Swedenborg as "divinely imparted and infallibly certain"—who have deified the man, and accepted the innumerable repetitions of his prolific mind as the certain emanations of immortal Truth. In their adoration, they unfortunately forget the imperfections of their self-proclaimed prophet, and hence invariably associate him with the Lord. It would seem that the world has had lessons enough in the fallacy of deification. Every religious chieftain, that ever lived, has always claimed personal exemption from error and other imperfection natural to man in the great system of universal progress, on grounds precisely identical with the enormous professions of Emmanuel Swedenborg—viz.: being a special agent for "the Lord" in the transaction of some mundane business in the theological field, and, consequently, being a particular favorite of the Lord, the Lord maintains him in a state of purity, and makes him a vessel for the introduction, into the great world of "sinners" about him, of infallible doctrines—doctrines, which, because of their direct emanation from the august source of Truth, must not be surveyed by reason or questioned by flesh and blood. This is the dogmatism of Swedenborg; and such is the voluntary deification of those, who accept his teachings with only their faculties of marvelousness, to which, however, they devoutly resign their Reason; or else they compel it very meekly and cautiously to perform the functions of a determined promulgator of a system which is claimed, at the commencement, to be direct from the Lord.

But there are hundreds of instances recorded in history, and many that were not deemed of sufficient importance to record, where men have set up a claim as high, and in the precise manner, as that erected by Swedenborg. We have Moses, and Joshua, and all the Bible authors; all the Priests and Bishops appointed by Constantine to vote the Hebrew writings, and other histories, canonical and divine; and Mohammed, and many of the Catholic clergy; the descendants of Joseph Smith—the dignitaries of the Mormon gospels and government; and very many chieftains among the Shakers, and among other sects, who hold miraculous inspiration to be possible to certain persons—the agents and favorites of the Lord.

It is on all hands acknowledged, that these personages are, and were, perfectly human; not exempt from sin and imperfection; not pure and immaculate, but possessed of different and peculiar personal characteristics—such as are, all over the world, in all ages and among all nations, the common inheritance and distinguishing peculiarities of humanity. But why do Christians believe in the perfect truthfulness of every thing which was spoken or written by the Bible authors? Why do they profess to believe that Constantine, and his convocation of Priests and bench of Bishops, were perfectly correct in deciding what combination of books we should regard as holy? Why do the Turks believe that Mohammed revealed the high and holy truths of Heaven? Why do Mormons believe in the perfect and entire infallibility of the revealments of Joseph Smith? Why do Shakers place their confidence in, and stake their lives and all their personal and temporal interests upon, the infallible truthfulness of Mother Ann's dispensation and revealments? Why do the receivers and disciples of "the doctrines of the New Church," as revealed by Swedenborg, believe that their self-proclaimed prophet was made the subject of supernatural and infallible revelations of religious truths—whose utterances are to be received as the voice of God to man? Again I ask, why do the followers of these respective religious chieftains,—who are acknowledged to have been human beings, subject to all the frailties and weaknesses common to other members of humanity,—why do their disciples, in view of all this conceded individual imperfection, believe in the unqualified infallibility of their utterances? Simply, because they adopt the professions of those chieftains, that "the Lord" was their especial guardian, and, consequently, that whatever they did, or wrote, must necessarily be regarded as unequivocally perfect.

And yet, the followers of all these religious masters indulge themselves in what they call *reasoning*; this is the manifest absurdity of all minds who have sold themselves, physically and spiritually, to the promulgation of some particular system of religion. It is an absurdity to exercise your reasoning faculties upon that which you believe to be infallible. If you are told, in 2 Kings ii. 11, that Elijah was seen going physically to heaven in a chariot of fire,—what do you say? Or, if you are told by Joshua, x. 13, that the sun stood still in order to prolong a battle,—what do you say? Or, if you read, in Isaiah, xxxviii. 8, that the sun was seen going backward,—what do you say? If you should read in those sacred records that it was a common thing to see stones dance, trees fly, and dead animals sing,—what would you say? Would you reason upon the probability or possibility of such occurrences? Nay; for, believing those accounts to be the utterances of Jehovah—the direct infallible revelations of "the Lord" through his favorite attorneys,—you will simply resign your reason; your powers of energetic and harmonious thought, your divinely inherited powers of comprehension, and say—"Well: it is above my comprehension, BUT IT MUST BE SO!" Again: suppose you accept the assumptions of Swedenborg that he was "led by the Lord;" that his knowledge was divine, supernatural, infallible—what would you say to any absurdity that he might utter? You would say: "Although I do not fully understand it, it must be so nevertheless!" Suppose, for example, that you should turn to one of his works, entitled "Divine Love and Wisdom," and read an old Chaldeanic idea of the origination of the animated world, which Swedenborg has synopticized in this manner:—"All poisonous serpents, scorpions, crocodiles, dragons, tigers, wolves, foxes, swine, owls, rats, mice, locusts, frogs, bats, spiders, flies, drones, moths, lice, mites; and all malignant, virulent, and poisonous herbs; did not derive their origin from 'the Lord,' neither were they created from the beginning, neither did they originate from nature, by her sun, BUT THEY ARE ALL FROM HELL." I say, suppose you should read this, while accepting the author as "led by the Lord," and hence saved from the commission of error—what would you say? Unquestionably, you would say, what Christians say constantly concerning the Apocalypse of John, "that it is entirely above your comprehension, but it must be true notwithstanding."

All attempt at reasoning on matters which are received as infallibly uttered, is manifestly absurd and even farcical. True, the high-born faculty of reason may be permitted to step majestically upon the eternal rounds of a theological tread-mill; or it may be most devoutly sold to some religious chieftain for the purpose of performing the functions of a menial in the promulgation of certain tenets; and it may be allowed to exhibit in the theological circle, which is eternally marked out and defined for the devotee, as much genius, as much consecutive reasoning, as much close logic—sound judgment and deduction—as much method, coolness, sobriety, dignity, symmetrical thought and harmony of proportions—as much penetration and logical analysis, as the disciple is pleased and able to employ; but, after all, what does all this pyrotechnical manifestation of talent amount to in the issue? Nothing! absolutely nothing more, than the splendid discharge of the functions of a menial to some fixed theological system and standard of infallibility; to which Reason is devoted and laboring in absolute bondage!

Men first accept, without reason, the author and the foundations of a system of moral philosophy; then they show a vast amount of logical consistency and profound reasoning. It is not the existence of any false logic subsequent to the acceptation of a religious system that I complain of; but the total absence of the dictations of the faculty of reason, when the system is first received. You seldom hear a Christian ask—"Is the foundation of my religion reliable? Did man actually fall? Was he, in fact, more perfect in the beginning than he now is? Did Moses write Genesis? Did Christ die as a martyr for his opinions? Or, did he suffer for me, to satisfy the justice of his heavenly Father which had been infringed upon by mankind, and thereby opened a door for human salvation? I say, you seldom hear Christians ask such questions. But why do they not? Because they dare not,—yea, they are so accustomed to mental slavery that they dare not,—exercise a particle of reason on the soundness of the foundations of their faith. But after the soul is chained to a theological system—after it is sold into slavery, and incarcerated in a spacious prison, with an extensive yard but insurmountable walls—then the *Reason-principle* is allowed some healthy exercise in tilling the ground; keeping up the fences; repairing breakages; handing water to those who thirst for it; and in maintaining an attractive and harmonious external appearance in order to induce travelers and wayfaring men to take up their abode in their magnificent mental slavery institution. Hence, subsequently to the reception of a religious system, you always see the bondmen very busy in "harmonizing Genesis with Revelation;" and commentaries succeed commentaries; notes on the Gospels succeed sermons; and, then, there are others, who, knowing the proverbial ignorance of laymen on points of historical differences and scientific antagonisms, in connection with the professions of the infallible system of religious faith, are very expert in their show of reason in the efforts to "harmonize Nature with Revelation!" And so, the bondmen exercise their understandings! Verily, in this position, the sublime faculty of REASON is, as a menial in the house of a religious chieftain, bold and dignified in the exhibition of its powers within certain fixed limits; but, beyond those confines, it were dangerous to venture!

Upon an interior examination, I find the most vigorous and talented minds frequently deceived as to the extent to which they think they exercise their reason. Especially is this true of those who have simply changed from one set of theological tenets to another. For instance, "upon the most rigid inquiry," says Professor Bush,* "I am satisfied that Swedenborg's system is true. When candidly surveyed, it answers all the demands of my intellect and my heart. It commends itself to my best reason, as given of God and worthy of all acceptation; and so believing, I dare not confer

* See page v. of the "Introduction" to the Memorabilia of Swedenborg, edited by Professor George Bush.

with flesh and blood!" Now what does all this mean? or, rather, what does it demonstrate? Most conclusively, it shows that this disciple of the Swedish seer had never once analyzed the ground elements of his faith in the miraculous and supernatural. He never asked himself whether the foundation of Swedenborg's theology was a veritable record of infallible Truths. Before he could make a "most rigid inquiry;" before he could satisfy his "best reason" that "Swedenborg's system is true;" it was certainly first indispensably necessary to analyze the *basis* of Swedenborg's complicated superstructure,—viz., the Primitive History! But did he do this? Nay; his mind was all ready for the acceptation of the new seed. His faith in the infallible; in the absolutely supernatural; in the miraculous; had not experienced or suffered the least disturbance. Hence by a "most rigid inquiry" he means, not a strictly logical and profound analysis into the beginning principles of his theological faith—into the basis of the Word, upon which Swedenborg's system stands—but, he means, that he examined Swedenborg's disclosures with strict reference to their coincidence with the "letter and the spirit" of the Word. Here is no philosophical penetration —no deep analysis—no far-reaching psychological foresight or research; but it is all subsequent reasoning! Again, this talented disciple of Swedenborg says—"If Swedenborg has uttered truth relative to the Spiritual World, it is because God enabled him to do it." Here the supernatural doctrine is accepted totally. "It is a truth," he says, "entirely transcending the reach of the native faculties of man." That is to say, no human being can see, think, or write, such truths unless he be "led by the Lord," and transcendently illuminated by the influx of the Supernal Spirit.

But here the question arises—how could this disciple of the Swedish seer, satisfy his "best reason"—supply "all the demands" of his "intellect and heart"—all "the central convictions" of his soul—by a "most rigid inquiry" into a system of truth which is "entirely transcending the reach of the native faculties of man?" Surely, a truth, which is above the "native faculties" of the soul, can not be "enthroned" in the intellect or reconciled to the emotions of any "heart," no matter how pure and exalted that mind and heart may be.

In this connection, I am impressed to inform you, that, to the end that you may become deeply acquainted with the principles of psychological science, it is of the highest importance that you bestow the strictest attention and thought to the present intellectual analysis. The operations of the human mind, like the ever-changing scenes of the kaleidoscope, may be differently seen on every new turn which we give it. Upon every revolution, new thoughts will appear in new connections; and old thoughts or educational impressions will, by the same revolutionary laws, so change their positions and manifestations, that, to the unmetaphysical or undisciplined thinker, it becomes exceedingly difficult to trace out scarcely any similarity between them and what before seemed to occupy the mental dominion.

Hence I solicit your undivided attention to the points at issue, because I feel it to be of the utmost importance, to your mental discipline and spiritual development, that you learn to comprehend the principles of psychology as they apply to the solution of many and various problems connected with the religious operations of the human mind. It is for this purpose, I feel impressed to say, that I bring before you the case of Baron Swedenborg, together with the peculiar mental manifestations of those, who, by instituting, as they suppose, a "most rigid inquiry," have satisfied their "best reason" and "all the demands of the intellect," that their prophet is an infallible teacher; hence, worthy of all consistent deification. "And believing so," says the disciple of this teacher, "I dare not confer with flesh and blood." That is to say, having viewed and analyzed a system of religious and theological Truth—"a Truth entirely transcending the reach of the native faculties of man"—the mind "dare not" any longer exercise its own God-given powers of understanding, but sells itself entirely to the *dicta* of the infallible teacher, and yields to "the most sacred obligations on the score of announcing" his stupendous revealments to the world! In this capacity, what a display of philosophical reasoning do we behold! How majestically the talented devotee stands in the court of his prison-house! How gracefully he bows before, not the "loftiest genius that humanity has ever enrolled in her ranks," but before "the accredited messenger of God,"—a man! In all this I behold no reasoning—no truthful analysis—no intellectually chemical test applied to the foundations of the religious conviction, but simply a strong semblance or show of, or an attempt at, reasoning which would be as likely to psychologize the reader as it did the intellect which "dare not" any longer "confer with flesh and blood." Nor is this all. I perceive in all this a deep and somewhat beautiful illustration of psychological principles which lie at the basis—which form the basis itself, in truth—of much theological faith in the human world, which but few have been able to successfully resist.

LECTURE XIV.

ON THE MORAL OR RELIGIOUS MANIFESTATIONS OF THE TRANSITION STATE.

In the preceding discourse, I gave an introductory description of the *Transition State;* and then proceeded to consider the causes of deification, and the self-psychologization of those who, by not fully comprehending the laws and diversified functions of the human mind, induce a faith upon their understanding, and who suppose, at the same time, that they received it only upon the most rigid test of reason. As a faithful type of this universal fallacy, I was impressed to select the case of Baron Swedenborg. In this you may see mirrored forth the precise position which many of you most probably occupy with regard to Moses, or Isaiah, or Paul. It is, therefore, essential that you observe well the looking-glass which will thus be held before your gaze, to the end that your knowledge of mankind may be permanently enriched and increased.

In the first place, let me remind you, that, when a human being is accepted as an infallible revelator—as an unerring teacher of heavenly truths—there is an end to all reasoning upon the probability or possibility of the reality of his revealments. The mere show of reasoning is equivalent to a farce,—it is almost a sacrilegious treatment of divine things,—an insult to utterances of the Lord through his chosen vessels. "Admitting the possibility of such communications as Swedenborg claims," says Professor Bush, "the question of their probability is the pivot on which the whole controversy turns; and this can only be determined by weighing the probable reasons in the Divine Mind for granting them." Now, can this be denominated reasoning? What does he mean by "admitting the possibility" of such professed communications? Why, he undoubtedly means the intimate—perfect—miraculous—supernatural—unphilosophical—unreasonable connection which "the Lord" established between himself and the illuminated soul of the seer with the avowed design of instructing mankind with a third edition of infallible revelations; for these are Swedenborg's claims. Now, with such a foundational admission as the foregoing in the mind to begin with, what an unsound method it is to attempt to decide "the probability" of such communications by "weighing the probable reasons in the Divine Mind" for permitting their development. Assuredly, there can be no absurdity more glaring after analysis than this. Think of the inconsistency of this position, for one moment, and you will perceive that nothing could be more illogical, and yet so seemingly sound and legitimate.

Suppose, upon "weighing the probable reasons," no very satisfactory "reasons" could be discovered for such a new development of infallible doctrine. What then? Would the intellect, whose "demands" had been fully satisfied, reject the "communications" as not altogether reliable? Far from it! But why not? Because he has sold his judgment,—his reason, his understanding, so completely, that he "dare not" any longer "confer with flesh and blood;"—he does not see Swedenborg any more as a man, physically and mentally constituted as other men are, but he sees "the Lord," the "accredited messenger," and himself as "the agent" of announcing his revealments to the world. Hence this disciple says—in speaking of the infallible truth emitted through Swedenborg—"It is a Truth entirely transcending the reach of the native faculties of man. * * * It was designed for propagation. It must be proclaimed in order to be available to the ends for which it was given. This Truth has come to me, and throned itself in the central convictions of my soul; it brings with it the most sacred obligations on the score of announcing it to the world. The trust is holy, and through the grace of Heaven I hope to prove faithful to it."

Let it be understood that I am not impressed to criticise this brother's language as is the method among those who know comparatively nothing of the fine sensibilities which prompted its use; but I am delivering to you a course of philosophical lectures on the psychological laws of the human mind, and therefore select such language and illustrations as will subserve the purpose of their elucidation. It is time that man should comprehend himself. For the greater his knowledge the greater his power. It is expressly to this end, I repeat, that I bring these psychological cases before you on this occasion.

The mind, unless it be exceedingly well constituted and harmonious in the performance of its functions, will easily deceive and constantly psychologize itself. And no man is so thoroughly satisfied of his own entire sanity as he who is unfortunately insane. But why is it so? Simply, because he does not make a true investigation into the peculiarities of his own state. His impulses are his laws—the incoherent whisperings of his own thoughts are the voices of the invisible agents of Jehovah,—and thus, he is psychologically held in mental bondage to certain sentiments; with perfect confidence that he, more than any one about him, has weighed all his convictions in the balance of a candid reason.

These remarks I do not apply to the solution of Swedenborg's psychological state, but particularly to the condition of those who think they exercise their best reason in deciding upon, or in accepting certain points of, a doctrine, in cases where the foundation is admitted without a question—viz., that the revelation is wholly and unqualifiedly infallible. With this admission fixed in the mind, what matters it whether you can see any "reasons in the Divine Mind" or not? Suppose you do not see any, what then? There is no choice—no alternative! The ingredients of the alledged infallible, or supernatural, revelation may all, more or less, conflict with and jar your current experiences and reason; nevertheless, you have nothing to say,—no arguments to weigh,—nothing to harmonize and reconcile with the known laws of Nature; but you must acknowledge, as Christians every where do, with regard to their faith in the miraculous, that you "can not comprehend it, but it must be true notwithstanding."

You surely perceive that there can be no *pure* reasoning on a supernatural basis. Of Swedenborg's revealments, Professor Bush says—"Their truth can only be made apparent by their intrinsic character, and their character must be thoroughly studied in order to be understood." Again, he says—"Taken up by fragments it must appear broken, incoherent, and frequently absurd. Surveyed entire, it is consistent, harmonious, and grand beyond description." Now what does all this mean? He previously says that Swedenborg has "uttered truth relative to the spiritual world" which is "entirely transcending the reach of the native faculties of man." To this psychological absurdity I solicit your attention. Let me ask—Can the intellect be satisfied without comprehension? Nay; for the mind can rest only upon adequate evidence. Again—Can the intellect understand any thing which is incomprehensible? Certainly not! If, then, the supernatural relations of Swedenborg are beyond "the reach of the native faculties of man," how can Professor Bush truthfully affirm, that, on surveying them entire, they appear "consistent, harmonious, and grand beyond description"? The inconsistency of such an affirmation is surely self-evident. Furthermore, Is a revelation, which man can comprehend, above man? Certainly not! But why not? Because any thing which is comprehensible by the human mind can not be any more great or spacious than the power which comprehends it; on the same principle that a quart of water may be held by a quart measure; but should the measure be unable to embrace the quantity of water which is presented, then could the vessel truthfully say,—that "it comprehends it all'? I think you perceive the argument. It is so self-evident. If the mind understands the alledged truths or revealments of Swedenborg, then those truths are not supernatural; neither are they above the internal abilities of the human mind, in certain high states of transitional illumination, to accomplish or unfold, and that in a cool, consecutive, logical, lucid, severe, symmetrical, and admirably harmonious manner, too, with which, it is very unjustly alledged, Swedenborg made his multitudinous disclosures. But suppose the mind does not comprehend all these disclosures; then can that mind assert the uncomprehended portions to be Truths? How does he know? At best, it is but a generous inference—an admission of the possibility—that those relations are veritable. According to this principle, it appears evident that he who could make himself believe, that those supernatural relations satisfied all the demands of his intellect and heart—commended themselves to his highest reason as given of God and worthy of all acceptation—is surely in a transitional state between the influence of education and the psychological captivity of a prevailing doctrine or theme of thought. You perceive here a show of reason; but no pure reasoning. You behold a seemingly logical display of analyzations, deductions, and conclusions; but you only see, in fact, the semblance of these indispensably essential properties of a pure and healthy argument.

It will be observed that all reasoning concerning the teachings of any revelation which is claimed to be, or admitted in the commencement of the "inquiry" to be, supernatural, is all absurd, farcical, seeming, spurious! I am impressed to say, and I know full well that the subject will warrant any strength of assertion, that there can not be any pure reasoning, or any exercise of the consciousness of intuition, upon a supernatural foundation. But here, in order to prevent any misconceptions among you with regard to my position in the premises, let me say that I am impressed to esteem nothing as supernatural in the sense with which this term is employed, by all believers in the miraculous, to signify things, events, and actions which are above nature, or not within the scope of the operations of the established and known laws of Nature. I believe in no suspension, transcendsion, contradiction, or variation of, no superaddition to, no supernatural interference, on the part of Deity, with any of the principles of his own constitution. On this head, you will find my impressions explicitly defined in the second volume of the Great Harmonia.

But it may be said—"Although we can not comprehend the supernatural, we may nevertheless exercise our reason upon supernatural developments." True, you may exercise your reason, but to no purpose,—especially if you commence by admitting the supernatural as the foundation of your faith. Suppose, to illustrate this position, you take a miraculous revelation as the basis of your thought and argument. Well: with this settled conviction in your mind—which you think satisfies your intellect and heart—suppose I should ask you this question: Do you believe that God is perfect? Without thinking of the supernatural revelation, a single moment, you would readily respond, from the consciousness of your soul—"Yes: God is perfect—I know he is perfect." But how do you know he is perfect? Forthwith you would exercise your reason and say—"I know it by myself—I am finite, he is infinite—I am imperfect, he is perfect—my heart tells me this." But did you ever see God? "No." How, then, do you know there is a God? "I know it in my soul—the fields, flowers, firmament, demonstrate the existence of a creative or formative Power." But how do you know that God is infinite? "Why, he could not be God if he were not infinite?" How do you know this? "My reason tells me this truth." You believe, then, that there is a God; that he is perfect; that he is infinite? "I do, from the center of my soul." Do you, also, believe in a supernatural revelation from this same God to man? "I do." But if you believe from the consciousness of your soul, and from the dictates of your best reason, that there is a perfect and infinite God; then do you depend upon that supernatural revelation for your faith in these things? "No." But suppose your miraculous revelation did not coincide with the promptings of your soul—suppose it taught you that God is neither perfect nor infinite, but passionate and locally visible; what would you say? "O, I can not comprehend it, but I should nevertheless believe it to be true." Then you would ignore or repudiate reason in adopting an infallible revelation? "Certainly." But why? "Because, a supernatural revelation is expressly designed to do for us what reason can not do." But you believe in a perfect and infinite God without the assistance of any book, do you not? "Yes." Then you believe in the highest and most important thing in pure theology without any supernatural revelation? "I most certainly do." And, yet, if your infallible revelation should most positively contradict the convictions of your heart and intellect, you would consequently repudiate Reason and adopt the Word? "I would." Very well: now I will convince you that your supernaturally inspired revelation not only proves that God is neither perfect nor infinite, but that he is self-contradictory.

But let me say, that I do not at all associate the God of any known supernatural revelation with that Great Positive Divine Mind who lives in, and governs, the universe with an unchangeable government. On the contrary, I am impressed to regard the God represented in all sacred volumes as the legitimate offspring of the undeveloped and unprogressed intellect of man in ages bygone. Let this be remembered in order that you may not confound my position with that occupied by a believer in a supernatural disclosure, with whom it may be supposed I am indulging a conversation.

Understood thus, I will now proceed to show that the infallible revelation of all Christendom not only disproves what you suppose your "heart" and "intellect" teach you, but that it equally disproves and contradicts itself.

First affirmation—see Genesis i. 31—"God saw every thing that he had made, and behold, it was very good."

The contradiction—Genesis vi. 6—"It repented the Lord that he had made man on the earth, and it grieved him at his heart."

Now, I ask, does this appear like the infallible revelation or utterance of a Being which is acknowledged to be without variableness neither shadow of turning? I solicit your attention to the facts as they appear in the English translation of a book which is regarded as an unalterable production of "the Lord," through his holy prophets and divinely inspired penmen. Remember, I do not do this to excite any derision, prejudice, or obloquy in your minds toward a book which is honestly esteemed by thousands as a "Holy" production. Nay: far from it. I simply desire to urge you on to the "being a law unto yourselves;" to develop and strengthen your hearts and intellects to the most dignified, harmonious, and energetic growth; to the end that you may be superior to all derision, prejudice, superstition, and doctrinal vagaries which now swarm and sicken the civilized world. All assertion and denunciation I regard as the mere breath of the lips—it amounts to nothing. It is one thing to indulge ridicule—but it is quite another thing to confute with sound arguments. I have been thus particular to explain to you my position and motives, and it would be a sad, unnecessary, and dishonorable thing in any one of you to misconceive or misrepresent me in this investigation. I will now proceed.

Second affirmation—see Ezekiel xviii. 20—"The son shall not bear the iniquity of the father."

The contradiction—Exodus xx. 5—"I am a jealous God, visiting the iniquity of the fathers upon the children," &c.

Third affirmation—Leviticus xix. 13—"Thou shalt not defraud thy neighbor, nor rob him."

The contradiction—Exodus iii. 21, 22—"When ye go, ye shall not go empty; borrow of your neighbors and guests—gold, silver, and raiment; ye shall spoil the Egyptians."

Fourth affirmation—see Genesis iii. 9, 10; also Exodus xix. 19—"Adam heard the voice of God in the garden," &c. "Moses spake and God answered him by a voice," &c.; and, in the thirty-third chapter, twenty-second and twenty-third verses of Exodus, it is affirmed that God has hands, and a face, and back. But observe—

The contradiction—in fifth chapter of John, thirty-seventh verse—"Ye have neither heard his voice at any time, nor seen his shape." Again, in fourth chapter of John, twenty-fourth verse, it is said—"God is a spirit." And then—which makes the affirmation of Moses appear wholly contradictory—Luke says, in his twenty-fourth chapter and thirty-ninth verse, "A spirit hath not flesh and bones."

Fifth affirmation—see third chapter of Lamentations, thirty-third verse—in speaking of the Lord, it is said—"He doth not afflict nor grieve the children of men willingly;" and, in first Chronicles, sixteenth chapter, forty-first verse, it is plainly affirmed—"His mercy endureth forever." But all this saying, about the Lord's unwillingness to afflict the children of men, is plainly contradicted in the Lord's command to Moses. In this you will find—

The contradiction—see seventh chapter of Deuteronomy, second chapter, sixteenth verse—"Smite the nations; utterly destroy them; and show no mercy nor pity unto them." In 1 Samuel, v. 9, it is said—"He smote them with emerods, with a very great destruction." And elsewhere it is recorded—"He cast down great stones from heaven and killed them." See Joshua, tenth chapter, eleventh verse—"Their infants shall be dashed in pieces, and their women shall be ripped up," &c. Now, what can be more savage and ungodly than these records of "the Lord's doings"? Surely, the commonest sympathies of the human heart are far more divine than the attributes of such a God as is here represented by one and all of his alledged holy prophets. During our late war with Mexico, the most infuriated warrior did not even suggest such barbarous cruelties as are described in this infallible revelation, as suggested and performed by the Lord himself! But see the—

Sixth affirmation—to be found in thirtieth Psalm, fifth verse—"His anger endureth but a moment." The same author says elsewhere—"The Lord is gracious and full of compassion, slow to anger, and of great mercy." And Daniel says--ninth chapter, ninth verse—"To the Lord belong mercies and forgivenesses, though we have rebelled against him." Now, I desire your strictest attention to this point: that the Lord is not "slow to anger," that he does not get over his anger in "a moment," nor is he merciful and "full of compassion;" for, by reference to the sixth chapter of 1 Samuel, nineteenth verse, you will see that the Lord gives to the affirmation of David—

The contradiction. In this chapter it is related that the Lord, for the simple act of looking into the ark, *slew fifty thousand and seventy inhabitants.* In the thirty-second chapter of Numbers, thirteenth verse, it is related that "His (the Lord's) anger was kindled; and he made them wander in the wilderness, (not for "a moment" which is the period that David sets to the duration of "his anger," but for) forty years, till all who had offended him were consumed;" and, in the twenty-fifth chapter of Numbers, fourth verse, it is related how "He (that is, the Lord,) commanded the heads of the people to be hung up against the sun, to turn away his fierce anger." Are these contradictions to be explained away by an ingenious and clerical reading of the text? Can it be said that these inconsistencies will not appear when the whole is read in its stupendous connections? Can these contradictions be repudiated on the ground of "garbled extracts" and misrepresentation? Can it be said that every part is so intimately connected and blended with every other part, that an adequate view of the whole is indispensable to a just estimate of the minor portions? Nay; this can not be said of a supernatural revelation. The parts must be just as distinct and infallible as the whole. And furthermore, let it be borne in mind, the quotations refer either to fact or to principle; and the contexts are precisely to the same import and purpose. Hence, the affirmations and contradictions are opposed to each other,—fact for fact, and principle for principle,—and the plea of unfairness can not be brought to bear upon these plain propositions which are put into our minds by the very revelation in question. I will confess that these contradictions will seldom appear to him who reads the whole; because there is not *one* in five thousand persons possessed with the critical discrimination of mind which is required to detect the positive or relative absurdities in the system under consideration.

Let me place one statement of fact in opposition to another, and you will see my meaning.

Seventh affirmation—see Genesis xxxii. 30, also Exodus xxxiii. 9–11—where it is said, "I have seen God face to face," &c. "The Lord talked with Moses, and spake to him face to face, as a man speaketh to his friend." Now, this is a simple text—requiring no figurative or correspondential interpretation. It is plain English language, and every educated man can read it for himself. And now, let it be observed that—

The contradiction is just as plain, and to the point, which is affirmed in the same book of the Old Testament. See Exodus, thirty-third chapter, twentieth and twenty-third verses—where it is said, in contradiction to Moses who affirms he saw God face to face —"Thou canst not see my face"—"no man shall see me and live"—"my face shall not be seen!" It is well to observe, in this connection, that no biblical logician or accepted scholar can make it appear that this is not a positive contradiction of fact—an hypothetical fact that God was seen by Moses "face to face," and the contradictional fact, that "no man" can see God's face "and live;" and, in the mean time, it would not be just to pass over the affirmation of St. John, which contradicts Moses, that "God is a spirit," nor the still stronger affirmation of St. Luke, that "a spirit hath not flesh and bones," which demonstrates the Mosaic record of seeing and conversing with Jehovah exceedingly apocryphal, and far, very far from our conceptions of what an infallible relation should be. Having thus given you an illustration of what I mean by biblical contradictions in point of fact,—which is only one of twenty thousand errors which I could furnish you in case it was deemed necessary,—I will now give you an example of what I mean when I assert this so-called infallible book to be also contradictory in point of principle.

It will surely be conceded, that any thing which refers especially and explicitly to the great attributes of Jehovah must of necessity be classed among the category of statements which are identical with principle. To illustrate my meaning:—Any thing which refers to historical occurrences—to the number of an army—to deeds of cruelty—to horrid massacres—to points of genealogical and chronological history, &c., are properly denominated "facts," and the correspondential contexts are termed "contradictional facts;" but any thing which refers particularly to the divine character and attributes, or to certain laws which the Lord is alledged to have instituted for the unerring government of mankind, is to be classed among "principles," and the contexts or manifestations of those attributes are to be denominated "contradictional principles." Now, in accordance with this definition, which the most erudite commentator will not undertake to repudiate, I will furnish you with a few contradictions in point of principle. See the—

Eighth affirmation, concerning the intrinsic *disposition* of Jehovah. Ezekiel says, in his eighteenth chapter and thirty-second verse, "The Lord has no pleasure in the death of him that dieth." But how positively does Joshua give to this amiable disposition on the part of "the Lord" a startling contradiction! Behold, for illustration—

The contradiction in the tenth chapter of Joshua, twentieth verse; where it is said—"The Lord hardened their hearts, that they might find no favor, and be utterly destroyed." Here you perceive, the holy prophet asserts that the Lord does take "pleasure in the death of him that dieth;" because he "hardened their hearts" with the express design to keep them from the mental state which deserves "favor," thus the more perfectly to accomplish their "utter" destruction! But, for another illustration, see the—

Ninth affirmation, which refers to God in the exercise of his lenient disposition through his will or omnipotence. Thus, we read, in 1 Timothy, second chapter, fourth verse, that "He willeth that all men should come to the knowledge of the truth and be saved." But observe—

The contradiction. In 2 Thessalonians, second chapter, eleventh and twelfth verses, it is distinctly and positively asserted that "He shall send them strong delusion, that they might believe a lie and be damned." Now, friends, how can you reconcile this contradiction with the admission of a divine and infallible revelation? You can not evade this point honorably; you can not honestly deride this proposition; you can not refer me to Dr. Adam Clark's, or to McKnight's, Campbell's, Scott's, or to any other biblical scholar's commentary for an explanation. You can not furnish a literal signification of one passage and a spiritual interpretation of the other. For we have an English translation of an infallible "word,"—the accepted nomenclature is exceeding simple and plain,—and all intelligent minds can read "the word" as well as Swedenborg,

McKnight, or Clark can, and can also as easily decide upon the consistency or rectitude of all biblical statements. What position, then, are you to take, when you read a positive contradiction? Timothy asserts that the Lord "willeth that all men should come to the knowledge of the truth and be saved;" but does he "will" all men to know the truth and be saved, when he announces his most positive and settled determination, through the same book, that he will —yea, stronger than this, that he "shall—send them strong delusion," (that is, a positive psychological, irresistible influence,) "that they might believe a lie," and, consequently, have their damnation made positively certain by the same Lord who desires, and wills it, that all should know the Truth and be saved? I know it is claimed that this is to be done, very generously and mercifully by the Lord, in order to test the soundness of those who think themselves already among "the elect;" but this thought is so insulting to the goodness, omniscience, and omnipotence of the Living God, that I stop not to descant upon a proposition so profoundly unreasonable and irreligious.

But let me again ask you—"What position will you take when you read these positive contradictions in a volume which is venerated by you as the *plenum* of celestial and infallible Truth?" Your reply is anticipated. You have accepted the foundation without a question; your heart and your intellect believe in a perfect and infinite God without consulting your infallible revelation; but, when you do consult the household God, and read the doctrine, that God is not infinite nor perfect; that he was seen locally; that he frequently manifested anger and furious passion; that he made his alledged prophets and apostles reveal contradictory things concerning facts and principles,—I say, when you consult these things, what do you think? Most distinctly you confess,—"I do not understand these supernatural mysteries—these surpassing arcana of the great triune God—but they must be true notwithstanding!"

That is to say, you have sold yourself to an incomprehensible faith, hence you suspect yourself—your reason, intuitions, instincts, soul; and can say, with Professor Bush, that, "Believing so, I dare not confer with flesh and blood." If I have not anticipated your replies correctly, or the actual foundations of your faith in the supernatural and miraculous, then I desire to be rectified in these particulars to the end that the human mind may be still better comprehended. A mind, which is thus believing in the infallibility of any revelation, is, most positively and unequivocally, psychologized by a religious faith to begin with; then he is psycho-sympathetically magnetized by the thoughts of the author, or authors, of his faith; so that he begins to imagine that his "heart," his "intellect," and the "central" intuitions of his soul are all "convinced" of a faith which is "beyond the reach of the native faculties of man;" and, then, in the exercise of his "best reason," he is in the transition state between misdirection and liberty, between bondage and freedom, between using the eyes of his leader and the proper use of his own powers of discernment!

From the foregoing, let it not be inferred that I am creating a question as to Swedenborg's versatility of talent, his veracity, or spiritual illumination. The *reality of his intercourse with the spiritual world* I am not permitted to doubt. But the great and paramount question to be established in regard to Swedenborg, and in regard to every other champion or representative of supernaturalism, is this: "Can there be any *pure reasoning* upon a supernatural or irrational basis?" If there can not be, then we are compelled to account psychologically, or upon *ontological* principles, for this universal fallacy or faith among mankind. To give this explanation, the case of Baron Swedenborg was selected as the best modern *type* or example of supernaturalistic faith, accompanied by the semblance of philosophical reasoning. And Professor Bush was chosen also as an illustration of the *Transition State*, in which the mind is neither so free, nor so able to reason, as when the individual is in the more advanced conditions, hereafter to be considered. The supernatural system of faith must be analyzed. And who among you can say, but that Swedenborg's *mission* is not so indissolubly connected with the spiritual or mystical *coming of the Lord*, as with the great question of *naturalism* and *supernaturalism*, which seems to press this Age for a thorough and perfect solution? It is oming to be seen that social improvement depends very much upon a rational verdict.

Friends, there is a new philosophy in the world! There is a new covenant of Man with Reason! It is not the resurrection of an old scheme, born in Greece and laid to sleep in the lap of Rome, and now exhumed under a new title and differently recommended. Nay; but it is a stupendous development of God's Truth through the ten thousand avenues of Nature and humanity,—a deep, strong, heavenly strain of music which is yet destined to lead human souls into dependent groups around one common center of harmonious sympathy. There is a new-born thought on the altar of the human heart—a toleration, and genial goodness, breathing like the warmth of a universal spring over the tender buds and unfolding sensibilities of man's immortal soul!

LECTURE XV.

THE TRANSITION STATE OF MIND, AS DEVELOPED AMONG RELIGIOUS CHIEFTAINS.

Those who heard the discourse on last Sabbath evening, will doubtless remember the presentation of certain passages of the Primitive History, which were positively contradictory in themselves, both in point of letter and internal signification. And there were two conclusions, legitimately developed from the premises, which were frequently urged upon your attention; first, that there can not possibly be any pure reasoning upon an admitted basis of supernaturalism; in other words, upon a foundation, which is lost in the dark depths of incomprehensibility; second, that the contradictions referred to,—which were exceedingly weak and unforcible when compared with many others contained in the same book,—demonstrate that those accounts originated solely and entirely with human beings.

These positions are very distinct and easily comprehended. But the question is—Are they true? This interrogation was mainly answered in the preceding lecture; wherein it was shown, that he who takes for granted the professions of any religious chieftain, that he is a particular favorite of the Most High, and especially called to reveal infallible doctrines, has virtually resigned his mind to the government of another. Therefore, that he who placed himself in such a position had trammeled his own soul, and chained his reason to a theological system, and hence was free to exercise his understanding only within certain well-defined limitations. And it was further shown, that an infallible revelation must not contain contradictions, or inconsistencies in point of fact or principle; but, inasmuch as the system under investigation *was proved* to contain those evidences which demonstrated its fallacious and imperfect character, it was consequently concluded that the work is wholly and unqualifiedly referable to the operations of the human mind.

This position is very comprehensive and essentially important. It throws a great responsibility upon the source of my impressions,—which I am impressed to cheerfully acknowledge and accept,—because, as you will very readily perceive, there is a stupendous amount of explanation demanded from me on all sides, and which I must be expected to furnish to those who conceive their faith, in the miraculous and supernatural, mortally injured by the assertions made and positions taken.

For example, I must explain to the Turks how Mohammed received and wrote his religion, i. e., if I repudiate the doctrine that he was infallible and supernaturally inspired; the same explanation is demanded by Christians concerning the prophetical and other writings of their so-called infallible penmen; the same explanation is demanded by the Shakers, who regard, most devoutly, the system of faith and social government which rests upon the Bible and upon the equally infallible allegations of their female leader; the same explanation is demanded by the followers of Joseph Smith, who was esteemed as the express agent of "the Lord" in the revealment of an additional amount of infallible truth, beginning where the Bible leaves off, and continuing the narrations of supernatural histories and doctrines up to the present time—thus converting all past revelations into the Mormon system of faith; and lastly, and more positively and peremptorily than all the other sects, the followers of Swedenborg demand an explanation of his transcendental revelations and profound unfoldings of the literal, spiritual, and celestial senses or significations of the Word.

But why do these different sects require these explanations?

Why do they clamor about a satisfactory solution of the processes and operations of Isaiah's, David's, Mohammed's, Smith's, or Swedenborg's mind, while these religious chieftains were engaged in the development of their so-called infallible revelations ? They demand these explanations, because they know comparatively nothing of the powers and psychological laws natural to the human mind. They have no insight into the principles which govern the soul. In a word, the followers of these several religious chieftains are reposing their heart's confidence upon the professions of their leaders, because they are ignorant of the mind's laws and hidden qualifications. In the commencement, a supernatural faith is adopted; and, then, the habit becoming permanently fixed in the mind, it is very easy to accept the subsequent relations of persons who recommend themselves by claiming a relationship to supernatural revelations and influxes. That is to say, a mind that has never ventured to question the accounts of Moses, Joshua, or of Aaron,—that has not felt the first sensation of mental independence sufficient to interrogate the reliability of the professions and testimonies of the religious characters and chieftains of antiquity,—such a mind, is all prepared to believe the analogous professions of Mohammed, Smith, or Swedenborg. These characters simply claim for themselves what Moses and Joshua claimed—viz.: to have been particular favorites of the Lord—to have seen, and walked, and conversed with him, and to have been the divinely appointed vessels for the revealment of infallible truth. And the mind that can accept the professions of one as true, can as easily receive the claims of the other. Because, from the moment you adopt, without an analytical investigation, the belief that a human being, constituted of flesh and blood as we are, and subject to all the frailties and imperfections consequent upon such a material constitution, can bring forth infallible truth, you open the flood-gates of innumerable absurdities, and expose your souls and understandings to the vagaries of sympathetic minds, and also to the impositions of ambitious and designing men. Now I am impressed to say that, he who understands the constitution of the human mind, and has a general comprehension of the principal laws which control the mental organization, could never be psychologized into the erroneous belief, that the Lord selects certain individuals as the agents of an infallible and supernatural revelation.

But the sects demand an *explanation* of the causes and motives which actuated their chieftains to proclaim to the world such astounding professions. Again, let me remind you that no person, or follower of these respective leaders, would feel the need of any such explanation if his mind was familiar with its own laws and hidden qualifications; hence I attribute any such personal need to personal ignorance. If man comprehended man, then all the phenomena natural to prophetic and exalted minds could receive an easy and exceedingly simple solution. But as it is—the human mind is so manifestly ignorant of its own intrinsic constitution and principles—that, when I shall furnish the plain and philosophical explanation to those who clamor most for it, it will be seen that they do not at all comprehend it, and hence a continuation of their thoughts in the channels of supernaturalism and miracle will be just as certain as it was prior to the psychological solutions which I may offer.

What an inconsistency is this! for minds to believe in the mere professions of their religious chieftains—and believe in much that is profoundly absurd and incomprehensible—while, in fact, they do not know scarcely any thing of the beginning principles of knowledge, which are based upon the constitution of Nature and the laws of Mind. When I assert that these followers are ignorant of psychological principles, I am aware that I run the risk of provoking from them a supercilious smile, on the supposition that the deep foundations of their faith are utterly misunderstood and misrepresented. But of their ignorance the world will most certainly be convinced; not so much by any thing which I may write, but, inevitably, by the progressive development of intuition, reason, and science. It will be ultimately seen that no religious chieftain ever held converse with "the Lord," or revealed infallible truth; but the laws of psychological science will shed a new and simple light upon the structure and functions of the human mind, at the expense of much unhealthy reverence and mental slavery that now retard the higher progressions of man.

In accordance with my impressions, I now proceed to affirm that all religious chieftains known to the world—Moses, Isaiah, Paul, Mohammed, Zoroaster, Smith, Swedenborg—were all, more or less, in what I term a *transition state* of mind, which is midway, or intermediate, between mental slavery and liberty,—or, rather, a state in which the soul is strongly sympathetic with hereditary impressions, with educational convictions, and with prevailing forms of belief, while, almost at the same time, the mind exhibits a kind of consistency and independence of thought in proportion to the preponderance of the orderly faculties in the mental structure.

In this place let me say, that, by classing Moses with Mohammed, and Joseph Smith with Baron Swedenborg, no disrespect is intended to either party. I am made conscious of a vast difference between these religious chieftains in point of the purity of their respective characters and in the comprehensiveness of their genius. Of this I may hereafter speak. But when Christians claim for Moses, Turks for Mohammed, Mormons for Smith, and the New Churchmen for Swedenborg, that their favorite prophet was divinely inspired and supernaturally endowed to reveal infallible truths, then it is not I who allude to them in connections which may be esteemed by their followers as dishonorable. Nay; but they stand before the world just as I have classed them. The professions of Mohammed are just as worthy of a candid investigation as the corresponding professions of Moses; so, likewise, I esteem the high and incomprehensible claims of Swedenborg as much deserving of our candid attention as the analogous presumptions and assumptions of Joseph Smith. Yet, in all this, I make a vast difference between these characters, their relative developments of truth, and their pedantic claims to infallibility. In the matter of professing to be the agents and selected messengers of God to man, these religious chieftains place themselves on the same identical platform. In this respect, one is deserving of just as much honor and investigation as the other; and no more on the score of hypothetical conscientious endearments or educational predilections.

Without further preliminary remark, I proceed to consider the psychological phenomena which characterized the state of Emmanuel Swedenborg; not, however, with any intention of considering the quality or quantity of the truths which he is supposed to have perceived, comprehended, and written, but with the already avowed design of furnishing a philosophical solution of a state of mind which could entertain a belief that the Lord gave it the power of revealing ideas, which are very improperly alledged to be entirely above the reach of the native faculties of man.

Let us commence with Swedenborg's own affirmation. He says —in a letter to Dr. Detinger—"I can sacredly and solemnly declare, that the Lord Himself has been seen of me, and that he has sent me to do what I do, and for such purpose has opened the interior part of my soul, which is my spirit, so that I can see what is in the spiritual world, and those that are therein; and this privilege has now been continued to me for twenty-two years." Now, this is a wonderful belief—a wondrous profession for one human being to make before a world of individuals constituted like himself! Again, I solicit the candid attention of Christians to this point, and to all the points which will be discussed in the progress of the present explanation; because the whole case is a fine mirror in which they can view themselves most accurately and comprehensively. The claims of Swedenborg are no less wonderful, miraculous, or supernatural—perhaps, no less unreasonable and superstitious—than those claims set up by all the accepted prophets and seers of Christendom. Think of this declaration! A human being, constituted just as you are—under the absolute necessity of eating, sleeping, taking out-door exercise, and of submitting to all the mental and organic laws of mundane life—declaring, and that, too, most sacredly and solemnly, that he had seen the Lord and that his interior nature had been opened by the Lord in a supernatural manner! This is surely a most startling and miraculous, but not a novel, declaration for one individual to make before the world. It is not novel, because it is the uniform and invariable assumption or profession of every religious leader and chieftain that ever stood before mankind.

To prevent misunderstanding, let me again define my position in the premises. I do not object to, nor am I impressed to undertake to controvert, the statement of Swedenborg that he had seen into the Spiritual World; for this power, as I have before said, is the constitutional or natural inheritance of every individual member of the human race, and hence is not a supernatural exercise of the inward spirit. But what I am deeply moved to consider as unsound and fallacious, is, his profession that the "privilege" of seeing into the spiritual world was *granted* to him for many years by the Lord himself. You will observe the position assumed. It is that Swedenborg's psychological condition *was not a natural* and consequent result of certain physical harmonies and mental sensibilities on his part, but a supernatural operation performed upon his most interior being by the particular manipulations of the Lord of heaven! This is his own solemn profession. In his letter to the king, he says—"The Lord our Savior manifested himself to me in a sensible personal appearance, and commanded me to write what has already been done; and was afterward graciously pleased to endow me with the privilege of conversing with spirits and angels. It is not in my power to place others in the same state in which God has placed me. * * * This knowledge is given to me from our Savior, not for any particular merit of mine, but for the great concern of all Christians' salvation and happiness." Now this is a solemn declaration; and the ground taken is substantially identical with that assumed by all religious chieftains in all ages of the world among all nations.

This position is fatal to all efforts to personal progression on the part of the unprivileged classes of mankind. It would be presumption for a plebeian character to assert that the Lord had most graciously pleased to grant to him the "privilege" of conversing with spirits and angels. Yea, verily! But let a nobleman—a finely educated and esteemed patrician—set up a claim to heavenly privileges on the score of an embassador admitted to the courts of a celestial aristocracy, and he is very likely to be believed in after years by those who are already well prepared for it, with a strong faith in the absolutely supernatural and miraculous.

If Swedenborg had confessed, what he discovered a few years prior to his decease, that he was not wholly infallible, then his followers would not so readily take his theological system as the foundation of a bold, aristocratic sectarianism. But without impeaching the honesty of this chieftain, I may here assert, what I know to be true, that he felt consciously impressed that the foundation of his system, and the principal minutiæ of his propositions and conclusions, were reliable, and therefore felt convinced, that, although there were defects which demonstrated his disclosures to be essentially human in their derivation; nevertheless he had devoted his life to the exposition of a good cause, and thence derived his self-justification to secrecy as to the import of his subsequent discoveries. It would be rather humiliating to a patrician mind to confess himself mistaken for nearly a whole life-time. The uniform modest, unostentatious demeanor of this talented Swede—the total absence of any show of pride of position or claim to merit—has much to do in recommending his professions to the intellects and hearts of many Christians. This certainly is an attraction in any human being. But it is precisely what all Christians try to exhibit before the Lord in order to receive his favor. In plain language, this is a species of theological merchandise—an affected show of deserving nothing for the express purpose of obtaining great spiritual riches from the Giver of grace to the unmeritorious heart. Now, all that can be claimed for Swedenborg on the score of his uniform humility is this —he had in his own mind the means of self-justification, the nature of which he never disclosed to the world.

When a giant is caressed he looks as mild as the morning and gentle as the playful child, but urge him to combat and his form will ascend like a colossus and his gigantic arm will swell with a mighty strength. So with Swedenborg, when considered in relation to his supernatural claims. When viewed adoringly, he says to you in substance—"Do not believe me simply because I have seen Heaven and Hell—have discoursed with angels—and been admitted to the precincts of the Divine Presence. But believe me because I tell you what your intuitions will tell you, if you will calmly listen to their voice. In your soul you will see the principles which, from their very nature, must result in just such eternal actualities as I disclose to you." Now, this amiable disposition, on the part of a moral or theological giant, who knows he has you in his power, may be deemed highly attractive to some minds. But let us see whether he will remain thus passive and beautifully unpresuming, when his testimony is questioned. Suppose, after consulting my soul and nature, I should say to him—"I can not believe in your professions respecting the 'favors'—'grants'—'privileges,' &c., which you affirm to have obtained from the Lord. I can and do believe that you occasionally saw into the spiritual world—that you sometimes beheld, and conversed with, spirits and angels; but I do not believe that you, or any other being that ever breathed on earth, was instructed by 'the Lord' *himself* to utter infallible truths to mankind." What, think you, would this unassuming giant say in reply? He would not rise in his strength immediately, but he would, with his mind swelling with a reviving conception of his certain infallibility, reply most positively in this manner, (as he did in his letter to the king,)—"If any doubt shall remain, I am ready to testify, with the most solemn oath that can be offered in this matter, that I have said nothing but essential and real truth without any admixture of deception." Ponder this for a moment. An unassuming man! Declaring that he had wrote nearly thirty years nothing but the truth—no error, no imperfection, no mistakes. Now, what am I to say? I have said that I do not believe in his supernatural ecstacies of mind, nor in his infallibility. But what can I say, admitting his honesty, when he is ready to take the "most solemn oath" that he had wrote "nothing but essential and real truth" for several years? Does he still remain the same unassuming man? Does he still very modestly counsel me to consult my intuitions and my highest reason, and let them decide? If he did, it would be an unparalleled example of modesty and meekness in the theological annals of the world. Moses, Joshua, Isaiah, Paul, St. John, Buddha, Mohammed, Roman priests, and Joseph Smith, might each and all have learned a valuable lesson in the method of a gracious and genial humility, with the vast back-ground of a settled conviction that they were infallible teachers instructed by the Lord himself. What majesty there would be in such meekness! What a mighty giant might live beneath the tender deportment of the playful child! But how disappointed am I in this! Every religious chieftain professes to be God-favored—God-privileged—God-appointed! You may very carefully question your intuitions and consciousness whether Moses, or Jesus, or John, or Mohammed, or Luther, or Calvin, or Swedenborg, or whether any other religious leader, did or did not reveal the unalloyed truth, according to the Lord's particular appointment; you may question just so long as your consciousness harmonizes with what they teach,—but when you feel to disagree with them, What then? The answer is plain. Do you question their honesty? Not at all. Very well: on this admission these religious Generals erect a "most solemn oath" that they have uttered nothing but perfect and infallible truth by divine appointment and permission. Now what can you say? Are you free to reason upon a supernatural basis? Are you free to be led "rationally and in freedom" in matters pertaining to religious systems of faith? Are you in a condition to exercise man's highest prerogative, in deciding upon the intrinsic truth of a miraculously delivered revelation—viz., your reason-principle? Swedenborg is exceedingly mild and affable to your intuition and consciousness until they remonstrate against something of his asserted claims,—But what then? Why, he sacredly and solemnly declares "that the Lord himself has been seen of me, and that He has sent me to do what I do;" and this declaration is made not less than twelve hundred times, here and there, throughout the entire mass of his theological works; which are so repetitious with regard to their contents that, without the least disrespect to his genius, it may be truthfully said that he renounced all interest in the world of literature about him, and derived his mental subsistence and enjoyments wholly from the vitals of his own religious cogitations.

Again I say, there can be no pure reasoning upon a supernatural basis. The admission into your mind, that Moses or Mohammed, Smith or Swedenborg, were divinely and miraculously inspired of God—that they were honest, and rendered infallible by the especial manipulations and psychological operations of the Lord—is an admission which cripples your abilities to stand on your own internal prerogatives, and renders your attempts at reasoning as palpably trivial as the efforts of a lame man who would walk without his crutch and other dependencies to which he has become accustomed. But how shall I proceed to convince an ignorant man that he is not wise? How shall I prove to the believer in supernatural revelations and personages, that he does not reason analytically? How shall I open the eyes of the morally blind, and cause the spiritually lame to stand up before their God, on their own feet, and walk uprightly in enlightenment? Most willingly I confess that these things can not be instantly performed; for all changes depend upon time and the favorable operation of surrounding circumstances. In this way all the so-called miracles were accomplished. Hence I act understandingly. In the ultimate extermination of all unhealthy superstition I can not be disappointed. It is just as inevitable as the disappearance of catamounts, wolves, snakes, and lizards before the steady march of civilization. Hence individuals—and I among the number—can only shed all the light they possess on the surrounding darkness. If there be a moral wilderness to overcome; if there be theological wolves and bears to hunt; if there be unwholesome marshes to discover and purify in the great territories of the religious world; most certain am I, that it is the duty of every man, who is not intellectually blind and spiritually lame—those who can see for themselves and walk on their own feet—to turn out upon harmonial principles, to set about the high calling of making the wilderness to blossom as the rose!

But could I persuade a fixed Jew, a Lutheran, a Calvinist, a Shaker, a Mormon, or a Swedenborgian, that he is not altogether reasonable,—that he is not working in *the best field* and in the very best possible manner? Nay; far, very far from it! In viewing Swedenborg as the type of all religious chieftains or teachers of infallible doctrines, and his followers as the most perfect representatives of all sectarians who lay high claims to the profoundest reasoning, I am but doing what the entire case most distinctly suggests to the mind. Now I do not hesitate to affirm that the keenest intellects and purest hearts among the receivers of "The doctrines of the New Church," are not the logicians and analytical thinkers they are occasionally apprehended to be. True, they are exempt from the ordinary forms of enthusiasm, and they do not indulge as a general thing in common sophistries in the application of their superficial and arbitrary science of correspondences; simply because any mind that calmly submits to be psychologized and to be rendered psycho-sympathetic by reading the heavy statements and innumerable repetitions of this self-proclaimed prophet, is certainly in no danger of ever becoming conspicuously enthusiastic. To prevent any misunderstanding, I am here impressed to say, that Swedenborg is to be regarded as the author of many truthful revealments. On an examination of his various writings, you will find many historical, scientific, philosophical, metaphysical, and spiritual truths, which place this writer far up in the gallery of lofty geniuses that have, now and then, bloomed in the broad fields of humanity, like Century Plants,—but so occasionally, that the adoring world can not forbear the bestowment of the supposed honor of deification.

Notwithstanding Swedenborg proclaims that he is God-sent about twelve hundred times, and makes a most sacred and solemn oath that he has revealed "nothing but essential and real truth;" yet his followers say—"that the question must be first of all determined, whether Swedenborg was in truth made the subject of supernatural revelations." Now here is a show—yea, merely a display—of reasoning, at the expense of calling into question the honesty of their prophet's constantly repeated attestations! He says "the Lord himself" held him in perpetual relationship to goodness and truth, and enabled him to do all that he performed. The same claim is set up by Moses, and all religious chieftains before and since his generation; and what is the follower to say? The professions of the chieftain must be regarded as reliable, or else you call in question his moral character. From this, all disciples invariably shrink; and hence there is an end to all pure and sound reasoning concerning the foundations of their faith. For if I should affirm, which I most distinctly do, that Swedenborg was not supernaturally inspired to reveal infallible truths, then his disciples would peremptorily demand from me an answer to these interrogatories:—"Do you, sir, doubt the honesty of Emmanuel Swedenborg? Can you account for the profound and stupendous disclosures of this author, without admitting that he was, according to his own oft-repeated affirmation, instructed to do all he did by the Lord Himself?" I answer that I can; and I shall appeal to the principles of psychological science for an adequate solution of his case. "The receivers of his doctrines," says a talented disciple, "confidently affirm, that a fair and candid survey of the psychological evidence in the case is decisive of the fact of a supernatural illumination." That is to say, Swedenborg was vastly superior to other members of humanity, and his condition was *above* Nature; hence it was supernatural! Now I am deeply impressed with this thought, that the human mind can get at a great quantity of real truth by simple processes—by honest-heartedness, by observation of Nature, by intuition, and Reason. Therefore I am willing to adopt the assertion, that "it is possible for the mind, when conducted thither by appropriate evidence, to rest in the absolute assurance of truth on certain great points of our psychological being." And Swedenborg perpetually refers the reader to the facts of science, to consciousness, to Reason, to goodness and truth, in order to sustain and verify his multitudinous positions. But suppose some of his positions do not harmonize with the facts referred to—What then? No matter; you have no alternative, nothing to debate and decide. For there stands the "most solemn oath" of a man whose moral character is unimpeachable, that he has been "instructed by the Lord Himself" and has revealed "nothing but essential and real truth without any mixture of error." Thus, your position is easily defined. You must do one of two things: either reject his claim to infallibility, and then use your Reason in studying the works of a lofty and rare genius; or, reject your reason, and accept his claims to infallibility, and henceforth set bounds to your own sphere of thought and progress. There are no alternatives in this case; the same may be said of all who pretend to rank themselves among the believers in miraculous and supernatural things.

I have said that I can explain Swedenborg's psychological condition, and the origin of his disclosures, without impeaching his honesty or accepting his perpetually urged claim to a supernatural illumination of mind. This I will do in my next discourse, according to my impressions.

But as a preface to this solution, let me remind you that Truth is always simple; whilst Error is compound and generally incomprehensible. A wonderful matter, if it be a truth, is always found to rest upon a very simple and plain foundation. It is only error which hath its foundations in darkness, and turrets clothed in black and gloomy clouds. While mankind are heterogeneous, so will be their explanations. The undeveloped or unbalanced brain generates a corresponding mind, and then the latter, in its manifold operations, indicates the actual condition of the individual. Hence men and ages are quite analogous. Discord begets discord; although it often promotes and suggests harmony. As men become enlightened, their thoughts assume simplicity. The countless pagan gods or mythologic deities are but the embodiments of ignorance and forms of imaginations. Pythagoras was *more* progressed than the pagan priests, and hence was less complicated in his impressions and philosophy of nature. Enlightenment destroys mystery and complicity; and opens the door to grandeur, resting upon simplicity. Men will more and more lose sight of the supernatural or unnatural as their perceptions of truth become enlarged by experience and spiritually illuminated. And it comes to me as a prophecy, based upon the immutable laws of progression and knowledge, that *all Truth will ultimately be seen as a unit*—or, that ONE GRAND PRINCIPLE will be found to constitute the *Alpha* and *Omega*—the "All in All"—of the material and spiritual universe. If we follow Nature to her deepest recesses, and search far and wide for the principles whereby she conducts her stupendous operations, we shall discover in the end, that a few—a very few—simple truths lie at the foundation of all her vast developments. You may rest perfectly assured, that, when you get a complicated explanation of any thing, you have not got the entire truth. The experience of the entire world is, that all certainly discovered truth is exceedingly simple in its nature, and so easily comprehended, that even he who runs may read it. On this beautiful principle of simplicity, every thing is made and existing. The pulsations of the human heart occur on that principle whereby planets are made to roll in the broad expanse of the immeasurable infinitude!

LECTURE XVI.

CONTINUATION OF TRANSITIONAL MANIFESTATIONS AMONG RELIGIOUS CHIEFTAINS.

It will be remembered, that, the subject of the last lecture was particularly concerning the claims to infallibility which are set up by all religious chieftains, known to either the heathen or Christian world. And as a very faithful type of this class of peculiarities, common to the characters under consideration, I was impressed to select the case of Emmanuel Swedenborg, the very talented Swedish philosopher and psychological theologian.

A portion of the last discourse was also especially devoted to the consideration of the fact, that there can not be any pure analytical reasoning upon an admitted basis of supernatural inspiration. Because, by admitting the honesty of the minds who profess to be the subjects of such inspiration, you are either compelled to reject your reason and accept their professions as truth, or you must furnish a clear and consistent explanation of the problems presented. In accordance with my impressions, I will give you my solution of Swedenborg's psychological state in this lecture; and the same explanation will apply very generally to all honest religious chieftains that ever appeared on the stage of the world's vast theater. It is, however, deemed necessary to first show you how unreliable all human testimony is, particularly when taken in connection with professions to supernatural illumination of mind. In this I do not mean to repudiate the validity of human testimony and experience in the aggregate; for in this respect I esteem them exceedingly valuable as the foundation of much confidence and healthy inference · but I simply

17*

call in question the soundness of human testimony when it is associated with any thing which pertains to the miraculous or supernatural.

Allow me to solicit your attention to this point or peculiarity among all receivers of an infallible teacher : I allude to the powerful effort which is made to connect him with something wonderful and essentially divine—to include him in a category of supernatural personages and arrangements. The consequence of which is, to cut off all proper or natural sympathetic connections between a religious leader and the heart of humanity; thus to erect the chieftain into an object of profound reverence, as endowed with deific attributes and supernatural characteristics. Or if a connection is at all allowed to exist, it is based upon some divine and incomprehensible affinity with man by the mere wearing of a human body. Thus the Jews venture to regard Moses as a human being on the ground that he possessed many things in common with other men. And so it is every where, among all terrestrial inhabitants. Every religious leader and teacher is esteemed as a little lower than the gods —he must be a God manifested in the flesh, not upon any philosophical principle of universal incarnation whereby all visible things are physical embodiments of divine elements and essences, as, for example, minerals of Motion, vegetables of Life, animals of Sensation, and man of Intelligence; not so; but he must be a link in a supernatural and incomprehensible chain of celestial designs, and hence *above* nearly every thing which is human and consistent with mankind's current experience. This is the error of the world—the mistake of ignorant and credulous men. As I have said, such an error as that of deification is invariably committed by those whose minds are all prepared for miraculous disclosures by a strong and undisturbed faith in the unqualifiedly supernatural and mysterious.

Christians are generally exempt from this charge, because the most enlightened among them, who pass for good sound orthodox believers, are the veriest skeptics in all spiritual things. They have no light upon psychological subjects; no accepted theories concerning the state of the soul after death; no principles of scientific inquiry and analysis; no distinct and healthy views of the spiritual world; or any decided faith in the substantial existence and growth of the soul subsequent to its emergement from this life into another sphere of being. But those among Christains who are not much enlightened,—who are ignorant in the main,—believe most devoutly all which the other class merely profess to inculcate as religious truths. Hence I make a vast distinction between the teachers and the receivers of popular theology. But there is no such difference between the believers of Swedenborg and those who employ their talents in the promulgation of his theological system. They are, like the first apostles of Christianity, perfectly united in the main points of faith. And they, one and all, concentrate their efforts to supernaturalize their leader and identify him with a train of heavenly designs and miraculously endowed personages.

With the express design of recommending the high claims of Swedenborg to the Christian world, Professor Bush commences, in his usually vigorous and logical manner, to examine the prophecies of the Old Testament—of Daniel especially,—and succeeds admirably in showing that the second coming of Christ, in spirit, occurred about the time when Swedenborg arose in his prophetical character. Thus he begins, logically and biblically, to elevate the developments of his chieftain into the sphere of the holy, deified, and supernatural; hence also the medium himself to a corresponding plane of reverence. "We have seen," says this talented disciple, "that the grand reason alledged by Swedenborg as justifying his mission is, that the sublime event of the second coming of Christ was at that time in a special manner ushered in, and that he (Swedenborg) was raised up to be an accredited herald of the "New Jerusalem that cometh down from God out of heaven"—of which he was to be the divinely authorized expounder. That is, Swedenborg takes his "most solemn oath" that he is a divinely appointed and infallible messenger of God; and then this talented disciple brings his powers of biblical criticism and of prophetical interpretation to bear upon the Christian world, and demonstrates,—that is, if you will simply admit the premises,—that his prophet is precisely and scripturally what the latter so frequently alledges on his own behalf. It is claimed by Swedenborg that Christ had his second coming at the end of the year 1260, when the Roman empire began to sicken and waste away. This second coming was altogether quiet and unobserved by the world—it was spiritual. Hence this invisible circumstance would have most probably passed by entirely unnoticed had not Swedenborg made his appearance. Hereon he erected for himself a mission, and presumptively identified himself with one of the most celestial and august dispensations that could possibly enter the sensorium of the most ambitious religious chieftain.

And on these grounds Professor Bush enters upon his biblical criticisms—displays an amount of moral and intellectual attainment in oriental knowledge which Christians would do well to regard—and beautifully paves the way for the acceptation of Swedenborg's revealments, by proving that *they are as* reliable, supernatural, and infallible as the utterances of any personage connected with the Old or New Testament. And I confess that I fully believe the last idea to be truth; indeed I regard Swedenborg as a great improvement on all prior religious chieftains in the matter of talent, truth, comprehensiveness, beauty of conception, and harmony of statements. But Professor Bush's position is vastly different. He accepts the professions of Swedenborg, and then makes the Bible prophecies to bend and sanction those claims; and thus links his prophet with the high commissioned immortals of the skies. In clinching this opinion upon the mind of the disciple, the Professor says—"And if the second coming has thus stolen upon the world unawares, we perceive nothing unreasonable in the idea, that its appointed harbinger may have come equally incognito, and that the Elias [Swedenborg]—the John the Baptist—of the new economy, may have ushered in the footsteps of his Lord, fulfilling his ministry as a kind of "Vailed Prophet," shrouded in an obscurity which is destined ere long to break away, to be succeeded by a flood of celestial light that shall illuminate the earth." Now, how vastly superior is this theological case to any thing among what are called evangelical Christians! I think they would do well to educate themselves in it. But I quote it simply to show how prone all disciples are to deify their favorite chieftain; at the same time to show how the receivers of Swedenborg accept his professions as worthy of all confidence, and, then, make out a biblical case of demonstration accordingly.

But I have asserted that human "oaths" and testimony concerning things of a supernatural character are not at all to enter into our faith, because they are not reliable. Without impeaching the honesty of any religious leader, however, who professes to miraculous inspiration, let me call your attention to the testimony of several chieftains known in common and sacred history.

Let us begin with Zoroaster, the great Persian theological reformer; who originated and gave rise to the doctrine of antagonistic deities—Arhiman, the evil god, and Ormudze, the god of goodness. And it would be but just to say, that this author also originated the popular doctrine of a physical resurrection and day of judgment, which is believed in Christendom as an important part of the supernatural revealments of the Bible. Zoroaster professed to be inspired above his fellow-men by the mercy of the god of goodness, whose name was Ormudge. And sublimely says, in the beginning of his bible—called the Zeuda Vesta—"Gratitude, greatness, and glory be unto Him! The all-merciful, the all-beautiful, the all-perfect! Who, in the plenitude of his unutterable goodness, has opened the deep wells of my being in which He hath poured, with a most merciful hand, the sweet perfumes of paradise and the holy oils of a knowledge, which exceeds my strength and that of any genii of the mountains, or that of any man or woman or brute, which hath a place any where in the dominion of the All-merciful! The inexorable decrees of the All-merciful could be known to his elohims (or dependent subordinates) only through me, the chosen servant of the All-beautiful and the All-perfect. Glory, greatness, and gratitude be unto Him—the perfumer of my body and the giver of all the oils of knowledge unto me—the Controller of all good and the Great Enemy of the wicked genii of the darknesses."

Such were the professions of the great Persian prince, Zoroaster, who lived and wrote before the beauty and intelligence of Greece were known, and long before there was any thing like the Bible which we deeply regard. Now what can you say to this? Was Zoroaster honest in putting forth this claim to infallible and boundless knowledge? Certainly! Then why not accept him as a divinely appointed messenger of Truth?

For the present I will leave you to answer this question as best you can, and proceed to notice the professions of another religious chieftain.

Moses set up a claim to miraculous inspiration, which he urges constantly in his writings, but in language far less sublime than the professions of Zoroaster. By this inspiration he claimed to have written, or, rather I should say, it is claimed by his translators for him, that he wrote the Pentateuch, or first five books of the Primitive History. It is said in the fifth chapter of Amos and seventh verse, that "the Lord will do nothing, but he revealeth his secret unto his servants, the prophets." Now were Moses, Joshua, Aaron, and Amos perfectly honest in the presentation of their claims? Most assuredly they were. Then, why not accept them as infallible teachers of Truth?

Again, let us hear the professions of that religious chieftain known as Mohammed. He also claimed to be inspired of the Lord of Heaven, and hence his revealments are regarded, by those who believe his declarations, as infallible, supernatural, and divine. It is even absolutely denied by Mohammedans that their Bible—the Koran—originated with their prophet. They look upon it, as Swedenborg teaches his followers to regard those portions of the Word to which he fixed a spiritual and celestial sense, as of divine origin—not made by men; but eternal and uncreated, originating in, and proceeding from, the very essence of truth as it is in God. But hear him describe his mission. In the second volume of his Bible, two hundred and eightieth page, he says—"In all soberness of mind and fervor of thought, Mohammed declares he was called by God to be his holy prophet. Verily, God sent him to be a witness of truth; a bearer of good and merciful tidings; a repudiator of threats; an inviter of the faithful unto God; to be unto the world a shining Light." Now,—as Professor Bush says concerning the correspondingly sober claims of Swedenborg,—"this certainly has the air of being uttered by an honest man, and especially when viewed by the side of what is said in the immediate connection," namely: "Unto Mohammed appeared the holy angel Gabriel, in all the seeming of the human form, and caused, in a wonderful manner, the uncreated Koran to descend on his heart; and confirmed, by the merciful permission of God, all which was before revealed through Mohammed, his prophet, and gave many directions and good tidings to the faithful."

There is no sophomorical strain exhibited in this language; no proclamation of an insane man; no show of an immoral fabrication; no display of brain-sick reveries and rhapsodical expressions; no evidences of delusion, imposture or fanaticism; but it is cool, modest, straightforward. The lofty assumptions of the infallible Papacy—the gentle claims of Swedenborg—the oft repeated profession of Moses—and the more sublime declaration of Zoroaster—all, are very simply and beautifully expressed, and set up, in the Koran.

Do you believe that Mohammed was honest? I certainly do. Why not, then, take him as an infallible teacher? But the Turkish religion is objected to on the ground that it is bathed in blood, and that it is cruel and promulgated by threats and the sword, and thus proves its human origin! Who makes this objection to the Koran? The Christian! The old saying is here very applicable—"He who lives in a glass house should not throw stones." Upon a thorough interior examination of the contents of the Koran, I find nothing inferior to the Christian scheme of salvation and proselytism. In truth, the constitution and threats of the one resemble very closely the peculiarities of the other. I say this without any fear of a successful contradiction.

Let me refer you to a few parallelisms. In the Bible it is said—"He that believeth on the Son hath everlasting life; he that believeth not the Son, the wrath of God abideth on him." Again, "If ye believe not that I am he, ye shall die in your sins." Again, "He that believeth and is baptized shall be saved; but he that believeth not shall be damned." Now I desire you to observe that the Turkish religion is inculcated on identical grounds, with corresponding threats and penalties attached to its cardinal essentials. In the first part of the Koran, one hundred and sixth page and elsewhere, you will find the following language: "Verily, those who disbelieve our miracles and our wonderful signs, such will surely be cast among the unfaithful, to be broiled in the raging fires of hell! They who disbelieve the chosen prophet of God, and heed not his tidings to the faithful, they shall be broiled in hell; and as often as their skins shall be well burned, God will give them other skins in exchange, that so they may obtain the sharper torment and the more fearful agony." This is pure popular orthodoxy; and it is taught in the Koran by a religious chieftain whose professions to divine inspiration are just as cool, simple, and unfanatical as the claims of any teacher known to the Christian world.

See, for example, the exact correspondence between the claims of Daniel and those of Mohammed, respecting the inspiration derived from the angel Gabriel. In the ninth chapter of Daniel, twenty-first and twenty-second verses, it is said—"While I was speaking in prayer, the man Gabriel, whom I had seen in the vision, being caused to fly swiftly, touched me about the time of the evening oblation. And he informed me, and talked with me, and said, O Daniel, I am now come forth to give thee skill and understanding." But Mohammed testifies, and in just as honest language, that this same angel Gabriel came to him and laid the Koran upon his heart!

Mohammedanism began to flourish about six hundred years after the commencement of the Christian dispensation. Why not, then, claim its founder as a link in a chain of mysterious and supernatural events inseparably connected with the world's salvation? This honor is claimed for every religious chieftain by their learned followers; which is illustrated in the biblical demonstrations of Professor Bush, that Swedenborg was the prophetical Elias—the God-prepared and God-sent herald of a new dispensation in the form and method of the salvation of souls.

But the testimony of Ann Lee—an illiterate, industrious, and honest woman of Manchester, in England—has an equally sound claim upon your credence, to be accepted as a supernaturally appointed and divinely inspired mind. Her testimony is far better supported by others than the testimony of the principal Bible authors. After a season of agony and prayer, this honest woman became, she alledged, fully imbued with the Divine Spirit. She had extraordinary power and energy given unto her, and testified that she had received a full and infallible revelation concerning the original fall of man and concerning the peculiar means of his redemption. Her profession was so honest, her declarations so straightforward, her inspiration so self-evident, that a large number of highly intelligent individuals acknowledged her as their religious chieftain, and consequently she was soon esteemed as their spiritual Mother in Christ.

You will observe that the declarations of all religious leaders are to this effect: that the Lord of Heaven had especially prepared and appointed them to do something indispensable and wonderful in the business of saving souls. And yet every subsequent revelation is very likely to cóntradict and subvert the main characteristics of all preceding disclosures, alledged to have been sent by the Lord to his dependent creatures. This point should not be overlooked. But if you should undertake to question the truth of their assertions, then comes forth a "most solemn oath," from each and all, that they had revealed "nothing but essential and real truth," during the period of their supernatural illumination. What can you say to this? Can you doubt their honesty? Oh, no. Then how can you explain the communication of contradictory revelations from the same unchangeable God? But you say,—Zoroaster, Mohammed, and Ann Lee were either deceiving or deceived, while the Bible authors and Swedenborg were truly inspired. Now this is very unreasonable. The testimony of one is just as sound as the other. Daniel affirms that the angel Gabriel came to give him skill and wisdom; and Mohammed affirms that the same angel came, direct from "the Lord," and laid the Koran upon his heart. You have no other proof, than this statement, that either circumstance occurred; and I maintain that you have no more reason to question the truth or honesty of one chieftain than the honesty of the other. The cases are parallel.

But let us observe what the principal author of the Hindoo bible affirms with regard to the source and perfect infallibility of his disclosures. In the first part of the second division of the Shaster, I find the following beautiful language, uttered by Krishnah, the loyal son and supernaturally endowed descendant of the great Paramah, the Hindoo God:—

"The high mountains remain steadfast, but more lasting is the Spirit of the world. He changes cruel and malicious men into vultures and creeping things; yea, of wicked men he makes beasts, camels and dromedaries, for the faithful to work and punish with sticks and stones throughout their lives. All this knowledge, and all contained in this book, is from the unseen, steadfast, ever-working Spirit of the world. He is the unknown—the unacknowledged. He gave me all the knowledge of his heart—I can see, talk, and obtain all knowledge from the Spirit Kalif, whom no other eye can discern. His Palace is embowered in trees of gold—his music is made and heard by the beautiful and the faithful. All this I am obliged to tell the faithful—for I am the receiver of his knowledge—the great avenger of all murderers, slanderers, prodigals, wicked, and covetous men."

Now here we see another religious chieftain professing infallible and boundless knowledge; and, as Professor Bush would very conscientiously affirm, respecting the claim of Swedenborg, "This certainly has the air of being uttered by an honest man." * * * "There is too much obvious truth, of the profoundest import, to allow the idea of their being merely the product of the religious frenzy even of a great and pious mind." Do you believe that this loyal Son of the Hindoo God was honest? Most certainly! Why not, then, accept him as an infallible teacher—the foundation link in a spiritual and supernatural chain of miraculous events? I may here say that I perceive an individual who is now contemplating a work of this nature: to show a providential chain of inspiration, commencing with the first indications of religious sentiment, with the express design of linking the whole category of theological professions, which I have mentioned, with the Doctrines of the New Church. Thus, being even more ingenious than the author of those doctrines themselves. Such a book, should it appear, will add another proof to the vast quantity of evidences already obtained, that disciples are invariably engaged in something like the deification of their chieftains.

But let us hear the professions of Joseph Smith, made in all soberness and simple-mindedness. "While I was praying unto God," says he, "and endeavoring to exercise faith in the precious promises of Scripture, on a sudden a light like that of day—only of a far purer and more glorious appearance and brightness—burst into the room." * * "In a moment a personage stood before me, surrounded with glory." * * "This messenger proclaimed himself to be an angel from God, sent to bring the joyful tidings, that the Covenant which God made with ancient Israel was at hand to be fulfilled; that the preparatory work for the second coming of the Messiah was speedily to commence; that the time was at hand for the Gospel to be preached, in all its fullness, unto all nations, that a people might be prepared for the millennium reign. And I was informed that I was chosen to be an instrument in the hands of God to bring about this glorious dispensation." Now let it be remembered, that Professor Bush calls this calm, honest, straightforward, unextravagant declaration of Joseph Smith, "the veriest babblings of fanatical delusion in the form of Mormonism;" whilst he affirms Swedenborg's relations to be "consistent, harmonious, and grand beyond description." And yet, the professions of these two religious chieftains—no matter how distasteful the truth may be to you—are precisely identical; only Swedenborg was more comprehensive and hence correspondingly presumptive. For instead of seeing an angel of God, who came to prepare him for the new dispensation, he is vastly more elevated, and says—"The Lord our Savior manifested himself to me in a sensible, personal appearance, and sends me to teach the things relating to the New Church—which is meant by the New Jerusalem in the Revelation." All this is proved conclusively,—Swedenborgians suppose,—by Scripture, whilst the sayings of Joseph Smith, who was just as cool, deliberate, prayerful, and scriptural, is most positively denounced as the "veriest babblings" of a fanatical delusion. Now, there are two things much needed in all this: first, pure reason; second, pure honesty. By the first it would be seen that the profession of any human being to miraculous inspiration is alike deserving of proper respect, on the ground of the psychological phenomena which such a mental state discloses to us, thereby increasing our knowledge of man; and by pure honesty—that is, the absence of an ill-begotten prejudice—the claims and teachings of every religious chieftain would receive from us a fair and candid investigation.

In the lunatic asylum lives a man who declares most positively, and would make a "most solemn oath" in the matter should the prevalency of doubts require it, that "the Lord" forbade him stepping from the front door and enjoying the fresh air. Now, I ask, do we accept this man's testimony and believe his claims to divine direction? Oh, no! Why not? Because it is altogether improbable. But do you doubt his honesty? Certainly not! Where, then, can or will you go for a truthful explanation of the origin of his solemn and sacred convictions? You would go to his mental state; yea, to the condition of his mental structure. In this we will find, perfectly and invariably, the true solution of all the theological problems under present investigation. But here let me be rightly apprehended. I do not undertake to affirm that all the claims of religious chieftains to miraculous inspiration and perfect knowledge, are invariably referable to insanity or mental aberration; but I mean that all such claims can be explained by a proper application, to the cases presented, of the many and various laws and impulses which control the mental constitution of man.

In this connection I am impressed, in order to perfect our investigation, to bring before you the professions which the *speaker* once made to perfect knowledge! This claim I put forth while very young, in the commencement of my experience in the magnetic field, with an honest heart, but in consequence of *two* mental conditions: first, my ignorance of the boundlessness of the universe, and even of the existence of a spiritual world as I now understand it: second, the far-reaching vision which I had of the broad territories of this earth, and the ease with which I could read a thought, see a person at a distance, and examine the interior of many things that were before great mysteries to my mind. So many wonders and visions, although limited in their nature and scope, broke upon my mind with such unspeakable distinctness and luster, that I, in the year 1844, in a brief lecture, made the following declaration to infallible and perfect knowledge:—"I possess the power of extending my vision *throughout all* space—can see things past, present, and to come. I have now arrived at the *highest degree* of knowledge which the human mind is capable of acquiring. I am master of the general sciences—can speak *all* languages—impart instructions upon those deep and *hidden* things in Nature which the world has not been able to solve," &c. Now, I confess, this declaration, as Professor Bush would say, certainly has the air of being uttered by an honest man. Yes, honest, but, at the same time, profoundly ignorant of the boundlessness of "all space,"—ignorant, of the innumerable "things" which pertain to "past, present, and to come," —ignorant, of the "highest degree of knowledge to which the human mind is capable" of ascending,—ignorant, of the scope of the "general sciences,"—ignorant, of the multiplicity of "languages,"—and about as ignorant of the "hidden things" which the world could not "solve" as the generality of mankind. And I here also confess, that the more I see of space; the more I examine the hidden things of Nature; the more I contemplate the unmeasurable infinitude in which rolls the incomprehensible universe; the more I gaze upon the planets, analyze the constitution of the human mind, and understand the eternal laws of progress; the more my mind is illuminated with the high influxions of light and truth from the inner life, the more do I shrink from the authorship of such rhapsodical and pedantic language as that to which I have called your attention. While such a profession to infallibility is now amusing to me, it, at the same time, demonstrates the fact, that in case a religious chieftain is honest-minded, his claims to perfect knowledge and miraculous inspiration are based wholly upon his greatest foe,—namely—upon his own ignorance!

In consequence of man's ignorance of himself—of his own inherent laws and mental constitution—he has unconsciously glided into much absurdity and unhealthy fanaticism. Dishonesty and Ignorance, the twin-born of unprogressed minds on the earth, have peopled the religious world with millions of false and pernicious doctrines—each, claiming to be the particular development of the Lord through his chosen prophets and gifted messengers. This is truth, and I am impressed to urge it upon your minds and lives; without, in the least, fearing the displeasure of those who, being already prepared by an undisturbed belief in the miraculous and supernatural, have simply changed old forms of religious absurdity and theological superstition for new forms and modifications thereof now before the world. There is not a sect in Christendom entirely exempt from this charge—the charge of ignorance, under the cloak of a popular education and a display of biblical knowledge. The world will progressively outgrow these doctrines of supernaturalism; but while the car of progress is tardily rolling onward, it is certainly the duty of every man, who can see for himself and walk for himself, to assist in augmenting its locomotion.

But here the question is asked—"If you do not admit Swedenborg's claims, how can you explain his far-sightedness—the comprehensiveness of his disclosures—the endless variety of his correspondences,—the close, discriminating accuracy of his scientific statements?" I reply, very briefly. On examination, I am moved to take the positions that follow, respecting the psychological case of Baron Swedenborg.

I confess, to begin with, that he was the most comprehensive mind—the loftiest genius—that humanity has ever enrolled in her ranks. All this I trace very easily to the laws of hereditary influence—to the psychological facts connected with his history prior to his birth, which I shall disclose upon some future occasion. Hence he was, while in the rudimental or ordinary state of mind, a very peculiar and comprehensively inquisitive man—analytical more than synthetical; more comprehensive in particulars than in generals. His mind had unusual traits in it—commonly called originality of character. And in the scientific and philosophical fields of research he was particularly a lofty genius. He was usually very mathematical and precise in his analysis; consequently, having reached a few veins of vital truth in science, it was remarkably easy for him to widen and vary his inquiries, and also to anticipate many of the scientific, philosophical, astronomical, and physiological discoveries of more modern times.

Here let me remind you, that I am not now criticising this author's philosophical or theological works—this I will do very probably hereafter; but I am now tracing out the causes of his subsequent professions to miraculous inspiration and infallible knowledge; and, I repeat, this general explanation applies equally to Zoroaster, Moses, Mohammed, Joseph Smith, and to all other religious chieftains, both male and female, that have played a part in the drama of this earthly existence.

It will be remembered, by those who know any thing of his early history, that Swedenborg's scientific and other researches were of an exceedingly outside or material character. They consisted principally of inquiries into Chemistry, Metallurgy, Mechanics, and Finance; the construction of Ships, Docks, Dykes, &c.; the Invention of Stoves; the Rise and Fall of Swedish Currency, &c., &c.,—with astronomical and correlative examinations, in which he was always more or less successful. Now, let me remind you that Truth is invariably simple; I appeal to your consciousness to sustain this assertion. I say this to prepare you to receive the statement, that Swedenborg's mind became fatigued with his hard and physical studies; as the palate rejects an article of food which has been long used without its proper accompaniments. Hence he gradually became metaphysical; then psychological; then theological; then religious. His mind was not impulsive; hence he progressively and quietly passed from material to spiritual themes of thought, and, being an industrious man, he paved the road all along with such works as "Intercourse between Soul and Body"—"Principia"—"Outlines of the Infinite"—"The Worship and Love of God." The latter work is the last Bridge which he built between philosophy and Theology. And when he arrived at the theological side of the channel, he cut loose from nearly every thing which had before held him to *terra firma;* and immediately began to contemplate a new and extensive field—the theological—which he felt to be sufficiently large for his mind, and very refreshing, as a change of occupation would be to any individual fatigued with monotony and materiality. He saw, like Constantine, that no harmony could exist in Christendom without an infallible standard of faith. Present confusion among Christians arose principally, Swedenborg thought, from the many and various readings of a Book which he had no doubt was in and of itself infallible. He thought that if a sense could be fixed to it—indorsed as heaven-given—the New Jerusalem would certainly come. He was first psychologized with the *undisturbed belief* that the Word was holy and infallible; only needing a proper interpretation. And the belief that he could analyze and harmonize and bestow a triune sense upon the Word became so strong in his mind, that this also psychologized him into the faith the Lord himself must have imparted the conviction ; and so, he boldly and constantly asserted it. He was perfectly psycho-sympathetically magnetized by the conviction which I quote from Professor Bush's own acknowledgment; viz.: "In Swedenborg's *own estimate* the development of the Internal sense of the Word, as the grand instrumentality for promoting the ends of Divine Love and Wisdom in the regeneration and salvation of men, formed the paramount purpose of his illumination." Certainly it did! And being perfectly justified by a conviction, no matter how induced, so high and important as this, he put himself to the work of writing an infallible Revelation of the Word! But I am not impressed to deny that Swedenborg was mentally enlightened by much clairvoyant illumination, and saw angels, and the Spiritual World—I believe that he did have occasionally such high and good perception. But I explain his claims,—that the Lord gave him especial instruction, and identified him with a vast scheme in the salvation of men,—wholly on the ground oft ransitional psychology. That is, his mind fluctuated between the influence of education and the superior impressions, which flowed into his understanding, occasioned by his intimate mental relation to the purely spiritual state. He vibrated constantly between two extremes—between reality and supposition; and he saw into "Heaven and Hell" *inferentially* and *analogically*, (not literally,) just as Milton saw the Prince of Darkness and the splendid compartments of pandemonium.

Before dismissing this extraordinary illustration of what I mean by a transitional state of mind, as based upon a fine rudimental condition and as carried through a psychological and sympathetic state, I will show you that Swedenborg acknowledges his state to be as I have described it—viz.: a state which is neither ordinary nor extraordinary—a blending of both—"a certain state," as he expresses it, "which is mediate, between sleeping and waking," in which "he did not know whether he was fully awake or not." He says "This manifestation of the Lord is more excellent than all miracle." * * * "To me, it has been granted to be in both spiritual and natural light at the same time." This statement is his own, and very generally applies to all the various religious chieftains referred to. It is the state in which hundreds have been when they thought they had truthful visions and saw God. Just in proportion to the blending or mixture of these ordinary and extraordinary conditions, will be the imperfection of each; hence each is unreliable. Therefore I do not question the honesty of Swedenborg, in order to furnish a solution of his peculiar state. But most distinctly do I affirm that his mental condition was psycho-sympathetically induced, and that, so far as his general illumination is concerned, he was in a transition state between the natural and spiritual, between slavery and independence of thought, and he consequently manifested *both* partially, but neither absolutely. The theological works of Emmanuel Swedenborg, like the teachings and records of all religious chieftains known to sacred history, must be accepted rationally, and studied as prodigies in the sphere of psychological science, and as deserving the profound attention of all students of the phenomena of mind. They all have much to recommend them:—morality, depth, order, wideness of thought; much pure analogy; and more of healthy inference.

We can not possibly do ourselves more injury, and the author of a religious work more injustice, no matter what his pretensions than to accept his teachings as infallibly true in their particulars. We can at best only obtain from a person, (even when exceedingly well illuminated,) the great general principles of truth. Because the *particulars* of his thoughts will necessarily partake, more or less, of the peculiar idiosyncrasies and individuality of his own mind. Hence, concerning the teachings of Swedenborg, I affirm and repeat that there is, in their particulars, too much obscurity, ambiguity, and spiritually inflated conception, in his psychological or religious works, for them to be of any particular utility to the social and moral world at the present time. But I am moved to defer a critical examination of this author's works to some future period.

In closing my remarks upon this head, it is deemed proper to remind you that God is no respecter of persons. His providence is general and universal, embracing the low and high—the animal and the human—the falling sparrow and the ascending seraph. His inspiration is universal; illuminating every thing according to its condition and capacity. His laws are unchangeable; operating the same every where and at all times. His revelations are universal. And just in proportion as we unfold the sensibilities of our minds, and arrange all the discordant elements of our being into a musically harmonious order, will the joy, and light, and wisdom of the the higher spheres flow in and convert us more completely into the heavenly image.

LECTURE XVII.

BEING AN APPLICATION OF PSYCHICAL LAWS TO EVERY-DAY LIFE.

The principles upon which the human mind exists are exceedingly simple; but the external manifestations thereof are innumerable and various, because they are changeful as the rolling sea. The sea is in itself immutable. But its elements are ever changing, and its face invariably indicates the deep, inward commotions. A far-reaching calm is now upon its countenance. Not a reverse breath moves its depths. The sun sends its brilliant rays far down into its reflective surface. A soft tranquillity pervades the entire body. It is so still, so abandoned to quietude, so calming to the feelings and thoughts of the contemplating soul, that you lie carelessly down in your bark, and pass into a sweet, confiding slumber.

You dream of a changeless, stormless, harmonious sea. In your imagination, you behold one vast plain of crystal water,—calm as an angel's face. Vessels glide to and fro most beautifully, as by a magic power; disturbing not the broad surface of the still waters; neither arousing the reposing crew from their peaceful slumber. In truth, the prevailing tranquillity is so profound that you can not any longer dream; and your sleep becomes thoughtless as a summer morning.

But, anon, your repose is broken by the tempestuous throes of the mighty deep! The once calm and tranquil sea is now convulsed with an elemental storm; and the whole is one vast scene of confusion and disorder. Vessels are thrown from side to side as by the ruthless hand of some frenzied giant. The once slumbering crew are now rushing from spar to spar with the speed and confusion of fright. And you start to your feet amazed, confounded, disappointed.

Thus it is with the human mind. The human face is now calm as a morning on the Nile. Not a wave of trouble is visible upon its surface. Every feature is soft and subdued. No passion stirs the placid fiber. The sturdy muscle is reposing in a deep sleep. The soft, friendly eye is swimming in the element of tranquillity. And the countenance is mild as an angel's eye. The calmness is apparently so profound, so unwavering, so immutable, that you can not any longer withhold your confidence. You gaze upon the face with delight. The contrast between it and others—your own, perhaps—is so vivid that you can not but love it. You fall asleep. You dream of a quiet, serene mind. You behold, with delight, a soul as tranquil as a day in the land of spirits. You repose the utmost confidence in the safety and changelessness of such a mind! And your slumber soon becomes a dreamless condition.

But, lo! an unpleasant sound vibrates upon your ear. You start to your feet, and behold a horrid transfiguration. The once soft feature, the placid nerve, the reposing muscle, are now all disordered and furrowed with discordant emotion. You are not expecting this storm of passion, and hence are not prepared for the painful shock. O, how unnatural! It seems like a ruthless hurricane in a land of flowers. In the tempestuous mind, thought and expression are simultaneous. The thunderbolt and the lightning fall together. Passion has ascended to its zenith. The coruscations of the intellect are fierce and terrible. The once quiet and holy countenance is now repulsive as the troubled sea, which casts up mire and dirt. Alas, your confidence is injured. You dare not again slumber; although the human face is again peaceful as the evening star. The eye may swim in the pool of affection, the soft surface may move with joyous smiles, the tongue may speak the music of love in your listening ear; nevertheless, you dare not again slumber—you dare not rest the tenderest emotions and elements of your being upon the bosom of a soul so tempestuous.

This is only one revelation of the human mind; not so much a disclosure of the elements and principles of which the mind is compounded, but, more particularly, a manifestation of one of its innumerable moods. Now you can not but believe that an angel is in reality calm—always full of joy, love, and wisdom; never a troubled sea, casting up mire and dirt—i. e., angry words and profane language. You believe that an angel is the very impersonation of heavenly tranquillity—that it is immutable in its feelings and affections. Yes, you believe it. But can you explain the existence of such uniform quietude? Can you explain the depth, sources, and immutability of an angel's harmony? Is an angel exempt from disturbing causes? Is there nothing to interfere with its peace and tranquillity? Are there no contrasts from which to extract happiness and instruction? Can you justify yourselves in the indulgence of passion on the ground of your inharmonious environments? Nay! An angel has eternal contrasts before it; yet it is as quiet as the Sabbath of the happy soul. And you, my friends, should not altogether justify your tempestuous natures by reference to surrounding influences. But rather say that you are ignorant of yourselves. An angel is calm and happy, because it is wise as to the existence, nature, and proper exercise of its immortal attributes. This is the great secret! The will-power of an angel is always exercised through the diamond avenues of Wisdom. A wise will is very powerful. The passions of the soul must live in eternal obedience to this indwelling Master—the wisdom-attribute.

If you desire calmness in the midst of a storm, then study the wonders of the inner universe; learn the laws by which it is controlled. You are yourselves universes in miniature. A countless number of unities enter into the composition of your being. You are, when individually considered, a thousand universes in one. You are the masterpiece of the material creation; and yet, you are but a mere link in a chain—a mere clasp—to an endless concatenation of physical and spiritual entities which flow from, and spirally return to, Deity.

Knowledge, combined with Wisdom, will enable you to put all enemies under your feet. The kingdom of Heaven is within you; the true king is only required. Allow your Reason to ascend the inward throne; place the scepter of interior power in his hand; yield all things to his exclusive and eternal control; and then, as certain as you have an existence, the angel will beam forth from your spiritual character and your actions will partake more of heaven than earth. The heavenly kingdom will now begin to unroll from the elements of your being; and you will begin to see how simple are the principles which govern your mind, and how accessible are the true means and methods of immutable happiness.

But happiness in this life is positively denied to us by the popular theology. Indeed, present happiness is regarded by the majority of Christians as evidence of depravity. Happiness is synonymous with wickedness. They say "this world is all a fleeting show, for man's illusion given," and regard every thing, which tends to increase the happiness of humanity, with the eye of suspicion. They talk about the pleasures of sin; about the subtlety and machinations of Satan; about the allurements and devices of God's eternal enemy; and, thus, they estimate almost every effort or scheme to improve and perfect the present condition of man, as preeminently sinful and satanic. They teach their children to repel every plan of human happiness as a devil's trap; and they strenuously ignore all means and methods of human comfort and enjoyment on the ground that this world must be made a "vale of tears," and "the cross" must be borne, or heaven will prove unattainable.

Theology, like a ponderous car, has rolled over the world for long centuries. Like the fabled Upas, it loads the atmosphere with desolation and death. Like a great Idol, as it is to many thousands, it has rolled its dark and destroying proportions over the weak and adoring multitudes. And in its track you will find the young and the innocent, the fearful and the noble,—all wrecked and abandoned to a miserable superstition.

It is my impression to give you this discourse parenthetically, as a kind of application of the ideas heretofore developed in the examination of the professed infallibility of religious chieftains. For it is already daylight. The great moral luminary is shedding its golden rays abroad over the eastern sky. The clouds are fast dispersing. From the night comes forth a brilliant day. From the decay of old trees springs up fresh and stronger vegetation. From the Tartarian gulf of ignorance and mythologic developments, there unfolds a world of knowledge, and the rudiments of a truthful theology. From the night of superstition comes forth a day of pure, practical religion. But, as yet, few can see the newly arisen glory. The horizon of a new era is illuminated; but only those who are aroused from the slumber of ages, can behold the new-born sun. The sleepers are not awakened. The dreamers are not disturbed; nevertheless there streams, through the lattice-work and interstices of their mythologic faith, the crystal rays of that glorious sun of religious freedom which shall know no setting!

It is with a grand joy which can find no expression, that I behold how perfectly all conceivable happiness is within man's power to attain. It will not come by his faith in the sinful nature of Adam, nor by believing in the immaculate purity of Christ. He can not truthfully expect to be condemned for Adam's sin, nor saved by the imputed righteousness of any human being. For the only true Savior is Wisdom. The more a man possesses and exercises of this interior prerogative, the more is he a Savior of the world.

The physical, social, intellectual, and moral world will be eventually harmonized and exalted by this eternal Savior—by this crowning Attribute of the Divine Mind. But the intellect is repelled and the heart is sickened by the features and professions of popular theology. It has not refined the affections of the spirit; neither has it developed the intellectual energies of man, nor improved his social condition. It is said that Christianity has civilized the world.

The civilization of this portion of the world is no more referable to the religious faiths and opinions of Christians, than the magnetic telegraph is referable to the thunderbolts and lightnings of Mount Sinai. For popular theology never informed the world of Astronomy nor of Geology; neither did it ever suggest the building of an ocean steamer, nor the construction of the powerful locomotive, which rushes through the fields of civilization like the terrible tornado, and yet, is as tame beneath the hand of the skillful engineer as the babe on the mother's bosom.

The laws of the land are superior to the jurisdictional methods of popular theology. Our best institutions and modes of government, our republicanism and general charity, are founded not upon the infallible teachings of any religious chieftain, but upon good wholesome maxims—such as have been derived from the moral aphorisms of Confucius, Lycurgus, Jesus, and Dr. Franklin. The Christian system, as a system, has not improved the heart and the life of man. It is the best Idol in the world for the weak and the morally debilitated to look up to and devoutly worship; but, considered as a system, it is absolutely detrimental to the progress and happiness of humanity. It is an Idol, because the professions of its founders—the religious chieftains—to perfect knowledge and infallible revelation of truth, are accepted by the honest-minded devotees as unequivocal. Hence the teachings of Nature and the dictates of an enlightened Reason are virtually set aside, or else compelled to bend and do homage at the shrine of the Idol—at the altar of a sublimated superstition!

It is a glorious work—that of harmonizing and elevating the world! But the church, with all its appendages of modern invention, and with all its instrumentalities of individual salvation, has not, neither can it, accomplish this elevation of man—this renovation of the social and moral world. You will surely agree with me when I say, that a period of twenty centuries is sufficient time to give any system of salvation a fair trial. The world is diseased; but the old remedies—the church appliances of prayers, laying on of hands, baptism, transubstantiational ceremonies, conversions, changes of heart, &c.—are no more applicable to the disease than bleeding, blistering, cupping, and calomel, are adapted to the promotion of mental vigor and to the development of physical comfort. I say the church and the priests have used their old nostrums long enough. The trial has been fairly made, the verdict of enlightened men has been rendered, and it is now time to apply the remedies suggested by the Harmonial Philosophy. That is to say, let Nature and Reason prescribe their own remedies, and we shall soon discover the true means and methods of individual happiness and of universal peace.

There is a spirit of truth abroad in the world, and destined to rule the earth, by which the mass of mankind shall be blessed, and which will make them heirs of the kingdom of heaven—the only universal and everlasting government that can possibly exist. In contemplating the destiny of mankind, we quicken our love for mankind—we place a higher estimation upon the individual members of the universal family. Our hearts overflow with that intense and expanded benevolence which tends to make man perfect even as his Father in Heaven is perfect. This universal love for man is perfection itself, to a great extent. For universal good thus becomes our own good—a good which we assist to develop among men, because it is realized in our minds, longed for by our hearts, and striven for by our energies. If we desire, we can trace out our own destiny in that of mankind. The full, perfect and proportionate development of our nature is the great end for which we should constantly and prayerfully strive. According to that principle of individual harmony whereby Jesus may have felt himself united to Nature and Deity—causing him to say: "I and my Father are one"—you shall be able yet to realize the high truth that it is the Divine Principle of Nature, God, who is working all progression; that he is in us and by us; in others and by others; he is all in all; the universal Spirit in which the whole material and spiritual universe is bathed and is blessed.

By the progressions of the Race to which we belong, you may expect to see many strong and stupendous revolutions in all departments of Mind. The authority of antiquity and tradition will lose its power. Absurd speculations will gain no foothold in the mind. The imagination will no longer be left to roam unrestrained in the dark regions of theological conjecture. And the chains of religious servitude which priests have fastened upon the mind, effectually preventing the proper exercises of reason, will be stricken off and thrown into that "lake" of ignorance and theological chimeras, in which also future enlightenment will "cast" the heathenish fables of Death and Hell.

Blended with the highest axiomatical principles of truth, and with many heavenly precepts, in the Scriptures, are to be seen the footsteps of a dark and dreadful mythology. Associated with the pure utterance of "Love ye one another," is that horrid speculation of the oriental tribes concerning the Tartarian gulf; or, entwined with the music of a sweet-toned divinity, you find the dark and dreary myths of an early period, when men were not developed in science and wisdom. A religious chieftain, although he may set up a claim to infallible revelations and inspiration from heaven, can not now affirm that the sun was made to stand still, because the imperial laws of astronomical science are too well understood to admit the remotest possibility of such an occurrence. But there are thousands who profess to believe that the Lord of Heaven did cause the sun to stand still, in accordance with the statements of Joshua. Why do they believe it? Simply, because a religious chieftain affirmed it! But Galileo discovered that the sun was and always had been stationary, and that the earth rolled harmoniously around it; hence that the statement of Joshua could not be true in any case. For if we explain the passage by saying that the phenomena appeared to Joshua's mind like the standing still of the sun, causing him to think and write it so; then we, at the same time, prove the chosen prophet of God to be fallible and subject to mental mistakes and imperfections of thought, like the generality of mankind. This admission would be fatal to any thing like an infallible revelation; for, after all, we would be compelled to read the Bible with a commentary of our own mental construction.

And so, in order to preserve the immaculate inspiration and truthfulness of the Old Testament sayings, and to escape the necessity of admitting the imperfection of Joshua's understanding, the Romish Church thought they would burn the astronomical truth by burning Galileo, or extinguish the truth by compelling the discoverer to renounce it. He did audibly renounce it; but did that save Joshua's statement from impeachment? Nay; far from it! The progress of mind soon developed the science of planetary revolutions, and the religious world was compelled to renounce the infallibility of the Bible reading. In the same manner, the science of geology has forced the priests and Bible-logicians to numerous concessions; and thus, the advancing intellect of man is daily gaining new victories over the myths and dogmas of the unprogressed past. And how invariably do we see the disciples of a false theology, and of a superstitious religion, flee to a popular subterfuge in order to escape the conclusions and consequences of a fair and dignified criticism! Astronomy and geology no sooner demonstrate the Mosaic and other biblical accounts erroneous, than the priests and craftsmen of theology commence a discourse to their congregations something like this:—"Brethren, this age is blessed, through the favor of God, with much scientific truth. Discoveries, valuable to the world, are being daily made; and worldly wisdom is being daily increased. But it is sad to witness the efforts of Satan, in it all, to bend and pervert the holy Scriptures to the discredit of religion. Oh, the ignorance of men! Oh, the depravity of the human heart! To prove by science that the Bible is not infallible—what a wicked attempt! But, brethren, we do not undertake to contradict the discoveries of science. Oh, no; we love them—we esteem them highly—we are grateful that, through the blessing of God, in his providence, he has seen it proper to send us these interesting disclosures. But, brethren, wicked men oppose them to the Bible because the *apparent* sense of the letter indicates the scriptural accounts of creation to be erroneous. This is wrong. Because the Bible is just as true as ever—it is God's word to fallen man; but we, poor sinful mortals as we are, have not understood the full sense of the word as it was originally given. For we now discover that, according to translations of the year 1620, and by the marginal notes of the great divine, Bishop So-and-so, and those of the Rt. Rev. Dr. Allright, who wrote, with the assistance of the original Greek and Hebrew notations of the still earlier Fathers of the church,—from these indisputable authorities we learn, that Moses did not mean that the heavens and the earth were made in six literal days and nights; but that the six days signify *six great epochs of time*, during which the successive geological stratifications occurred; as are indicated by that noble science. Thus, brethren, all we have to do is to read the Bible with an understanding heart, and there will be no discrepancies between it and the modern disclosures of science. Just believe the scriptural accounts to be infallible and perfect to begin with, and we can assure you, that, by praying to God for faith and a clear mind, you can make the Bible always harmonize with the developments of science, no matter what those developments are.

If an apostate should say, that the Bible is proved to contain errors by the teachings of science, then all you need utter in reply, brethren, is this : the Bible is true, sir, but we have not rightly apprehended the meaning of the authors. The contradiction is in the letter, not in the spirit. Wherefore? Because all truth must be in harmony; and inasmuch as the Bible is God's eternal word and science is also true, it therefore follows that the truths of Revelation and those of nature must agree, when properly comprehended."

Such are the miserable subterfuges of the popular church theology. The clergymen tell you to pray to God for a clear mind wherewith to understand his holy word; but the sciences of diatetics and physiology prove that, he has the clearest mind who consigns to his system healthy food, in proper proportions, associated with sound habits of sleeping and of out-door exercise. The desire, or rather the habit, has become so firmly fixed upon the mind to have some religious chieftain to lead us from Egypt to Canaan, from earth to heaven, that most people do not know how to reject their idols and turn to the attainment of truth through the soul,—through the intuition and the universe.

Of course, every religious book in creation can be changed and construed into new meanings by slight alterations in its phraseology. Priests and clergymen have no other trade than this by which to obtain a living. All their capital is invested in this business, and the stock goes at par just so long as certain doctrines are esteemed by the populace as essential to future bliss. But should, by any mishap, the doctrines of a devil (or a spirit of evil) and a hell be proved to be the coruscations of the Zoroasterian theology of Persia —the legitimate children of a crude and barbarous age; then the occupation of the evangelical priesthood would no longer be a despotic monopoly, as it now is, but a wreck of matter and of most miserable superstitions. Their stock would no longer go in the popular market. They would no longer be allowed to keep the keys of heaven. They would no longer be permitted to stand between the people and their Maker; for every body would then conceive of new ways of salvation and means of happiness.

These views of the nature and destiny of man, serve to remind us that our duties to ourselves, and our obligations to the generations which shall succeed us, are alike solemn and momentous. For science and philosophy are all embosomed in the human soul. And while we are applying the laws of Nature to the harmonization of ourselves and society, let us not fail to fulfill our obligations to those that shall come after us; let us impart to them high minds and healthy constitutions, for these are the greatest fortunes which parents can bequeath their children. Be true-hearted, reverent, and faithful—full of integrity in the performance of all things; be firmly determined to develop and apply the principles of Nature to every thing,—and the highest happiness will be the inevitable consequence.

How it improves and expands the soul of the mind to gaze, through the multifarious avenues of his existence, into the Spirit Land—a world of unmeasurable magnitude and of inconceivable attractions! By a law of universal sympathy, by a principle of a celestial Love—its inhabitants are joined into one grand system of unchangeable Harmony. It is impossible for discord to exist there. For each and all have a deep, high, all-comprehensive knowledge of the principles of every species of joy and Happiness. In accordance with these principles, they live most harmonially. Their obedience is apparently involuntary; they live in harmony with the great controlling Laws of the material and spiritual universe, as naturally as the planets revolve about the Central Sun.

The universal Harmonies of the spiritual world are based upon the principles of Love and Wisdom. When the mind, or the soul, of man abandons the corporeal organism, it leaves behind it on the earth, a vast variety of terrestial imperfections. On the earth, the antagonisms of human society are pre-eminently calculated to develop the evils of war, theft, licentiousness, and other moral discords. Children are born with defective, unkind, deformed, unlovely bodies and minds; born of ignorant parents, or of parents, who, by yielding to inordinate impulses, have disobeyed the laws of life, and the offspring must accept, and begin their present existence with, many predispositions to live wrong and discordant lives. Such are involuntary foes to the laws of moral harmony; and the consequences are constantly experienced by themselves and by all contiguous members of the human family. But what a consolation it is to know, that, when the motives or causes of war, theft, and wrong cease to exist, it is positively certain that the discords of life will then also have an end! This glorious result will flow from the progressive development of Love and Wisdom among the multitudes of earth. Men will learn to trust less to mythology for harmony of soul, and more to the Principles of Nature. It will be seen that moral health depends more upon a baptismal ceremony, which is practiced religiously every morning, than upon any form of church discipline. "He that believes" in the power of Love and Wisdom, "and is diurnally baptized" in the clear waters of some flowing spring, "shall be saved" from much pain and melancholy, sad dreaming, mental confusion and disease. It will also be seen, that moral health depends more upon physical harmony than upon the writings of religious chieftains or upon the prayers of the so-called contrite heart. The faith of the religious devotee can not move a moral or a physical "mountain" half so quick as drilling-irons, powder, spades and shovels in the hands of intelligent and properly remunerated men. And still it is said that we must not yield up our confidence in the infallibility of religious chieftains, because Christianity has civilized the Anglo-Saxon and American nations. But I deny the assertion, and say in reply, that the greatest agent of civilization was never suggested by any system of religion. It originated with the genius of mind. I allude to the blessed art of Printing. By this lever, the wide world is moved and shaken to its center. Parts are brought into the closest sympathy with the whole. The pulsations of Europe are felt in America, and when the heart of America is dilated with the great principles of Liberty, the art of Printing conveys its most delicate vibrations to the remotest extremities of the inhabitable globe. By printing, by physiology, by science, by commerce, by Wisdom, the world has been civilized up to its present state; and the popular system of theology has been dragged along by the side of civilization with all the pomp, deference, and display which is so uniformly bestowed upon some dependent but cherished Idol. This is no theory; it is the plainest statement of historical facts, of which every thing bears the most unequivocal testimony.

In conclusion let me urge you to get Wisdom. This is the great Savior. Know thyself. Be the simple-minded devotee of Nature's laws. Have a good and benevolent Reason for every thing you do. Never act from a narrow, selfish impulse. Be loving and tenderhearted. Always remember that happiness depends upon physical and mental tranquillity—upon individual and social harmony. Never do wrong. For while I speak, there are thousands of pure and loving angels looking upon us, desiring our speedy deliverance from discord and error.

LECTURE XVIII.

CONCERNING THE PHILOSOPHY AND PRINCIPLES OF SOMNAMBULISM.

STILL our theme is Man. His nature is still rife with mysteries. There are phases and moods in his mind which we have not as yet fully analyzed. But let us not get bewildered; let us continue to calmly investigate; let us not allow ourselves to become lost in a subject so complicated and sublime; let us examine the peculiarities of man's nature with a steady nerve and a serene mind; for in him we may find much that reminds us of the lower kingdoms of Nature, and much, also, which commands our veneration and conducts reason to the Central Wisdom—to the great *consilium*—of the universe.

In this investigation you have followed me very patiently. You have listened with the ear of intelligence; but yet you have not fully comprehended all the points of the argument, nor fully recognized the application of all the principles which the analysis has progressively unfolded. There is properly, however, no cause for complaints, because the subject has glided into your minds just in proportion to your degree of readiness for its reception. Still it is my impression that you can render yourselves more impressible to the influx of thought, and more capable of consecutive reflection, by a proper exercise of your own constitutional powers. When you come to see that you can find immutable happiness in knowledge; when you begin to feel that Wisdom is worth more to you than the golden banks of California; then you will know how to rightly direct and potentialize your innate abilities. When you have a firm faith in knowledge—in its beatifying and saving power—you will then seek Wisdom. When you believe that Wisdom is the great savior of the soul—that it will teach you how to Love, and to live, and to work, and to subdue disease, and to banish error, and to exterminate all ignorance and injustice—then you will have taken the initiatory steps upon that straight and happy path which is certain to lead the traveler to the kingdom of spiritual Harmony. It is to the end that you may progress in Wisdom concerning the powers and tendencies of your psychological natures, that I am moved to impress upon your minds the truths of spirituality as revealed in the general mechanism of man.

The preceding discourse referred especially to the human mind in what was denominated the *transition state*—a condition, midway between sympathy and clairvoyance. The phenomena of this transition state were shown to be many and various. Attention, however, was particularly directed to the religious departments, in which its external manifestations are more frequent and prominent. But at this stage of the examination, it is deemed essential to make a few remarks concerning the states of mind which precede the Transitionary condition.

You doubtless remember that the first, or ordinary stage, was termed the "Rudimental State;" the second the "Psychological State;" the third, the "Sympathetic State," and the fourth, the "Transition State;" but you may feel disposed to inquire—"whether I consider the psychological and sympathetic states as improvements upon the natural or common state of the mind?" I reply that I do not. No state is an actual improvement upon the rudimental; except good clairvoyance. The psychological and sympathetic states are deviations or side manifestations of mind. They do not result from the progressive operation of mental laws, but are incidental to the general play of the spiritual potencies, as the fruitless twigs on a tree are side consequences of, and incidental to, the main growth of that organism to the point of its culmination.

The mind in its natural state is capable of a high cultivation. In this state we find nearly all our poets, philosophers, and educated men. And although I have treated the psychological and sympathetic states as proceeding from, or as flowing naturally out of, the ordinary state of the mind; yet I have not designed to give the impression that the former were actual improvements upon the cultivated rudimental state. Because, if these conditions were in very truth superior to the ordinary state, in which we find the entire multitudes of earth, it would then become a strange problem—How vigorous and talented men could have their mental condition defined, since they are not clairvoyant, and yet are far more intelligent, as a general thing, than those who are in either the psychological or sympathetic conditions.

We shall be philosophical truly, if we will lay it down as a principle of mental science, that the sympathetic, psychological, transition, and somnambulic states, are simply concomitants and variations of the mind in its rudimental condition. It was affirmed on the very threshhold of these discourses, that the lowest of every thing in Nature contains the highest in a latent or undeveloped state. That is to say, when applied to this subject, the rudimental state is the dormitory of all the conditions which have been, or which may be, considered and developed. It has also been most distinctly shown that many individuals are naturally or commonly under something like a psychological or sympathetic influence. This fact is exhibited in religious meetings, in popular excitements, epidemics, panics, &c., as evidenced in the instances already related. But still more distinctly has it been proved that many individuals get into the transition state, which is a middle ground between reality and imagination—between something and nothing—between individuality of character, and its absorption by the over-mastering potency of surrounding minds or mythologies. Thus, how evidently was Emmanuel Swedenborg in a transition condition! He gazed in both directions—downward into the rudimental state and upward into the spiritual state—and in proportion as the two conditions were confounded in his mind his appreciation of either was materially and unfortunately impaired. But not only was Emmanuel Swedenborg thus impaired in the spiritual departments of his mind, but the same defect spreads over the whole field of supernaturalistic disclosures. Every religious chieftain that has, in the honesty of his inner conscience, believed and proclaimed himself to be supernaturally endowed, has been in what I term a transition state of mind, in which he could neither comprehend much of his own state nor the condition of those about him. This fact I have sufficiently illustrated in previous lectures. We will, therefore, let that pass, and return to the proposition that no condition is an improvement upon the rudimental state, except the truly Clairvoyant or Spiritual states, which will hereafter be examined in their natural order.

Recurrence to an original proposition is now deemed necessary. My impressions refer to the duality—or twofold mechanism—of the human mind. By interior investigation, I discover the innermost departments of the soul to be constructed upon positive and negative principles. These principles give rise to corresponding external structures. The principles of judgment or wisdom, being in and of themselves positive, unfold the material arrangements of the front brain, which is called the cerebrum; therefore this department of the sensorium is positive, and exerts a corresponding potency over all the remaining members of the physical economy.

It should be borne distinctly in mind, that, unless there existed, within the constitution of the thinking principle, a combination of elements which correspond to the brain, this organism could not have been developed. There would have been nothing to suggest and control its growth. Hence the true philosophy is this,—the positive brain is unfolded, because there was a spiritual brain behind it possessing a corresponding character and construction. Hence, too, in accordance with these principles, the negative brain was developed, which is called the cerebellum. And the same law lies behind or back of every other structure. For instance,—the external ear, which the material eye can perceive, is only a sign which the internal ear has put forth, in order to invite impressions from the objective world. So with the visible organ of vision. Its fair mechanism and delicate proportions may be considered as the external form of the spiritual organ of vision which springeth, in a corresponding manner, from the interior brain. When you see water rippling through the verdant meadow, you very naturally inquire as to its source. You can not understand effects unless you study causes. The purling stream inevitably suggests to your mind the idea of a fountain spring—the external effect must flow from some interior cause. When you gaze upon the full-blown flower, you simply see the visible form of invisible principles—principles, which were deposited in the little germ that seemed almost void of life.

The true philosopher never confines his investigations to the externals of creation. He must interrogate internal and hidden laws. The ear, the eye, the leg, the arm, the viscera, the brain—how came these structures to exist? Why are there two of each organ? Why are there two sets of muscles—the one to contract, the other to expand, and vice versa—when motion is commanded by the invisible potencies of the Will? Why are there two sets of nerves, or magnetic conductors, going to and from the sensorium—the one to convey life-principles from the brain to all parts of the body, the other to receive impressions from the external world and transmit them to the seat of Love and Wisdom—to the throne of government—which is the Brain? Why is the brain the highest part of the whole organism? Why is it placed upon a pedestal, and made to rule the body as the engineer governs the locomotive?

These are philosophical questions. And we should seek the replies in the very place where they are asked. The brain grows on the top of the body for the same reason that the rose unfolds on the summit of the stalk. It is the flower of the physical form; and it governs the body because it is the grand reservoir of motion, life, sensation, and intelligence. The double arrangements, visible throughout the body, are external manifestations of corresponding, but unseen, powers which enter into the constitution of the immortal mind. The body is possessed of various dualisms—such as two arms, two legs, two eyes, two ears, two brains, &c.,—because every thing in the vast empire of creation is originated, controlled, perfected, and maintained upon positive and negative principles. This is the order of Nature. But when we confine our attention to the human mind, we find a still more valuable reason for the existence of these double structures.

Not only do we find that the eyes, ears, limbs, brains, &c., are constructed and situated in the living temple with strict reference to the relative laws of positive and negative dynamics or moving potencies; but we also find the still more delightful truth, that these double forms are visible because there are corresponding forms behind or within them! Thus the law of cause and effect conducts us most deliberately to the soul. If a body moves, there must be therein a cause of motion. If a body is endowed with eyes and ears, there must be a cause of such organs in the very bosom of vitality. In accordance with this reasoning, I desire you to conceive the idea that the mind, which develops the organs of external sense, is itself provided with identical senses. These interior senses create and unfold the outward agents of perception just as thoughts clothe themselves in words; the words are the forms into which the thoughts incarnate their indwelling powers of vitality. You can not think without words; neither can the mind possess the principles of seeing and hearing unless they clothe themselves immediately with appropriate material vestures. This is a law of Nature; it applies to every thing in her every department of principle and sphere of external development. This conception of things I hold to be essential to a proper understanding of the phenomena of somnambulism, to which I intend presently to direct your attention.

As a matter of physiology, and with a design to assist the elucidation of this very interesting subject, let me fix your thoughts upon a few explanations. Somnambulism may be produced naturally, or it may be superinduced by manipulations. It matters not, however, how this state of existence is obtained; for the results or manifestations are invariably the same in character, but frequently different in degree. While some persons in this condition possess but little perception or powers of accomplishment, others manifest much more than their usual clearness of intellect and energy of muscle. But in nearly all cases, the same individual, when awake and when somnambulic, appears like two entirely different characters.

Here it becomes a very interesting question: "How can these totally different conditions be produced or exhibited in one individual?" The answer to this interrogation will, while it tends to increase our knowledge of mental physiology, do much toward making the future state of the soul a very comprehensible subject.

It is proper to preface this explanation with the proposition, which I have all along insisted upon, that the entire organism of Nature is pervaded with a spiritual or vitalizing Principle. It is diffused throughout all the wide realms of creation, like the medium of sensation which permeates the human body. The recent researches of several eminent experimental philosophers have done much toward making the existence of this unseen medium a matter of familiar demonstration; they have, to say the least, made it a subject of unmistakable probability. But aside from what physiologists have done on this head, I can assure you that there is a universal vital principle, which, while it establishes a means of communication between all bodies in nature, and is the great sensational medium, so to speak, which pervades the illimitable nervous system of the universe, is nevertheless far inferior to, and vastly different from, that celestial combination of elements which constitute the Divine Being. And yet, when man becomes highly cultivated in his affections and intellect, all elements will be invested with a diviner meaning, even to the recognition of the Supreme Being in their silvery depths. There will then be no more mere electricity, no more common magnetism, no more sunlight or material heat; for as man develops into the spiritual he will spiritualize the natural, and naturalize the spiritual, to the just estimation and equilibrium of both. The consequence of which will be a higher and diviner appreciation of those things which we now regard as the common and unsanctified realities of existence. Then, too, the general mind will esteem that which I have termed a universal vital Principle, as the sensational emanations of a Central Divinity.

The fluid in question is the grand vehicle of universal influence. In pervading and traversing bodies, it modifies them, and is equally modified by them in turn. When it circulates from one body to another, with the same quantity of power and velocity, these two bodies are maintained in harmonious relations one toward the other. It is also through the instrumentality of this general medium that our nerves receive sensations from surrounding objects or bodies. Let us all the while bear in mind the duality or two-fold organization of man. Let us think of his sensible and super-sensible state—his material and spiritual—his human and his angelic nature. The discoveries and developments of Animal Magnetism have demonstrated, most conclusively, that when the rapt poet has appealed to the unfettered energies, higher principles, and imperishable character and loveliness of our spiritual nature, he has not wasted his loftiest aspirations and measured expressions upon metaphysical abstractions and poetical rhapsodies, but upon a living, glowing, glorious truth which no imagination can exceed or talent exhaust! Man's present visible organization, being as it is the cradle of the spirit, is perfectly adapted to the objects and convolving circumstances of the external world; while his invisible being is preparing to unfold, as the flower from the bud, to rise above the sensuous conditions of this life into a brighter, purer, loftier sphere, where passion and judgment will have attained the summit of an harmonious concord. Thus the disclosures of magnetism inspire us with a deep, delightful faith; with a clear perception of a future destiny; with an exalted conception of the interior nature of man; and puts us in the possession of a knowledge of immortality which is more demonstrable than a distant country, which is as firm as the familiar principles of physiology, and as immutable as the laws that control the concentric firmaments.

Let us, then, keep our minds upon the two-fold nature of man. Let us remember that, besides the material or visible organs of sense, man is endowed with corresponding internal senses, of which the nervoús system is the magnetic flexus or wires which connect the interior being with the objective world. The nervous system may be considered a kind of mercurial bridge upon which the exact image of external objects and influences travel into the sensorium. The spirit thus holds converse with the outer world. The mind sees, the mind hears, the mind feels, the mind reflects; all else is blind—deaf—dead. But, as I have before shown you, the mind clothes itself in physical vestments, with senses adapted to the conditions of the present mode of existence; but owing to the exceedingly close connection between these two bodies, it is almost impossible for the common mind to discriminate between them;

hence the world is always in possession of a materialistic school of philosophers, who, while they attempt to explain the system and phenomena of mind on the hypothesis that matter and mechanism are inseparably allied, and fail, yet this school does much toward preventing the growth of sickly superstitions among the clergy. While the chemist and physiologist can not detect the presence of the spiritual body as distinct from the material encasement, the magnetic power steps in, separates the inner from the outer, and opens to our vision a magnificent arcanum and a universe of new truth.

In the power of magnetism, the same person may be made to appear like two individuals, both in his deportment and expression. Should, by any cause whatever, the external senses be confused, deadened, and closed, the internal organs of sensibility become immediately intensified in their capabilities, and alone perform the functions common to those of the external body. The vital principle, which before pervaded the external portions of the organism, is now transferred to the interior departments of the body, and conducts impressions of the most fine and delicate character to the mind. These impressions are very distinct and delightful, because the attention and sensibilities of the mind are no longer confused, diluted, benumbed, or distracted by the intrusion of impressions from the outer world, which is common to the ordinary state. This state is somnambulism.

Somnambulism may be philosophically considered as the incipient manifestation of the spiritual faculties, in contradistinction to those of the mere visible organization. It will be observed that somnambulism is not clairvoyance, except in a very inferior degree; yet it is the same in character, and is a state which can be easily cultivated into a high kind of mental illumination. It is very desirable, therefore, that, especially on the present occasion, you confine your thoughts to the simple manifestations of somnambulism; for, by a proper conception of this mental condition, you will find your minds perfectly prepared to accept all the phenomena of Spiritual Clairvoyance on the basis of a mental science which is just ascending to its appropriate position before the world.

Somnambulism is the first demonstration of the independence of the soul. It is clairvoyance undeveloped. The medical profession, however, foster a different theory; and the talented members of churches, and the chief rulers of theological science, appear to regard the whole subject with the most profound and reprehensible indifference, from which improper condition they will be eventually aroused, to the position of self-defense, by the superior intelligence of the masses that unfurl the banners of Progress! The medical professions, as a general thing in this country and upon the Continent, diagnosticate somnambulism as a disease of the nervous system. And Christians, who should make themselves acquainted with some evidences of the soul's immortality and individualism, are in the habit of treating such mental manifestations as the workings of the tender imagination. "We do not know," says the talented Dr. Hufeland, "either the essence or limits of this astonishing power; but every thing proves that it penetrates the depths of the organism, and the internal life of the nervous system; that it may even affect the mind itself, and disturb its ordinary relations. Whoever, then, undertakes to govern and direct this mysterious power, attempts a very bold and responsible task. Let him consider well that he is probably penetrating, as far as is possible, into the most elevated laws of Nature. Never let him enter this sanctuary without reverential fear, and without the most profound respect for the immortal Principle which he attempts to set in operation." Now this is the true spirit of inquiry—the true basis of a scientific investigation. But he who resigns the use of his reason, and consigns all philosophical topics to the medical profession and yields all psychological knowledge to the gentlemen of the gown, is not prepared to pronounce even the simplest opinion upon a subject which promises as much pleasure to the peasant as to the king. It takes hold upon immortality. It stands upon the watch-tower, and points the traveler to sublimer spheres. There are some who know the value of somnambulism as a demonstration of the soul's immortality. According to the opinion of a celebrated French author—M. Colquhoun—the study of the phenomena of human magnetism has lately accomplished more wonders, than all the preaching ever heard in France, by weaning many from the deadly errors of materialism and infidelity, and giving birth to a sound spiritual and religious faith. This author affirms, that "the state of somnambulism is one totally different from that of ordinary life,—a state, in which the animal sensibilities undergo an essential change,—a state in which the ordinary activity of the corporeal faculties is suspended for a time, and the internal instinct—the immaterial principle—the very soul itself—displays its unfettered energies, independently of the material organs." Wordsworth, the true philosophical poet, prophetically and very accurately described this mental conditon, before he had any practical knowledge of it, which he obtained on his ascension to the spiritual country. He calmly writes concerning this state, although wholly unintentionally, as one—

> "In whom the burden of the mystery,
> In whom the heavy and the weary weight
> Of all this unintelligible world
> Is lightened: that serene and blessed state
> In which the affections gently lead us on,—
> Until the breath of this corporeal frame,
> And even the motion of our human blood
> Almost suspended, we are laid asleep
> In body, and become a living soul:
> While with an eye made quick by the power
> Of harmony, and the deep power of joy,
> We see into the life of things."

Wordsworth, in thus undesignedly describing this state of the soul, has proved himself as sound a prophet of a divine reality as any Jewish Rabbi or Judean shepherd, whose sayings are incorporated in what we are educated to term the Holy Bible.

Somnambulism, whether natural or superinduced, has done more good, than all the sermons that were ever penned, in the field of human skepticism. Some intelligent author hath said, that "human magnetism is a natural cause, which explains all the effects formerly attributed to magic and witchcraft, as electricity explains the thunder, as astronomy explains the appearance of comets, as a knowledge of the different laws of Nature explains all those phenomena, which, in past times of ignorance, were ascribed to supernatural agents." The doctrine that an emanation of vital magnetism from one individual, directed by his will, may act upon another individual—just as an emanation from the brain acts upon the fingers—does not conduct us to the belief of the action of demons; on the contrary, such a philosophy effectually annihilates this miserable superstition, by teaching us most impressively to see in ourselves the efficient cause of many effects which were in more remote periods of the world ascribed to strange, supernatural, and chimerical potencies. A German writer, while his mind was swelling with gratitude for what the disclosures of magnetism had done for him in his skepticism, thus breathed forth his sentiments: "The phenomena of human magnetism are facts, which can no more be doubted, than can the reality of those meteoric stones which occasionally fall from the heavens. If there be any bridge—any connection—between this and the other world, any transition from the temporary life of the soul to the eternal life of the spirit, these phenomena must be capable of giving us some insight into the subject. They deserve, therefore, in spite of all danger of deception, our most serious attention; as it would be equally foolish, in the face of such amply attested experience, to deliver ourselves over to an all-denying skepticism, and to resign ourselves to a blind faith, in the case of every alledged phenomenon. Somnambulism affords us at least, in its already admitted facts, the incontestible proof that higher powers reside in man, which stretch beyond the narrow sphere of this rude sensual existence, and transcend the horizon of the human understanding entangled in its abstractions."

It should be remembered that somnambulism may exist, and yet the patient may not be able to obtain any impressions or knowledge from the Spirit Land. A person in this state, without the use of any of the external organs of sensibility, sees and distinguishes objects as distinctly as when awake and in his ordinary condition. But the difference between somnambulism and clairvoyance is this: while the somnambule is capable of moving about, by day or night, with equal if not superior confidence and security—carefully avoiding all objects that may happen to stand in his way; the clairvoyant, on the higher plane of perception, can survey as accurately, the interior of objects—not excepting the earth, the human body, and the soul—and even can extend his vision far into the life of things. But still higher is the Spiritual State, which I shall hereafter elucidate.

Some individuals are natural somnambulists; others are capable of it only while under the magnetic influence. And yet it matters not how the interior senses are opened, because the manifestations are the same as a general principle. While in this state, the patient performs things, of which he is absolutely incapable when in his ordinary condition. He frequently exposes himself fearlessly to dangers from which he would otherwise shrink with terror. He reads, writes, sings, plays, thinks, reflects, reasons, and performs a variety of the most delicate operations—both intellectual and mechanical—not only as if he had the complete use of all his corporeal senses, but as if the power, acuteness, and delicacy of his natural faculties were actually increased—which is the fact—in consequence of being emancipated from their organic thraldom.

The following interesting account originally appeared in the Manchester (England) Courier, and has been extensively copied in the public journals of this country as entitled to unreserved credence. It presents in a high degree of perfection, a phenomenon which in its general features is constantly occurring, and which may be witnessed by any one who will take the pains to institute the proper experiments on subjects duly susceptible. The explanation of the phenomenon given by Mr. Braid, as mentioned in the two closing paragraphs of the extract, does not appear satisfactory.

"On the 3d inst. Mad'lle Jenny Lind, accompanied by Mr. and Mrs. Schwabe, and a few of their friends, attended a *seance* at Mr. Braid's, for the purpose of witnessing some of the extraordinary phenomena of hypnotism. There were two girls who work in a warehouse, and who had just come in in their working attire. Having thrown them into the sleep, Mr. Braid sat down to the piano, and the moment he began playing both somnambulists approached and joined him in singing a trio. Having awakened one of the girls, Mr. Braid made a most startling announcement regarding the one who was still in the sleep. He said, although ignorant of the grammar of her own language when awake, when in the sleep she could accompany any one in the room in singing songs in *any* language, giving *both notes and words correctly*—a feat which she was quite incompetent to perform in the waking condition. Mr. B. requested any one in the room to put her to the test, when Mr. Schwabe played and sang a German song, in which she accompanied him correctly, giving both notes and words *simultaneously* with Mr. Schwabe.

"Another gentleman then tried her with one in Swedish, in which she also succeeded. Next, Jenny Lind played and sang a slow air, with Swedish words, in which the somnambulist accompanied her in the most perfect manner both as regarded words and music. Jenny now seemed resolved to test the powers of the somnambulist to the utmost by a continued strain of the most difficult *roulades* and *cadenzas*, including some of her extraordinary *sostenuto* notes, with all their inflections from *pianissimo* to *forte crescendo*, and again diminished to thread-like pianissimo, but in all these fantastic tricks and displays of genius by the Swedish Nightingale, even to the shake, she was so closely and accurately tracked by the somnambulist that several in the room occasionally could not have told, merely by hearing, that there were two individuals singing—so instantaneously did she catch the notes and so perfectly did their voices blend and accord.

"Next, Jenny having been told by Mr. Braid that she might be tested by some other language, commenced 'Casta Diva,' in which the fidelity of the somnambulist's performance, both in words and music, fully justified all that Mr. Braid had alledged regarding her powers. The girl has naturally a good voice, and has had a little musical instruction in some of the 'Music for the Million' classes, but is quite incompetent of doing any such feat in the waking condition, either as regards singing the notes or speaking the words with the accuracy she did when in the somnambulist state. She was also tested by Mad'lle Lind in merely imitating language, when she gave most exact imitations; and Mr. Schwabe also tried her by some difficult combinations of sound, which he said he knew no one was capable of imitating correctly without much practice, but the somnambulist imitated them correctly at once, and that whether spoken slowly or quickly.

"When the girl was aroused, she had no recollection of any thing which had been done by her, or that she had afforded such high gratification to all present. She said she merely felt somewhat out of breath, as if she had been running. Mr. Braid attributes all this merely to the extraordinary exaltation of the sense of hearing, and the muscular sense at a certain stage of the sleep, together with the abstracted state of the mind, which enables the patients to concentrate their undivided attention to the subject in hand, together with entire confidence in their own powers.

"By this means, he says, they can appreciate nice shades of difference in sound, which would wholly escape their observation in the ordinary condition, and the vocal organs are correspondingly more under control, owing to the exalted state of the muscular sense, and the concentrated attention and confidence in their own powers with which he endeavors to inspire them, enables them to turn these exalted senses to the best advantage. It is no gift of intuition, as they do not understand the meaning of the words they utter; but it is a wonderful example of the extraordinary powers of imitating sounds at a certain stage of somnambulism. And wonderful enough it most assuredly is."

In almost all such cases the external eyes of the somnambule are either exactly closed, or else open and staring—destitute of expression and sensibility; and "from the decisive experiments that were made," says a French physician, "in a great variety of instances, it appears clearly to be made out, that the faculty of sight neither was, nor could possibly have been, exercised through the medium of the usual organs of vision." All the other senses—hearing, smelling, tasting, feeling, &c.—are generally dormant or entirely suspended. The somnambule is also capable of answering distinctly any questions, of a terrestrial character, which may be put to him, and, occasionally, of sustaining a rational conversation. "One of the most remarkable characteristic circumstances attending this singular state of existence, and which is also found invariably accompanying the clairvoyant state," says a writer, "is this: on awaking, the individual who had thus insensibly performed all these astonishing operations, retains no recollection of any thing that occurred while he was under the magnetic influence." Cases of natural or magnetic somnambulism have become so common that it is deemed unnecessary to furnish any especial instances. Hundreds could be quoted; but almost every family knows, experimentally, something of the state, and much of its symptomatic peculiarities.

Apparent death is not always accompanied by a suspension of consciousness, for in some cases the mental faculties have been engaged in an exalted manner, a singular and well authenticated instance of which is related in the Psychological Magazine. "A young lady, after lying ill some time, to all appearance died. She was laid in her coffin, and the day of the funeral was fixed. When the lid of the coffin was about to be nailed down, a perspiration was observed on the body; life soon after appeared; at length she opened her eyes and uttered a most pitiable shriek. She said it seemed to her, as if in a dream, that she was really dead; yet she was perfectly conscious of all that happened around her in this dreadful state. She distinctly heard her friends speaking, and lamenting her death, at the side of her coffin. She felt them pull on the dead-clothing, and lay her in it. This feeling produced a mental anxiety which was indescribable; she tried to cry, but her soul was without power, and could not act on her body. She had the contradictory feeling as if she were in her body, and yet not in it, at one and the same time. It was equally impossible for her to stretch out her arm, or to open her eyes, or to cry, although she continually endeavored to do so. The internal anguish of her mind was, however, at its utmost height, when the funeral hymns began to be sung, and when the lid of the coffin was about to be nailed on. The thought that she was to be buried alive was the one that gave activity to her soul, and caused it to operate on her corporeal frame."

It has been asserted by several very honest persons, that they have experienced a consciousness of being out of the body.

Perhaps the clearest and most positive testimony to the fact, is that given by Dr. Adam Clarke, the learned Wesleyan, who, when relating his recovery from drowning, stated to Dr. Lettsom, that during the period of his apparent unconsciousness, he felt a new kind of life. These are his words:—"All my views and ideas seemed instantly and entirely changed, and I had sensations of the most perfect felicity that it is possible, independently of rapture, for the human mind to feel. I had no pain from the moment I was submerged; a kind of green color became visible to me; a multitude of objects were seen, not one of which, however, bore the least analogy to any thing I had ever beheld before." When preaching in aid of the Humane Society, at the City-road Chapel, in London, he said, 'I was submerged a sufficiently long time, according to my apprehensions, and the knowledge I now have of physiology, for me to have been so completely dead as never more to exist in this world, had it not been for that Providence which, as it were, once more breathed into me the breath of this life."

It has been my impression to furnish you the rationale of this incipient manifestation of the interior senses of the mind, concerning which you will each know more when you are raised in a spiritual body to the corresponding world beyond us.

A subject which takes our affections into its strong embrace, and empowers the reasoning faculties with a fresh proclivity to probe the deep depths of truth, must be approached and fostered with a religious reverence. When you approach it, I admonish you to trifle not, but take off your shoes, for it is holy ground. It refers to our deepest vitality. It touches gently the finest feelings of the mind, and throws a deep magnificence and a grand beauty over the whole arcanum of our future destiny! The double nature of man is proved to a demonstration. The external man corresponds to the internal man. And the eyes of the mind put on the material organs in order to see the external world. But magnetism, like an angel from the sphere of knowledge, plays upon the material sense—bids the living principle to go within—shuts the outer doors of the temple—locks the sentinels in the depths of sleep; and touches the spirit of wisdom in the soul, and, lo! the secrets of

Nature are revealed, and the human mind is illuminated with light reflected from a world of new realities.

Human magnetism is not forced to rely upon any one solitary and partial claim to notice and consideration. Its roots are running far beneath, and extensively throughout, the general ground of humanity. It holds the tendrils of many hearts in its power. And the noblest theories are forced to do homage to this new science, because its light is greater and more positive. It invests the temple of Nature with a new significance. It brings the planets nearer, and begets a friendship within us for their beautiful inhabitants. Beautiful and grand realities are being disclosed to us from the granite sides of creation, which were formerly prison-houses and the hiding-places of innumerable mysteries; and the black clouds that have for ages concealed from our vision the sweet joys which pertain to our future, are penetrated and removed from off the firmament's face which now smiles upon us like a new-born babe! "We stand," says a celebrated German physician, "before the dawning of a new day for science and humanity,—a new discovery awaits us, far surpassing any that has been hitherto made, which promises to afford us a key to some of the most recondite secrets of Nature, and to open up to our view a new world." In the simple phenomena of ordinary somnambulism we behold the glimmerings of a spiritual reality,—the incipient manifestation of a higher power. For, even so, in the bud we see indications of the coming flower; in the child the future man; in the man the angel, which is tending progressively toward higher and happier destinations!

LECTURE XIX.

THE MENTAL FACULTIES CONSIDERED IN RELATION TO CLAIRVOYANCE.

In the religious department of man's mental constitution are to be found some of the most mysterious laws of his nature. His mind, like his muscles, has expansive and contractive powers—faculties which receive and impart; ebb and flow like the ocean tides.

Phrenological science has discovered, classified, and named the mental faculties, and very truthfully, too, to a great extent. The mind is ascertained to possess faculties which guard and protect the whole economy, and faculties, also, which refine and expand all the subordinate sensibilities of the soul, and convey them upward to states and spheres which pertain to higher and holier existences. For instance,—while Alimentiveness, Secretiveness, and Acquisitiveness operate in the mental economy as guardians and conservators of the internal welfare of the individualism; Ideality, Benevolence, and Veneration act, on the other hand, as angels which open the blinded eyes of the mind, invigorate its aspirations, lead it out beyond the changeful earth, and point upward to that Eternal Mind, which lights with a brilliant glory the temple of the universe.

These contractive and expansive faculties of the mind preserve,—when they are properly developed and harmoniously exercised,—its health and equilibrium. While one group of faculties watch the personal interests of the physical and spiritual organism; the other group counteract the tendency to extremes, and teach the mind to expand its sphere of enjoyments as wide as the ocean of human existence. One combination of mental powers renders the individual exceedingly selfish and egotistical, while the higher combination causes the individual to forget self, as self locally considered, and expands his sensibilities to the sphere of all human sensation and sympathy. It matters not, however, how expansive the mental sympathies are, they may still all be summed up in the word, SELF—which is the center and circumference of the individualism. If the individual is unfolded enough to elevate his thoughts above the local wants and contracted desires of the body and mind, then he has simply expanded himself into a larger sphere of existence. The mind that has grown large enough to love the neighbor as himself, has then simply enlarged the scope of its individuality. It seeks its enjoyments in a wider field. Self has widened its circle so that the neighbor is embraced; but it is still self notwithstanding. This is a law of the individualism, and it is not possible to escape its legitimate workings.

The contractive faculties of the mental economy exert a strong restraining influence upon all the physical functions, while the expansive faculties act in the capacity of moral reformers. The latter give rise to all the high and magnanimous sentiments which dilate the soul. They originate also the religious aspirations, and urge the mind to seek its happiness far beyond the mere locality of the body and its selfish demands. They show that enjoyment consists, not in those little and trifling affairs which pertain to physical and merely personal comforts, but in the free and full exercise of the reasoning faculties in the boundless fields of humanity and nature. They likewise render the soul clairvoyant by opening its interior senses, which can detect and trace out the life of things. The truly illuminated mind is one whose contractive powers are constantly under the positive control of the expansive faculties,—just as the strong arm is big with muscle and with all the appendages which expand and give power. The conclusions, therefore, to which, on this occasion, I am impressed to lead you, are these: First, that a well-balanced development of the contractive and expansive faculties, is essential to individual harmony; second, that the religious laws of the mind are the magnetizers which tend to throw the whole spirit into a superior condition, and this state is far in advance of natural or induced somnambulism, which is generally esteemed as clairvoyance by those who have not separated the mental states.

Every man who subdues his egotistical and selfish propensities; who takes the government of his soul into his own reason; who rules within himself, a law unto himself—such, in very truth, are in a condition which may be truthfully regarded as pre-eminently "superior" to any other general state of which the mind is constitutionally capable. I will not now, however, anticipate too completely the "spiritual state" of the soul,—which I am impressed to consider familiarly on some future occasion,—because, naturally succeeding the "somnambulic state" is the "clairvoyant state," which I am more particularly moved to philosophically analyze and explain, if possible, to your full satisfaction.

One general source of skepticism and erroneous inference in regard to the phenomena under consideration, is, the custom of confounding totally different states, and estimating them all as "the mesmeric state," or "the clairvoyant state," &c.—thus frequently making the general condition accountable for each and every thing which may have resulted from a very superficial state of mind. The truly scientific mind would not allow such indiscrimination to characterize his observations. He would discover every variety of symptoms in the subjects of magnetism, which would indicate distinct degrees and states of mind. The state of clairvoyance is exceedingly rare, and, when developed by the volition or manipulations of another, inevitably depends very much upon the particular temperament of the operator, combined with the constitutional predisposition of the subject. "The best and most interesting cases of the clairvoyant state," remarks a French author, "are those which have occurred naturally—that is, without the employment of any artificial means. The inferior magnetic states are frequently mistaken for the higher condition of clairvoyance, which is a source of much error and skepticism." And the same writer goes on to say—that, "the alledged propensity to deception in common somnambulists has been conspicuously remarked by almost all observers of these phenomena,—especially in the case of females, which disposition has been generally attributed to their unhappy vanity and love of display. But I suspect it is owing, in a great measure, to the importunity or mismanagement of the operator, or of those in communication with the subject. This propensity to deception has never been known to occur in the highest states of clairvoyance, in which the faculties appear to be quite spiritualized. We can not, however, be too cautious in putting questions to somnambulists, or in taxing their powers too much, because they may themselves be deceived, and deceive others, without the least design. It should be remembered, also, that the thoughts and desires of the operator have a great influence on almost all somnambulists. In all cases, therefore, we should endeavor to discriminate as accurately as possible the precise state in which the subject may happen to be, in order to ascertain what he is capable of doing and seeing with a certainty."

It must be confessed, that, especially to the unsystematic and superficial thinker, the different magnetic conditions are extremely difficult of an accurate classification. Because the phenomena differ very much in different individuals, and sometimes even in the same individual at different times as the circumstances differ which attend the induction of the state. And besides this, the transition from one condition to another, from a low to a high state, and the reverse, is sometimes instantaneous and imperceptible. The states often manifest unexpected divergences and convergences—contractions and expansions—so that, in fact, it is exceedingly difficult to ascertain the boundaries, latitudes, and longitudes of a condition which,—because we do not yet know how to govern it,—makes so many angular revolutions on its magnetic centers.

Clairvoyance, as you probably all know, is a French term, literally signifying—*clear vision;* it does not imply any thing like a commerce of thoughts and wisdom from the world of spirits. Good somnambulism is manifested in individuals who can, without the use of the external organs of perception or sensibility, read, write, walk about, play, paint, perform delicate operations in mechanism, &c.; while good clairvoyance is indicated in persons who can see, in the same manner, but hundreds and thousands of miles through space and all material substances. Thus, it will be observed, that clairvoyance is but the complete development of somnambulism,—an extension and expansion of the same identical state. The clairvoyant state may be considered, even at this growth of the nineteenth century, as comparatively of very rare occurrence,—I say comparatively, because the inferior conditions are very numerous. Clairvoyance is a high state of mental exaltation. The faculties of observation are particularly lucid and illuminated; and yet, let it be remembered, this state may exist to a very high degree of accuracy, without the subject perceiving any thing actually spiritual or comprehending much of that which pertains to the world of spirits.

The truly clairvoyant mind is placed in a very peculiar relation to the external world. The individual is no longer a sensuous creature,—a mind depending upon the outer senses for thought, suggestion, reason, contemplation,—but he is already in an interior life where it is easy for him to see, to a great extent, into the hidden beauties and dynamics of Creation. He is also very intuitional. When once in this state, no matter whether it was naturally or artificially produced, he forthwith obtains a clearer knowledge of his own mental and bodily condition—is enabled frequently, with accuracy, to calculate the phenomena of disease, which will naturally and inevitably occur; and the subject can also determine upon the most appropriate and effectual application or remedies. In this state, the individual possesses all the powers of the somnambulist in a much higher degree of intensification and availability. Because while the ordinary "sleep-walker," as he is sometimes termed, has apparently only a portion of his mind under his own control, the clairvoyant is in the possession of all his voluntary powers of mind, except those which pertain to merely muscular motion; and even these are, in rare cases, entirely available to the subject's volition.

There is a world of psychological interest connected with the truly clairvoyant state. The psychometrician is generally one who does not enter any but the "sympathetic state," which I have considered in previous discourses. But between the veritable somnambulic and spiritual states there are a vast multitude of psychological phenomena which can not but arrest the attention of the most scientific thinker or metaphysician. These mental symptoms pertain especially to the universal lucidity of the high and perfect state of clairvoyance. It is a great study to observe, first in detail and then in combination, the contemplative abstractions of the surface-sleeper; then the ordinary vigil, reverie, and dreaming of the still advancing mind; then the very "deep sleep" which succeeds the process of common dreaming; then the transitions of the mind from inferior to superior states, in which higher dreaming, reverie, and vigil occur—such as characterized the mental state of Baron Swedenborg; and, finally, the high and truly clairvoyant state, in which the soul extends its vision far and wide over the fields of creation, almost totally irrespective of objects or distance!

The following is a good *test* of clairvoyance, taken from a recent work on Mesmerism by Dr. Gregory:—"At the house of Dr. Schmitz, rector of the High School here, I saw a little boy of about nine years of age put into the magnetic sleep by a young man of seventeen. As the boy was said to be a clairvoyant, I requested him, through his magnetizer, whom alone he heard, to visit mentally my house, which was nearly a mile off, and perfectly unknown to him. He said he would, and soon, when asked, began to describe the back room, in which he saw a sideboard with glasses, and on the sideboard a singular apparatus, which he described. In fact, this room, although I had not told him so, is used as a dining-room, and has a sideboard, on which stood at that moment glasses; and an apparatus for making soda-water, which I had brought from Germany, and which was then quite new in Edinburgh. I then requested him, after he had mentioned some other details, to look at the front room, in which he described two small portraits, most of the furniture, mirrors, ornamental glasses, and the position of the pianoforte, which is very unusual. Being asked whom he saw in the room, he replied, only a lady, whose dress he described, and a boy. This is ascertained to be correct at that time. As it was just possible that this might have been done by thought-reading, although I could detect no trace of any sympathy with me, I then requested Dr. Schmitz to go into another room, and there to do whatever he pleased, while we should try whether the boy could see what he did. Dr. S. took with him his son; when the sleeper was asked to look into the other room, he began to laugh, and said that Theodore (Dr. Schmitz's son) was a funny boy, and was gesticulating in a particular way with his arms, while Dr. Schmitz stood looking on. He then said that Theodore had left the room, and after a while that he had returned; then that Theodore was jumping about; and being asked about Dr. Schmitz, declined more than once to say, not liking to tell, as he said, but at last told us that he also was jumping about. Lastly, he said Dr. Schmitz was beating his son, not with a stick, although he saw a stick in his room, but with a roll of paper. All this did not occupy more than seven or eight minutes; and when Dr. Schmitz returned, I at once gave him the above account of his proceedings, which he, much astonished, declared to be correct in every particular. Here thought-reading was absolutely impossible; for neither I, nor any one present, had the least idea of what Dr. Schmitz was to do; nor indeed had Dr. Schmitz himself, till I suggested it, known that such an experiment was to be tried. I am, therefore, perfectly satisfied that the boy actually saw what was done; for to suppose that he had guessed it, appears to me a great deal more wonderful."

Every thing which I am impressed to affirm in this philosophical description of clairvoyance, is susceptible of the clearest demonstration by actual experiment; indeed I could quote facts innumerable in attestation of the points disclosed in this discourse. But this is deemed wholly unnecessary. The reader's principal desire, on this subject, must now be to know, how it is possible for the clairvoyant to see, without the organs of perception, as distinctly as we see with them, and to such an almost illimitable extent. Now here let me urge you to remember this fact,—that a person may be a good clairvoyant, so far as mere interior perception is concerned, without being much exalted in the intellectual departments of his mind. The eyes of his mind may be opened, but his understanding may remain entirely unexpanded. I have seen good clairvoyants who could see diseases in the living body, who could read thought, who could discern distant objects, who could see even the swelling bosom of the planet Saturn; and yet their understanding, or wisdom-principle, was so undeveloped that they did not know how to denominate the disease, nor how to discover the proper remedies, nor how to express the thought which they perceived, nor describe the objects or the planets which were plainly unfolded to the almost universal sweep of their vision. This fact will not surprise us when we recollect, that clairvoyance means simply "clear vision," without any reference whatever to the state of the understanding. You all very well know, that the Indian can see as far, with his natural organs of vision, over the geological manifestations of a country as the educated Professor A.; but the latter can easily understand those stratifications of rock which the Indian would pass by as things utterly transcending the available abilities of his intellect. So with some individuals who attain the truly clairvoyant state. They see things which their limited intellects will not grasp; hence frequently, in their descriptions, they utterly fail to impart a clear and accurate idea of that which they may perceive with the utmost distinctness. Hence it is that even good seers are occasionally led into misapprehension; not because of the suggestive influxes which some superstitious sectarians suppose emanate from evil spirits; but solely in consequence of a want of comprehension on the part of the subject. Let it be duly impressed, therefore, upon your understandings, that the clairvoyant state is not one which puts the subject in the possession of boundless wisdom, but a condition, properly speaking, in which the mind has a clear vision, independent of the external senses, to an extent always proportionate to the degree of the state, and the fineness of his interior temperament.

We come now more immediately to the question—how can this "clear vision" exist?

To fully elucidate this question, it is essential to first comprehend the nature of bodily vision,—especially its source and principles. But it will appear wholly unnecessary for me to repeat, what I have frequently alluded to throughout these discourses—namely,—that the outer organs of vision are constructed upon positive and negative laws; and that, from the universal exhibitions of a system of duality or twofold organization, it is but common sense to infer that the outer organs of vision, like all the other senses, are but the external form of interior correspondential principles, as words are the forms of thought. The source of ordinary perception is, therefore, very simple and easily understood. Here, then, let us commence our explanation. Suppose you desire to produce, through the agency of manipulations, the clairvoyant state. To accomplish this, you must first induce the magnetic condition. Let us now inquire—

What is the magnetic condition? It is a sleep produced in the body by overcoming the positive force of the system by the introduction of a power several degrees more positive.

What is this positive power? It is that portion of the spiritual principle—or the mind—which creates, maintains, guards, and transfers sensation throughout the body?

What proof have we that the sensational medium is identical with magnetism?

The most prominent demonstrations are the sympathies and antipathies; the likes and the dislikes; the inclinations and disinclinations; the attractions and repulsions; in a single word, the positive and negative principles upon which the soul always conducts its outer manifestations.

What may be considered a familiar illustration of the magnetic character of sensation?

Those things which act pleasurably upon the sensational medium are exactly adapted, in their positive and negative relations, to the medium with which their spheres come in contact. Those objects which attract the mind are positive to it to the full extent of the attraction; while those which repel it are, to the same extent, negative. It is, however, more exactly true to say, that the mind is enabled to discriminate between what is good and what is not good, or agreeable, by being surrounded by a magnetic coat of mail which seems as the medium of communication between the soul and the external world.

If the sensation of the body is closely allied to vital magnetism, and obeys the laws of magnetism, how can it be overcome in order to induce the magnetic slumber?

By disturbing the equilibrium existing between the mucous

and serous surfaces of the organism. That is, all sensation resides almost exclusively upon the external (or serous) surfaces of every organ, nerve, and muscle; because the internal (or mucous) surfaces of these structures are too positive to receive it; but, should you desire to produce the magnetic coma, then your operations should be directed to the transferration of the sensation from the outer surfaces to those of the internal.

How can this be accomplished?

Seat yourself in a position more elevated than your subject, who should be accommodated with a most comfortable posture. The object being to prevent all disturbing sensations from interfering with the main purpose, which is to equalize and identify your motives, feelings, temperature, and general condition. If any thoughts foreign to this purpose enter your minds, the object will be defeated. Evil intentions will dilute your efforts in proportion to their influence upon your mind. You can not employ this newly discovered power for any selfish, mercenary, or licentious purpose; it is above so narrow and corrupt a sphere! And if, in any instance, a person should profess innocence of crime, in consequence of a magnetic influence being exerted upon him at the time of his committing it, you may put the profession down to falsehood; for the person, in such case, although under the magnetic intoxication, is, notwithstanding, sufficiently in the possession of his own desires and powers of volition to do, or not to do, the deed of which he is known to be guilty. There is nothing in phreno-magnetism to warrant a different conclusion. In the matter of mere experiment, the subject can be induced to yield to the strongest sensation which may arise from the magnetic irritation of any one organ; but this can not be performed by the magnetic power, if, instead of an experiment, the operator has his will fixed upon the accomplishment of something which he knows, while willing it, to be clearly and absolutely wrong. The knowledge of the wrong weakens his positive power; and the subject is left to the exercise of his own desires, volition, and personality. This will be forever true; because this power is anti-physical, anti-selfish, anti-everything which is low, local or evil.

From experience I know this to be true; for I never entered the magnetic state when my mind did not strongly will the sleep upon myself,—my thoughts and desires being, at the same time, in complete sympathy with those of the operator; thus rendering my own mind instrumental in the production of the condition and also of its consequences. Hence, to produce the sleep, you must sit perfectly at ease,—dismiss all agitating and impressive thoughts, emotions, or speculations—do not pre-judge, or pre-theorize upon, any thing—be tranquil as possible in body as in mind—let the subject gaze steadily at some convenient object upon your person (the best thing I know of is a small breast-pin)—regard him or her visually and mentally with a fixed, and determined, and definite purpose;—do this for about two minutes. You may now breathe gently on the face and head. During all this time your hands should rest very easily upon those of the subject, thumb to thumb. After breathing upon the face, neck, and head—imparting, as far as possible, a calm, refreshing, and pleasurable sensation—then raise your hands very gently above the subject's head and bring them down, very softly brushing the sides of the head, and place them on the shoulders. Let your hands rest here about one minute. Then bring them down with a gentle sweep to the ends of the fingers, from which pass your hand off spirally into the air and return them, with the palms outward, to the head as before. These processes may be continued from twenty to thirty minutes. Sometimes it is necessary to lay your hand on the stomach. Manipulations, extending not only along the whole of the upper extremities but also down the lower extremities, are to some temperaments very essential to a perfect magnetism. It is necessary sometimes to magnetize at a distance of several feet; to nervous or sensitive temperaments this process is very soothing, refreshing and pleasurable. No muscular effort is necessary; all your movements should be easy, graceful, and not too rapid. Of this I will say more on another occasion;—when I come to consider the utility of human magnetism as a remedial agent in disease. The question here arises—

What changes are there wrought in the organism, by this manipulating process, should it happen to take effect?

"Of all instruments which we can employ," says La Place, "in order to enable us to discover the otherwise imperceptible agents of nature, the human nerves are the most sensible—expecially when their sensibility is exalted by particular causes. It is by means of them that we have discovered the slight electricity which is developed by the contact of two heterogeneous bodies." Yea, it is even so; for the magnetic power which the operator exerts upon the subject paralyzes the nervous centers in the eyes and their appendages, and overcomes the ordinary equilibrium of the general system. The sensational medium is repelled from the external surfaces to the internal surfaces, and the subject and the operator, so far as the positive and negative forces of the physical system are concerned, constitute one human body. And much of that principle, which, in the normal state, formed the medium of sensation, now goes into the cerebro-spinal centers and into other centers which pertain to the anterior, or front, portions of the brain. In consequence of the departure of the element of sensation from the surface of the body, the latter is left in a death-like, senseless, and profound slumber. And in proportion as the body is deadened the mind is enlivened; that is to say, when we are laid asleep in body we become a living soul, for the elements of the mind are then almost all absorbed into the brain, except enough to maintain the moderate performance of the organic functions.

When the brain is thus illuminated, the forehead is perfectly transparent. It appears like a window from which the soul looks out upon the fields of creation. All the upper portions of the face, including the bodily eyes, are also illuminated. These phenomena are not visible except to the mental vision. But what I desire you to see, is this—that good clairvoyants are generally not illuminated in the highest regions of the brain, but only in the base of the cerebrum, extending from the center of the forehead, around to either side, and downward to the top of the cheek-bones. This is the source or locality of the mental perceptions. But some subjects will place their heads to one side, or horizontally with the object to which their attention is directed, as if the vision came from all portions of the head at the same time. This is owing principally to the non-conformability of the perceptions, at first, to the universal medium of spiritual vision, which is electricity.

Clairvoyance implies the clear perception of things beyond the powers of bodily vision ; but it does not imply an understanding of the things observed. The front division of the brain is only illuminated. The organs of perception are principally excited by the flow of the sensational medium into them, which has been directed thither by the magnetic processes. The vision extends in straight lines when the distance is subjected to contemplation ; and yet, as with the bodily eyes, the interior perceptions harmonize very readily with the rays of light and electricity which play abroad in nature, so that the vision usually comprehends fully the half of a very large disc. A good illustration of the clairvoyant state, and of the character of the perceptions attending it, is given in a previous discourse, where I described my first interior view of Nature. Nevertheless the immediate tendency of this state is to enlarge the understanding, develop Love, invigorate benevolence, increase the wisdom-principle, and conduct the spirit into higher and larger spheres of contemplation. The discerning mind at once discovers the analogy,—yea, even the identification,—existing between the higher phenomena of magnetism and those states which characterized the Jewish prophets and all true pioneers of religious inspiration. In spontaneous clairvoyance,—which is identified with the state which is induced by the magnetic processes,—the eyes of the mind, the internal powers of vision, are wonderfully strengthened and enlarged, and there are no boundaries of time or space which can circumscribe their penetration. To the thus exalted mind, the old things pass away and all things become new; for, when properly regarded, the magnetic sleep is a spiritual repose, wherein the mind, elevated by contemplation, retires into the inner chambers of its own mystical nature, suspends for a time all commerce with the objective world, and exerts the noblest functions of its angelic organization.

Concerning the propriety of an anniversary in commemoration of the birth of MESMER, I have frequently been addressed as follows:

MR. A. J. DAVIS:

Dear Friend,—"I wish to call your attention to a matter that has long since suggested itself to me, and which also meets the united approbation of the friends of progress in the West—i. e., an anniversary in commemoration of the great event of the birth of Antonie Mesmer, who I conceive was the man that threw open the door, which has for so long a time shut mankind out from beholding that true light which is now shining forth, gladdening the hearts and illuminating the intellects of many. Such an occasion would call together the true and earnest seekers after truth, and serve to strengthen their faith with knowledge, and also cast abroad a new impulse by showing to the world that an assemblage of freed minds, such as this nor any other generation ever saw, could meet in 'Harmony,'—not for President making, nor for theological wrangling and warfare, but for the purpose of shadowing forth to our fellow-men how sublime are the effects of true spiritual light and knowledge upon mankind."

Yours Fraternally,

J. H. ——.

My impression on the above suggestion is this: Mankind are not yet sufficiently developed to cast aside the worship and deification of leaders and chieftains. [I will speak hereafter of the unnaturalness of such promotion or deification.] It is an evil, or mistake, which people fall into, without designing to do so. They can not keep in mind the difference between a *man* and a *principle;* the principle becomes entombed in the surroundings of the person; and thus, through ignorance and inadvertency, all days set apart for hero commemoration, uniformly result in discussion, divisions, and discord. The friends of progress, it seems to me, should have anniversaries. They should appoint a time for the celebration of some Principle—say, for example—the Principle of Progression, of Republicanism, or Liberty. Let the Convention be entirely free from particular reference to the birth or life of any one individual. This will utterly prevent local prejudices, and tend to expand the thoughts and affections of the people outwardly, into the universal sphere of being; and every mind will necessarily feel some general interest in the anniversary. Mesmer did not, according to my impressions, throw open the door to new truth in a manner which can be heartily approved of by an enlightened and spiritualized community. He *revived* simply what had been known, in different forms and under various names, for centuries previous to his birth. The nineteenth century is the time to open an anniversary in commemoration of a New Dispensation in every thing; which can, and should, be designated by the name of some universal PRINCIPLE, at once attractive and ennobling to every heart.

LECTURE XX.

CONCERNING THE PHENOMENA AND HISTORY OF CLAIRVOYANCE.

There is no disguising the fact, that human magnetism, and all the phenomena consequent upon its exercise as a peculiar agency in man's power, has been more or less known in all ages of the world. Every age has had its genius. Every era has its poet, its prophet, and philosopher. Every period has had its epitome—its perfect representation—in some particular individual. And in all exalted minds, both ancient and modern, the ascending and higher developments of human magnetism are, to my view, distinctly discernible.

In previous discourses I have alluded to the thought-reading, heart-discerning, event-seeing, and prophetic manifestations of Jesus. With these powers, we also see the operation of his strong magnetic influences among the sore, the lame, and blind. Occasionally, his cures were accomplished wholly through the "faith" of the patient; as in the case of the woman unto whom he said, "Daughter, thy faith hath made thee whole." And a Catholic priest is far more deserving of the title, "Defender of the faith," than George the Third, or than even any Protestant clergyman, because the disciple of Catholicism is generally treated, when he is either morally or physically diseased, through the agency of that "faith" which cured the woman of olden time. That is to say, that mystical power of the mind which is said to give, "to airy nothing a local habitation and a name," metaphysically or generally termed, "imagination," is the chief element played upon by the Catholic clergy, in connection with their strong magnetic influence, when they desire to raise from the bed, a palsied body and a weak mind.

The very physical character of the clergy generally,—especially those who, like an ambitious actor, depend upon "soul-stirring excitements" for success,—exerts a corresponding influence upon "the flocks" intrusted to their supervision and vigilance. If you will criticise closely and accurately the most influential lawyer, or politician, actor or clergyman, that comes within the sphere of your acquaintance, you will see, as a general principle, a large supply of muscular and physical substance. A "soul-stirring" speaker on the floor of Congress, or in the pulpit, is usually considered "a giant in stature as in intellect"—the first seems to be almost absolutely essential to a "successful career" in any department of public action. From this fact we are constrained to infer, that the "high calling" of the pulpit magnetizer, or the "loud calling" of the magnetic statesman and office-seeker, has more connection with human magnetism than with any "apostolic succession" or electional ordination.

We are fast learning to discover in ourselves the true causes of many mysteries. We may now invest what intellectual capital we possess in a "faith" which will not only make us "whole," but keep us so for evermore. It is better to believe in the principles of psychological science than in the dogmatic pretensions of any priest. It is better to believe in human magnetism than in the thirty-nine articles, which constitute the religious "faith" of thousands, who know, after all, almost nothing of true happiness. It is better to believe in the human soul, when exalted by purity of thought and harmoniousness of life and purpose, than in any creed in the wide world; for we have, by investing our faith in these natural things, the truth, and reason, and inspiration, and Nature, and the Universe on our side. While those who adhere to their educational prejudices, especially when those prejudices are proved absolutely to be grounded in the darkness of mythology, have nothing "on their side" but the old forms of faith, the ceremonies of idolaters, the dead pyramids of old superstitions, and the empty pretensions of educated clergymen, who, by the judicious exercise of their constitutional magnetism, draw many hearts into sympathy with their mystical institutions. But it appears—remarks a celebrated author—that there are persons, even of note, members of learned incorporations, fellows of royal and other privileged societies, professors in ancient universities, &c., to whom, at a certain period of life, the prospect of an accession of real knowledge, instead of being agreeable and satisfactory, is, on the contrary, rather unpleasant, painful, and very humiliating. Every man who then ventures to present them with novel facts or ideas, or in any way attempts to rectify or extend their notions of things, is regarded by them as an invader—a robber—an enemy—an antagonist, instead of being esteemed as an honest opponent, to what they have been accustomed to conceive to be their vested rights in religion, literature and science.

Goethe, the celebrated German poet,—who was a strong believer in Hellsehen, as clairvoyance is termed in Germany,—remarked upon a particular occasion, that when, from time to time, a man arises, who is fortunate enough to discover even one of the great secrets of Nature, ten others immediately start up, who industriously and strenuously endeavor to conceal it again from view. It is so, it always was, and, for a long period, it will continue to be. The confliction between darkness and light, ignorance and knowledge, appears to be interminable. The race of the obscurantists in politics, in science, in religion, and in literature, seems to be full of life and promises to survive even to the end of all investigation. To use the language of a favorite old author—"they are exceedingly angry with every one that hath outgrown his cherry-stones and rattles; they speak evil at a venture of things they know not; and, like mastiffs, are all the fiercer for being kept chained up, and fed, in darkness." Satanic agency is the cry raised by some popular minds against the toleration of human magnetism and clairvoyance; but the medical profession have another way—the supercilious pronunciation of the not very euphonious term, "Humbug"—in which they attempt to solve the difficult problems presented.

When men fail and fall vanquished, even with much truth on their side, Time conquers! In the year 1784, the French government issued a royal mandate to the medical faculty of Paris, requiring them to investigate the facts and pretended developments of human magnetism, and report the results of their examination. But the trial was brought before a prejudiced jury. The faculty had pre-judged the very censurable pretensions of Mesmer; who, because he could successfully exercise the magnetic power, assumed a mysterious demeanor,—thus adopting the pernicious custom of nearly all religious chieftains. The name of Benjamin Franklin, was affixed to the unfavorable report of the French Academy; but this was not right, because he was ill at the time, and could not have been present, though it must be conceded that he favored the general declarations of the prejudiced commissioners. But Franklin did not then know any thing of the higher phenomena of magnetism; hence his testimony can have no weight in this more enlightened day. In 1826, another commission was formed to furnish another report; because the first report had been proved unfounded in truth by the progressive developments of Time. The commissioners were now compelled to be more careful and impartial. The public stood ready to take the power of investigation, and right of judgment into their own possession. The jurors did manifest more nobility in their last examination; and the following were some of the conclusions to which they arrived. Their verdict:—

1. "It has been demonstrated to us, that sleep may be produced under circumstances in which the subjects have not been able to

perceive, and have been ignorant of, the agency employed to occasion the slumber.

2. "The real effects produced by magnetism are very varied. It agitates some; calms others; it usually accelerates the respiration and circulation; causes convulsive motions similar to electric shocks; a lassitude and torpor more or less profound; somnolency; in a limited number of cases, what was by the operators denominated, somnambulism.

3. "There usually take place changes more or less remarkable, in the perceptions and faculties of certain individuals in whom somnambulism is produced by the magnetic passes.

4. "It may be inferred with certainty that this (the somnambulic) state exists; and it is certain, also, that it gives rise to the development of new faculties which have been designated by the terms Clairvoyance, Intuition, Internal Prevision; and sometimes it produces great physiological changes—such as insensibility, a sudden and considerable increase of strength; which changes can not possibly be referred to any other cause."

These conclusions were published to the world by a Commission which had deep-seated prejudice, of a professional nature, against the science which the royal mandate required them to impartially investigate. They acknowledged the existence of human magnetism, the existence of somnambulism, and the existence of clairvoyance; which is all we can reasonably require. But let me, in this connection, remind the medical profession of more modern times of three particular conclusions of their French brethren:—

1. "We have met with two somnambulists professing the faculty of foreseeing acts of the organism.

2. "We have met with one somnambulist, (a female,) who could indicate the symptoms of the disease of three persons with whom she was placed in connection.

3. "Considered as an agent of physiological phenomena, or as a therapeutical means, human magnetism should find a place within the sphere of medical knowledge; and consequently medical practitioners should employ it, or superintend its employment, as it is practiced in the countries of the north."

The trial of the alledged facts and higher phenomena of human magnetism before the tribunal of the French Academy of Science, in the year 1784, is apprehended by most historians as unqualifiedly hostile to the whole subject. But this, like the signature of Benjamin Franklin to the report, is all a mistake. For the prejudice of the commissioners was arrayed principally, not against the physiological facts and psychological phenomena of magnetism, but against the false and pedantic pretensions of Mesmer. This man, although educated and degreed as a talented physician of Switzerland, was too fond of the marvelous to conduct himself like a free and unmysterious demonstrator of science. He no sooner discovered his ability to produce many physiological effects by the manipulations, than he became lugubrious and very mysterious in his deportment. And in 1777, when he left Vienna, and introduced himself to the best society, both literary and scientific, which he could find in Paris, he still carried about with him that imposing and wizard-like air which is frequently exhibited in the so-called evangelical orders of moral teachers. But he made many extraordinary cures. His fame spread throughout the influential departments of Paris. He made a great secret, (like some of our modern biologists and psychologizers,) of the magnetic influence, thus exciting a love of the marvelous in his followers, and charging them each one hundred louis for simply informing them how to conduct the magnetic manipulations. This very reprehensible course naturally excited the most resolute and well-founded opposition, among the medical profession, to Mesmer's pretensions. His methods savored strongly of imposition. His facts were too closely allied to fancies. He depended principally upon imagination for success. Scientific truths and corruptions were too intimately intermixed. In fact, Mesmer converted much of a sublime discovery into mere nonsense and quackery. And I can not feel it in my mind to denounce the French Commissioners for their hostility to such unwarrantable pretensions, any more than I can resist a feeling of disrespect and pity for those members of the clerical profession who assume the airs of a mysterious "high calling" and sanctity, so altogether false, unnatural, and manifestly quackish.

The decision of the French jury was, therefore, after all, not so much against the facts of human magnetism as hostile to the pretensions and theories of Mesmer. This places the subject where it belongs. At the same time, the disciples of magnetism, and the practitioners thereof, should learn from the fate of Mesmer, not to throw around the science any chicanery or mysteriousness,—such as selling secrets, making a condition of each sale that strict confidence shall be perpetually maintained, &c.,—because there is nothing but perfect freedom in Truth, at whose inexhaustible fountain every man in creation has an inherited right to drink freely, "without money and without price" forever!

I do not refer to Mesmer as the *author* or discoverer of magnetism. He simply revived a power which the most ancient inhabitants exercised; and which, in fact, has always been known, and exhibited in various forms, since the peopling of this globe. But modern history has obtained its data of Animal Magnetism from its appearance under the management of Mesmer. From his name the term "mesmerism" had its origin. And it is but wisdom,—I am impressed,—to allude to the trial of our beloved science by the French Jury of Physicians, as recommended by its leading pioneer in 1784; for, by so doing, we find that the commissioners were simply hostile to Mesmer and his theory, but not to the main facts and manifestations of magnetism; which, at that period, were necessarily very imperfect, and undemonstrative. In order to show you that I am not mistaken in this particular, I will quote a passage from the report in question, evidencing clearly that the commissioners did not doubt the facts of magnetism. Here is the passage:—

"It has been clearly demonstrated to us, in a manner the most ample and satisfactory, arising particularly from our own inquiry nto the phenomena of magnetism, that man can act upon man, at all times, and almost at will, by striking the imagination. It has also been shown clearly, that signs and gesticulations the most simple may produce the most powerful effects; that the action of mind upon mind may be reduced to an act (or science,) and may be conducted advantageously, when exercised upon patients who have the most implicit faith in the proceedings."

From the internal signification of this report, however, I think it appears evident that the commissioners were unanimous in the opinion, that all the mental and physiological developments of magnetism were attributable to the workings of the imagination. It matters not, however, what they referred the phenomena to, so long as the effects produced were acknowledged to be decidedly "powerful," and the "influence" conceded to be capable of a scientific recognition and administration. It is very vague, indeed, to refer any "powerful effects" to the imagination,—especially, when the difference between imagination and the laws of man's religious nature, are not yet fully defined. If persons can be made "whole" by faith, or have their raven locks whitened as the snow by the workings of the imagination, then we have discovered a power, which mind exerts upon matter, which is unspeakably valuable. Properly directed, such psychological dynamics may be a source of the most wonderful good to man. If a man is sickened by the imagination, gets the Asiatic cholera or small-pox; he is surely not actuated by an "airy nothing," but by a substantially positive power! Nay; there is, philosophically speaking, no such a thing as imagination! There is no such a faculty as fancy in the mind, for it is all mind—all soul—all spirit. And yet the mind is frequently misled—misimpressed—misdirected; which gives rise to those manifestations of faith and action which occasionally prove themselves to have been founded in chimeras. Fancy, therefore, is the mind misapplied or misimpressed; as when persons are very much frightened when there may be, in fact, nothing to naturally induce that condition. Nevertheless, the frightened mind, whether agitated by any adequate cause or not, acts as powerfully as it could when the cause is all-sufficient to produce the psychological state. Imagination, then, is the mind—nothing but the spirit of the internal—under an excitement founded perhaps in unreality which has simulated so close to reality as to be mistaken by the spirit for an adequate cause. This conclusion, then, is irresistible, that the Commissioners acknowledged the facts of magnetism; and instead of attributing all the manifestations to mere matter and mechanism, as materialists would, on the contrary, candidly confessed that the external effects were traceable to no other cause than the human soul while under a correspondential influence and power.

The utility of magnetism as a moral agent is very little understood; but there are some persons who know how to appreciate, and who have had the courage to acknowledge, the immense blessings flowing from its judicious administration. Concerning the delights arising from this unseen power, a clergyman, of England, possessing much talent and conscientiousness, thus testifies to the moral influence of magnetism in the case of his very much diseased friend:—

"The tranquilizing effects of the magnetic influence were manifested even unto the end of my dear friend's death. Yet he owed a deeper debt than this to magnetism! It had reclaimed him from the hardest infidelity! Of a singular organization, R. T.—my friend—the most amiable of human beings, approached the nearest to an Atheist of any one I ever met with. He seemed to want the very faculty, which says, at once—'There must be a God!' But in his last illness, then it was that a new principle supplied the defect of the original nature, more strikingly than if that nature had, from the beginning, appeared full of holy veneration. Who that then saw him, leaning over his Bible, as he sat for an hour or two in the evening, propped up on every side by pillows—calm, ven under the attack of periodical fever;—triumphing over mortal nfirmity and pain;—rejoicing, while we inwardly mourned;—and whispering patience and comfort to all around him;—who, that beheld this strength made perfect in weakness, but must have exclaimed—'The hand of Heaven is here!' This faith—this wondrous patience—this holy comfort springing out of tears—were, (as he himself confessed to me,) attributable, under Divine Providence, to the magnetic influence.

"From having seen phenomena, to which he could not refuse his assent, my friend was led, step by step, to recognize the mighty truth of the predomination of spirit over matter,—consequently of a Ruling Spirit creating and sustaining all things. 'I rejoice,'—touchingly, he said to me,—'that mesmerism should be the last remedy tried upon me—that it should prove successful in calming my pains; because it was the first thing that relieved me from the worst of all evils—that of an unbelieving heart.'"

This case should arouse the attention of our American clergy to the fact, that, more powerful and beautifully convincing than all the testimony of prophets and apostles respecting the future life, and the resurrection of the body of Jesus, are the developments of human magnetism to the spiritual wants of unbelieving but reasoning minds. It is my impression to bring before you the views and acknowledgments of minds in the old world. You can thereby see how many noble hearts have beat the pulsative elements of sympathy for that blessed science which is destined to cast a halo of spiritual knowledge over the entire world of civilization. And as we improve, the heathen of the islands will receive a corresponding impulse toward—Progression!

The author of a work, entitled *Facts in Mesmerism*, thus testifies of the physical as well as the moral benefits arising from this science:—"It is the peculiar happiness of magnetism not to be forced to rely upon any one solitary and partial claim to notice and consideration. Its roots are cast deeply and extensively into the general ground of humanity. Where the metaphysician leaves it, the man of science may take it up; and when science has gathered in its store of valuable facts, illustrative of all her noblest theories, it can still afford an ample harvest to him who would practically ameliorate the condition of his fellow-beings." Elsewhere the same author says, "The direct correspondence of magnetism with the nervous system, gives it a marked superiority over all such grosser agents as must reach that delicate frame-work of life by a circuitous route. Of all remedies, this alone pours its benefits direct upon the very springs of sensation; thus we possess a subtle means of acting efficiently upon that fountain-head of calamity and disease, to which neither drug nor couching-needle can find its way."

You may have heard it said, that the disciples of magnetism and of its higher phenomena,—somnambulism, clairvoyance, power of prophecy, &c.,—were generally derived from the weak-minded, the imaginative, and the credulous classes. But I will now furnish you with a testimony to the contrary, which our American dignitaries and medical men would do well to receive as a sufficient refutation of the charge. La Place, the astronomer and rigid mathematician, says, that, "the singular phenomena which result from the external sensibility of the nerves in particular individuals, have given birth to various opinions relative to the existence of a new agent denominated animal magnetism, to the action of common magnetism, to the influence of the sun and moon in some nervous affections; and, lastly, to the impressions which may be experienced from the proximity of the metals, or of a running water." * * * "We are," he says, "so far from being acquainted with all the agents of nature, that it would be quite unphilosophical to deny the existence of the phenomena, merely because they are inexplicable in the present state of our knowledge." It would be well, I think, for those of our American brethren, who denounce the claims of magnetism and clairvoyance without one examination, to repent themselves, and adopt some of that honest modesty of La Place, which enabled him to acknowledge that the wisest do not yet know "all the agents of nature,"—hence, that a denial of any such phenomena is eminently unphilosophical and absurd.

But let us look at the testimony of the celebrated Cuvier, whose opinion has much weight as a man of close discrimination: "We must confess," says he, "that it is very difficult,—in the experiments which have for their object the action which the nervous system of two different individuals can exercise one upon another,—to distinguish the effect of the imagination of the individual upon whom the experiment is tried, from the physical result produced by the person who acts for him. The effects, however, on persons ignorant of the cause, and upon persons whom the operation itself has deprived of consciousness, and those effects which animals present, do not permit us to doubt, that the proximity of two animated bodies in certain electrical conditions, combined with certain movements, have a real effect, independently of all participation of the fancy." In this connection, it may prove profitable to notice, particularly, the testimony of the author of an elaborate work on Human Physiology,—Dr. Elliotson, of England,—who says:—"I have now, for three years, carefully and dispassionately investigated this subject by experiments performed almost every day upon a variety of persons; and I do not only repeat my firm conviction of the truth of mesmerism, but also of the truth of many points in it upon which

I formerly gave no opinion." It is very evident, that the Doctor beheld more of magnetism than is admitted by the few itinerant psychologists of to-day; for he says—"The production of the peculiar coma (or profound sleep) by mesmerism, independently of all mental impressions, is a truth now admitted by a very large number of the best informed, acutest, and least credulous men in England." Another eminent physician says—"there is no longer any doubt, among those who have examined the subject, that in somnambulism the intellectual functions are not only very active, but frequently more developed than when the individual is awake." My impressions refer me to these remote testimonies as the proper historical beginnings of this particular science.

There is no longer any reason why some of our American scientifics and academicians should withhold their attention from a scientific philosophy, which walks among them, interrogating their repositories of learning, even while the sun shines forth from its zenith and the heavens emit no darkness. They can not still, with truth "on their side," affirm that "weak" and "credulous" minds constitute the only disciples; neither can they attribute all the phenomena to imposture or imagination; for they do not yet know "all the agents of nature." While the majority of medical men, and the generality of the clergy, turn aside, with a supercilious expression, from the candid investigation of these high manifestations of mind; that very eminent philosopher, Dugald Stuart, with much dignity of thought, says:—"Among all the phenomena, however, to which the theme of mind has led our attention, none are, perhaps, so wonderful as those which have been recently brought to light, in consequence of the philosophical inquiries occasioned by the medical claims of Mesmer and his associates."—But I will quote no further.

For the moral utility of magnetism, I refer you to hundreds and thousands of our own countrymen who have been led from physical darkness into spiritual light and joy, by its developments. And the same number can testify, of the physical utility of this science, in all parts of the world. Dr. Elliotson published a pamphlet entitled "Numerous Cases of Surgical Operations, without Pain, in the Mesmeric State;" from which you can glean the adequate evidence of the scientific, theological, and therapeutic utility of human Magnetism. Indeed, the shelves of the popular book-stores are literally studded with confirmatory publications concerning this unseen power.

The time has nearly arrived when the intelligent people of the United States will require a magnetic Institution, wherein the laws of psychological science and of human magnetism may be systematically administered to the sick and diseased. Magnetism has already accomplished so much for the souls and bodies of men, that, to longer deprive it of an appropriate position amid the established sciences, would be to deny to truth the possession of her just demands. An Institution is necessary to a proper administration of magnetism.

Let each one do all the good he can in the fields of suffering and ignorant humanity. The best preventative of disease, both moral and physical, is unwavering obedience to the established laws of Nature. But while there is suffering, let human magnetism play most energetically from your hands into its fountain-head.

LECTURE XXI.

CONCERNING THE SPIRITUAL STATE AND ITS EXTERNAL MANIFESTATIONS.

MENTAL illumination! I speak of no poetical fancy—no dream of the mind—under the influence of narcotics, opium, or stimulants. It is a high reality—a supremely superior condition. And yet it is a state with which but few are acquainted. It comes not within the sphere of every-day experience. It is that which brings the soul into close proximity with that "Interior Life," which holds perpetual commerce with the high, the holy, and the sanctified. I speak now of mental or spiritual illumination,—of an expansion of the expansive energies of the mind,—a subjugation of the material to the spiritual; the body to the soul!

You doubtless well remember what I have said concerning the states of somnambulism and clairvoyance. It was shown to be a fact, in mental science, that the somnambulic condition, is, properly and philosophically speaking, the first and lowest manifestation of the mind in the exercise of its spiritual capacities,—especially of the "eyes of the mind," which require no sunlight or artificial mediums of vision; but which see through the agency of a high species of terrestrial electricity. And it was also shown that clairvoyance is, properly considered, but the further development of the natural conditions and proclivities of the somnambulic state.

In all matters pertaining to these mental conditions, without any presumption, I may safely claim to be familiar; both by spiritual impression and personal experience. They are familiar to my mind as household words. They are not mere theories. They are not mental hallucinations, or the locomotive symptoms of nocturnal dreams; the principles of truth are flowing through them all. And when I speak of the laws, whereby these mental conditions are developed and regulated, I refer to nothing hypothetical or beyond the reach of human experience. The whole subject is present with me—a friend, with whom I hold the most delightful and confidential correspondence.

Nor are the manifestations of these states, however numerous and varied in different individuals, any strange or unexpected phases of mind to me; they all stand arrayed along the rectilinear line of natural cause and effect, and it is easy to pronounce a rational verdict upon a subject so absolutely transparent and comprehensible. But most of you are, perhaps, not thus experimentally familiar with the laws and workings of the human mind. Yet you all have experience of some description. The ordinary capacities of your souls, to say the least, are constantly called into action. Your very existence makes this inevitable. You must feel, and think, and compare, and analyze, and reason, and act; there is no alternative. Each one, consequently, possesses some absolute knowledge based upon experience. Every memory contains some peculiar picture; a concourse of people, a cluster of houses, a flock of birds, a combination of words. Each one remembers something particular; a word, a face, a song, a journey, a scene of infant years, a line of poetry. Each one has some experience of a mental nature; data, from which to commence a line of philosophical argumentation. Now, let me ask, how came these impressions so fixed upon your mind? Are they appended to, or daguerreotyped upon, your brain; the substance wrought up into living pictures? If so, how can you explain this department of your experience? If not, how can you explain the philosophy of memory? Your minds are ladened with wonders; mysteries, which you do not and can not readily comprehend. And why is it so? Because you are more perceptive than reflective; you discern more than you have time or the ability to understand. You are naturally more clairvoyant than spiritually illuminated; that is, you possess more clear perception than comprehension. You eat food which you can not digest. Hence, you have within you the proper means of continuous investigation, unassimilated. In this life—in this state of human society—your habits, and activities, and circumstances are all quite unfavorable to much success in self-investigation and culture. Therefore, you have much to learn when you attain the "spiritual state;" which will most assuredly be the consequence of a natural passage from this rudimental sphere into the Spirit Land. But let us now examine the causes and consequences of this condition, when attained prior to the event of physical dissolution.

First, let me remark, that the spiritual state—which I have heretofore denominated the superior condition—is the flower of clairvoyance! And I may here say, that in consequence of the infrequency of its occurrence, it might very properly be termed a "century plant," which blooms once in a hundred years. It is, in truth, the fruit of a large and beautiful tree; whose root is the rudimental state; whose body is human magnetism; whose branches are somnambulism; and whose buds are clairvoyance—in all its various divisions and developments. The spiritual state grows upon the summit of this tree as naturally as the peach succeeds the blossom, or the rose the bursting of the bud.

The causes of the spiritual state, where this state really exists, are mainly confined within the constitution of the mind. The individual must have an organic and hereditary proclivity to it. The temperament must be firm; yet high-toned and well-balanced. Vital and mental irritability are incompatible with this condition. A turbulent disposition can not enter it. The soul must be calm as the morning; the passions must be soft and tranquil as the evening zephyr. The soul must be full of self-integrity; and the very soul of Harmony must preside over the dominion of the sensibilities.

It is now proper to recur to the organization of the mind. Positive and negative principles are distinctly manifested in its construction. Its organic arrangements furnish the requisite demonstration. But let us regard, particularly, its expansive and contractive characteristics. In a previous lecture, I alluded to a class of phrenological faculties which possessed the qualities of contraction; while another class was endowed with expansive tendencies; the two, acting in harmonious concord, thus creating and preserving a spiritual equilibrium. All this has much to do with the spiritual state.

Generally speaking, you will find all mankind inharmonious,—particularly in the mental structure. The spiritual condition, it is said, is a great curiosity—a miracle—a wonder—a startling development. This is so because, simply, it is of rare occurrence. But think a moment. Look about you; inspect each other's countenances; interrogate each other's minds—what do you see? You behold dark expressions; eyes swimming in impatience; foreheads full of distortions; mouths that seem to have resigned all right and title to the empire of smiles! Cares, more weighty than pilgrim's package of sin, are saddled upon your minds; you groan with trouble and vexation. You live unnaturally. Your wants are seventy-five per cent. too numerous. You imagine unnatural gratifications; because your desires are unnatural. Your habits are expensive; because they are false. You are troubled; because you take upon yourselves too many superficial cares. You care more for the body than the mind. You are very particular about keeping clean the "outside" of the platter; all your sepulchres must be whitened. Cobwebs in the house are far more disagreeable than analogous substances in the mind. And thus you live! But what is the result? Why, you are all, more or less, unhappy—turbulent—passionate—inharmonious! You do not go into Harmony [or heaven] yourselves, nor let others enter. But you think the spiritual state is an impossibility—a wonder—a miracle—a supernatural condition. But why do you think so? Because it is so rarely exhibited. But think again; and let me ask—Is not an harmonious individual as great a curiosity—as great a wonder—as great a miracle? Yea, verily! For as society is constructed, as children are conceived and born, as human knowledge of Nature is limited; we find it exceedingly hard to secure to ourselves the kingdom of Harmony and its righteousness, with the sublime assurance that all the externals and happinesses of this life shall be added thereto.

You will, I think, cheerfully accede to this proposition: that the manifestation of the spiritual state is no more rare than the manifestation of a harmonious mind. For where you see the one you may safely look for the development of the other. The superior condition, like the diamond in the enamel, is set in the framework of individual harmony—harmony in the broadest and highest sense. Such harmony is the foundation, the germ, and the supporter of spiritual illumination. And you may rest assured, that men will become mentally exalted and spiritually minded just as fast as they subjugate the material to the spiritual; the body to the mind; the present to the future; the passions to the Reason-Principle!

The soul depends, for its equilibrium and organic harmony, upon the harmonial operation of positive and negative, or contractive and expansive, forces. The organ of Acquisitiveness would naturally load the body and mind with accretious and selfish luxuries; but Benevolence expands, or should expand, and in the same proportion, as the former organ contracts; thus the one supplies the individual with the "ways and means" of subsistence and of concentral development, while the other dispenses the superabundance, or all that can possibly be spared out of the internal economy, for the sustenance and benefit of needful persons. So, too, with Secretiveness and Ideality. While the former contracts and secretes the accumulations of Acquisitiveness, and maintains a strict vigilance and jealous care over the whole personality; the latter, (Ideality,) being an expansive organ, and closely associated with the efforts of benevolence, throws open the prison-doors and the miserly dens of Secretiveness, and exposes the richest possessions to the gaze and grasp of the child of want. And so with Alimentiveness and Veneration. The contractive propensities of Alimentiveness are carefully neutralized, and preserved from running into extremes of acquisition, by the expansive tendencies of Veneration. And so with Cautiousness and Hope. The dark, and suspecting, and jealous, despairing and disheartening influence of the contractions of Caution, is utterly overcome and maintained in a high state of mental equilibrium by the light, and cheerfulness, immortal youth, promising and future-illuminating expansions of Hope. I speak now of the well-balanced mind.

You have probably remarked, —for every student of human nature should,—that almost every person is in the possession of some general distinguishing peculiarity. That is to say, instead of seeing, as we should, well-balanced and harmonious characters, we behold minds which are distinguished by *one* of three general traits; which three every man should possess equally developed—viz.: a social nature, a religious nature, or an intellectual nature. It is a rare thing to meet these traits or departments of mind well and justly represented in one individual. When you meet with such a person, even if his harmony be of a low quality and of feeble tone, you have an abundant reason to anticipate something from him which will remind you of higher spheres. His state is measurably spiritual; and his rudimental condition possesses the distinct outlines of that which is assuredly superior.

But a character is defective which is not equally developed in these three departments. As children are born and educated, we see them exhibiting one of the three traits very conspicuously, but the remaining two only partially and lamely, as with those who are sent into "this breathing world, half made up;" disproportionably and wrong. In one person you will see a large development of the social nature, with but moderate intellectual and religious powers. Such a mind will manifest more love than wisdom. It is apt to "love not wisely, but too well." The ship has neither helm nor master. But the crew is heterogeneous, turbulent, beastial, and undisciplined. Full of misdirected love, full of impulse, full of passional-springs and energetic powers; but what fearful extremes and impetuosity! The elements are good; but they have no harmonious arrangements. Such a mind will be the object of love or unlove; will be either liked or disliked; for there is no alternative, simply because there is no middle ground upon which such a mental conformation can meet, and harmonize, with the main aggregation of individuals composing the world. The religious nature does not modify; the intellectual principle does not admonish, direct, nor govern. And, now, if there be one among you who has any thing resembling this structure of mind, I pray you to immediately set about the work of religious and intellectual culture. But let us look at another character.

In another individual you will see the religious nature, with but moderate social or intellectual powers. And what do we behold? The person is constantly idolizing and venerating something, which may be quite unworthy the deference bestowed. There is no middle position. Every thing must be converted into a religious meeting. Prayers must be muttered unceasingly. For Filial Love has gone into an extreme development. And the individual is more reverential than wise; more full of aspiration than capable of attaining; more likely to contemplate the distant eminence than to ascend its craggy sides; more disposed to think of Deity than understand him; more desirous of salvation than capable of "working it out" by the harmonious development of his interior being.

And, now, if any one among you has a disposition resembling this, try henceforth to change it by unfolding the social and intellectual departments of your nature. But let us look again.

Another individual is possessed with a high intellectual development, with but moderate social and religious faculties. And what do you see? You behold a person who "runs every thing into the ground." Cold, unloving, selfish. He is fond of ceremony; but every thing must be clear as silver, bright as an icicle, and uniform as the walking beam of an engine. His words must be used economically. Every thing must be strictly understood; and pleasures must be treated hydropathically. He is fond of steel; the head of his cane must be steel—hard, bright, firm! He must have bright buttons on his coat, too; for any thing covered is altogether too warmly clad. Take, for example, the aristocratic Englishman. How cold and stately! How many sterling qualities set in a steel frame! How practical! How replete with economical methods; how particular about having "A place for every thing, and every thing in its place;" how ostentatious; how full of living faith in the saving power of the Horse-Guards; how literally and prosaically he converses; how impregnated with gravity; what clean parks and aristocratic lawns; what a cold, stately residence; what a model household! Constitutionally arrogant and overbearing; self-conceited and self-righteous to the last degree; with just enough conscience to admit the mere probable truthfulness of the maxim, that another individual has a right to live in happiness and breathe the common air. In saying this, I do not by any means design to conceal the numerous exceptions to this general principle; for I can, now and then, perceive a man quite modest, easy-mannered, affectionate, and naturally noble and dignified. But looking over the entire nation, and taking a psychometrical view of the English character, as a whole, I can not but see the cold, steelish, economical, aristocratic, gruff, and constitutionally selfish and political nature of the people. They have more light than heat; more Wisdom than Love; more Intellect than religious or social sentiment. They are full of centralism, conservatism, assurance, and Individuality; which are based altogether upon the Intellect. But the warm, loving, tender soul—where is that? Ah: it is all absorbed into the intellect; the sunbeam is frozen in the icicle; the blushing flower is buried in the chilling snow! And do you find any person, of this intellectual caste, entering the Spiritual State? They have clairvoyants; but no spiritually enlightened. Do you find their religious and social natures in harmonious concord with their intellect? Nay: verily! There is a want of organic harmony; the mind is not rounded and symmetrical; the desires are not permitted their full and energetic play through the wisdom-principle; and the consequence is this: you do not hear of any such person entering the "Spiritual State,"—for this state and the state of harmony are equally rare and wonderful. They are inseparably connected—and mutually dependent.

The Spiritual State is rare because the conditions and circumstances indispensable to its development and existence are as infrequent and as little comprehended. The social, the intellectual, and the religious departments of the mind must have a harmonious representation and influence in and upon the individual A person, with a prominent development of one only of these elements, may be a very good clairvoyant—a seer of the interior and the distant,—but such a person can not enter the superior condition. For this state signifies an opening of the interior understanding as well as an exercise of the interior perceptions. In this condition the spirit not only sees, but seeing, it also comprehends. The Love and the Wisdom principles have an harmonious play; they act for, upon, and with, each other. In the "Spiritual State," the mind sees, the mind hears, the mind reasons, the mind understands. The whole interior Man is concordantly exalted. The perceptives, the retentives, the reflectives, the contractives, the expansives, the socials, and the religious faculties are—one and all—in a high state of exaltation. But unto the religious faculties, the social and the intellectual elements are harmoniously subordinated. And yet the illumination of all the faculties is equal in the Spiritual State.

This state is to all men attainable, because the conditions are possible to all. The intellect must not be merely and exclusively cultivated, neither the social nor the moral faculties; for if one of these is permitted to transcend and influence the others, then the mind is not prepared for an influx of heat and light—i. e., Love and Wisdom—from the superior circles in the Spirit Land. For to every state and degree of mind in this world,—(especially when the mind is on its true path of progression and proper development,)—there is a corresponding state and degree in the world of spirits. I would not be understood to teach the doctrine, that states of mind, which give rise to discords, corruptions, licentiousness, profanations, unrighteousness, &c., have analogous types or prototypes in the spiritual country; nay, it is quite different; I mean to teach this truth: that all the distinct and ascending states of Love* and all the degrees and progressive states of Wisdom, have, in the second sphere, their complete and perfect likenesses or correspondential representations. That is, in the Spirit Land you will find twelve general societies; six will represent the different developments of the Love elements of the soul, and the remaining six, the different developments of the attributes of Wisdom in the mind. But in this lower sphere where social and individual interests and activities are all, more or less, discordant and confused, conflicting and deforming to the soul, the Love and Wisdom attributes are frequently thrown out of all due proportions—giving rise to extremes and inversions †—which, happily, do not extend their vigor

* See Great Harmonia, Vol. II. Chapter on Moral Cultivation.

† See Vol. II. Moral Cultivation.

and proclivities into the world which succeeds the event of physical dissolution. There is nothing there,—no state, no influence, no want, no poverty, no beastiality, no depravity, in the Spirit Land,—to suggest, stimulate, or perpetuate the deformities of the soul. Hence, it is only the different progressive degrees of Love and Wisdom in the human mind that have their exact counterpart in the Land, to which we are all fast hastening.

And when the human mind is truly in the Spiritual State,—which corresponds to death on the outer and to harmonious mental development in the interior,—then the spiritual world will pour its blissful Loves and Wisdoms into the perceptions and understanding of the illuminated soul. The spiritual world does not come to us; but we go to it. When the human mind has attained a point or degree in its development, which is in harmony with the laws, the desires, the Loves, and the Wisdoms of the Spirit Land, then its inhabitants are ready to introduce the heavenly light and celestial heat of their own souls into the prepared soul on earth. And yet the prepared soul may not be in any one particular as high or as good as the source of his influx, for the pre-requisite is individual harmony,—not the degree so much as the condition.

When the mind is substantially in the Spiritual State, the upper portions of the head are beautifully illuminated! The superior divisions of the social and the intellectual faculties are glowing with a bright, mellow light which centers in the moral faculties, and this light glows and extends upward about four feet; the upper portion of which light is generally about twenty inches in diameter, and variegated as the rainbow—indicating the different loves and wisdoms which are excited by the illuminations. Now let it be remembered, this light is derived wholly from the interior elements of the soul. When the body is de-magnetized, or rendered comparatively insensible, by the transferration of the positive power from the external to the internal surfaces, then the life of the body flows up, measurably, into the mind, and the elements of the soul receive a corresponding elevation. (This was fully illustrated in the Chapter on Death—See Vol. I. Great Harmonia.) Into the bosom of this light,—the heat of which a sensitive hand can detect above the subject's head, when the Spiritual State really exists,—flow the breathings of the love circles or of the wisdom circles, just as the law of use may at the time prescribe. The profoundest thoughts and contemplations may be introduced into the thus illuminated mind, accompanied perhaps with the most useful and otherwise appropriate language; though the latter is not always associated with the forms of the influxes.

The individual whose mind is in the Spiritual State, is not altogether dependent upon the Spirit Land for revelations of truths and great thoughts; for, possessing both the somnambulic and the clairvoyant powers, associated with the still superior power of understanding what is perceived, the individual is capable of penetrating or probing deeply into the constitution of Nature. His vision extends far and wide; transcending all mere imagination; and inspecting things and realities, which the most vigorous and artificially excited fancy could never approach. Sciences and philosophies; things real and things imagined; existences which swarm this earth and those which enliven the stars of distant realms; human beings in the temporal body and those in the immortal organization;—all are within the grasp of the vision of the illuminated, and, to a certain extent, they are as comprehensible. Hence, the mind that receives no direct influx from the Spiritual world, is nevertheless capable, while in the Spiritual State, of investigating a wide field of thought and of giving utterance to many valuable and supersensuous truths. Indeed, it is thus that the Spirit Land develops the human mind which, in this state of life, is capable of being "caught up into the third heavens," and there permitted to, voluntarily, meditate upon the stupendous arcana of the spiritual habitations.

Here it is deemed necessary to remark, that the spirit, although it appears to, yet does not leave the body permanently until after death. The reasons I have already given.* But the mind is so exalted that the body presents all the outward appearances of the spirit's desertion, and the subject is frequently himself deceived on this very point. The ability to see Russia, or the planets, or other places and things, is so perfect and unmistakably clear, that, for the time being, the mind is liable to think itself altogether there, at the locality of the vision, in propria persona. A clairvoyant can see Russia; but to see into the constitution of things, and to give any thing like a truthful revelation of the laws, &c., which control them, the mind must be in the Spiritual State. Let it also be remembered, that in some peculiarly organized minds, spiritual impressions may be enjoyed without the spiritual perceptions; and vica versa, as in cases of good clairvoyants.

The Spiritual State is a religious condition. All true prophets and seers of the olden times were mainly in this exalted posture;—an attitude supremely heavenly in its character,—one which the mind is naturally inclined to accomplish, when left to follow out the living laws of intuition and Nature. At this point I am impressed to recommend this attractive subject to your best contemplations.

In the next lecture, I design to impart some impressions concerning "plenary" inspiration. For the present I have nothing more to utter on the philosophy of psychology and clairvoyance. The subject has been practically divulged in the foregoing pages; and it is probably all that I shall ever write upon it. I have imparted my own experience in some instances, and adduced the corresponding testimony and analogous experience of others; all of which comes

* See a pamphlet by the author, entitled "The Philosophy of Spiritual Intercourse," pages 127, 130, 136, et. seq.

very naturally under a harmonial and explanatory system of cause and effect. History is very explicit in its assurances of a knowledge of magnetism among the ancients; also, that the entire procession of gifted men, prophets, and seers, were subjects of what we now term Clairvoyance, or the Spiritual State. In this investigation, the names of many seers, who have distinguished themselves before the world, I have been obliged to omit for the purpose of devoting more space to philosophical explanations, and to the exposition of principles. It is presumed that the enlightened reader will not demand a greater array of facts in magnetism, as the world is now blessed with an abundance. The great leading and paramount object, throughout this course of lectures, has been the development and classification of the natural and spiritual laws which disclose and control the alledged phenomena.

LECTURE XXII.

CONCERNING THE PRINCIPLES AND CAUSES OF TRUE INSPIRATION.

According to the delineations in the last discourse, the spiritual state was shown to be the highest condition which the mind can obtain in its present rudimental and corporeal sphere of existence. It was also shown that this state of mental exaltation depends invariably upon certain harmonious conditions of body and mind.

The conditions which are essential to this state, although superior to the common plane of every-day life, and vastly different from those generally observed, are, nevertheless, completely within the power of mankind. This state is pre-eminently religious—not in the sense that the moral feelings and faculties are developed at the expense of the social and intellectual propensities and powers; but that the whole soul,—including all its feelings, affinities, friendships and multifarious relations to the external world,—is elevated and unfolded into the religious or spiritual sphere of human existence. At this point man forms a conjunction between the rudimental and second spheres of life; and it is solely in consequence of this meeting of the two spheres in the human soul, that stands thus on the apex of the material world,—from which elevation commences the spiritual sphere which leads off into Infinitude, and opens with its endless variety of scenes before the prepared vision,—that the mind is capable of realizing its connections to the thus united spheres, and uttering, from inspirations flowing from the two sources, the great principles of truth which belong to both departments of existence.

This mental condition, although every way superior to the ordinary plane of human states and experiences, is nevertheless perfectly natural and attainable to every person. It may be enjoyed by an individual in the full possession of his outer consciousness, and hence without the artificial magnetic sleep; but such a result is the work of steady progression on the part of the mind, from all the ordinary teachings, tastes, and attractions of life, to a high state of personal harmony, consonant with the great general principles and attributes of the Divine Spirit which animates the temple of Nature. The thus exalted intellect is a medium for the transmission of *no especial* and isolated current of inspiration, but its illumination, like its condition, is general, and hence expands in all directions. This is so because all the faculties and mental susceptibilities are equally refined, harmonized and spiritually exalted. The spiritual state, therefore, may justly be denominated a *spiritual resurrection* of all passions and attractions of the natural man, into the moral and intellectual departments of the mind, which instinctively and understandingly lay hold upon the things belonging to a world of more perfect knowledge. The causes and paths which lead the mind to this state are simple and easily understood; as will be seen as I proceed to lay before you the philosophy of inspiration. I now desire to call your undivided attention to the consideration of this particular subject.

Inspiration is a term derived from the Latin, *inspiro*, which means to draw in, or inhale. This is the meaning generally attached to the word by theologians. My impressions however refer me to a different signification. I employ the term as significant of a state of mind which enables the individual to have retrovisions and prophetic perceptions, accompanied with an illumination of the understanding or reasoning principle. True inspiration is based upon psychological principles. Like every thing else in this universe of progression and development, true inspiration is of various kinds and graduated by innumerable degrees, as regards quality and quantity. It is super-sensuous, but not super-natural. It is the illuminating presence and influence of God in the soul; it is co-essential and co-extensive with the constitution of the human mind; and yet, in consequence of the prevalence of social inequalities, ecclesiastical materialism, and individual imperfections, a high and universally applicable inspiration is enjoyed but by a very few of the earth's inhabitants.

First: I will now briefly explain the view of inspiration, entertained by the Catholic and Protestant systems of religious faith. These sects regard inspiration as entirely above the reach of the human faculties of thought. It is regarded as a supernatural action of the Divine Mind upon the human will and understanding. It is believed that the Lord selects and prepares certain prophets and apostles to be the recipients and exponents of his will; and then, by an immediate conjunction, which the Lord supernaturally establishes between himself and the chosen vessels, the latter are enabled to speak and write the Divine Will without any mixture of error or imperfection. The Catholic regards all inspiration as a direct result of the action of God upon the world; he does not believe that the whole human family is inspired by the Divine Mind; but that all plenary inspiration is confined to the Bible, to the Pope, to the Priest, and the Church. The Protestant does not admit so much communication with the Divine Spirit, but thinks that all inspiration which is orthodox and supernatural is to be found within the letter and symbols of the Sacred Scriptures. He believes that the Divine Mind disclosed his will to the Bible authors, completed through them all communications from the supernal courts to man; and on perfecting the New Testament, he closed all private and particular correspondence which had existed between himself and the earth's inhabitants. Thus it is distinctly evident that the two systems of faith which now divide Christendom have their foundation upon the supernatural and incomprehensible.

Second: I will now proceed to consider the trammeling, enslaving, and pernicious influence which the above sectarian idea of inspiration inevitably exerts upon the human mind. The first perceptible effect of this partialistic doctrine, is the generation of a religious despotism which the multitudes are educated to receive with an unreasoning faith, and to love and protect with an unflinching reverence. The majority of Christendom grow up with the conviction that the Supreme Being will communicate to none, except to specially chosen favorites and supernaturally appointed mediators and attorneys. This idea trammels the soul in its aspirations after light and knowledge, because it teaches that the portals of the heavenly citadel, and all the avenues leading from God to man, were closed up and eternally locked at the event of the formation of the sacred canon. The soul that would be advanced in spiritual happiness and high religious culture, is dogmatically forbid the privilege of uncovering its head to receive the light which is streaming forth from the bending firmaments; but is constrained, nay, absolutely commanded by the dominant theology, to retreat into the mazes of the past, *there* to read and contemplate, without daring to question, what men have written and tradition has preserved. The mind being thus trammeled, fears to cast off its fetters, it can not advance; for it is educated and compelled to linger on the deserts of the remote past whose atmosphere is peopled with the phantoms of a Tartarean theology, and with the distorted and sickly forms of decaying superstition. If the aspiring mind of to-day would seek the immediate presence and illumination of heaven—if it would bathe, refresh, and invigorate itself in the Spirit of God—it must retreat into the labyrinths of ancient sacred temples and walk on arid ground; which vague tradition asserts to have been supernaturally blessed and sanctified; there to breathe forth prayers and worship in the midst of the fossil vestiges and hypothetical divinity of semi-barbarian ages.

The aristocratic despotism, generated by this ecclesiastic and partialistic notion, is the most gigantic and insurmountable obstacle to individual progression and enlightenment. A generous democracy is frequently chilled in its natal hour. The flower of liberty is plucked with a ruthless hand from its native soil by despotic and dogmatic minds, who have the unblushing arrogance and misfortune to consider and proclaim themselves to be God's vicegerents. The spirit of a universal republicanism, richly impregnated with grand and philanthropic objects, and contemplating in its sweep the universal liberty and happiness of man, is frequently arrested in its flight from heart to heart, surrounded by the soldiers of the king, bound in chains and hurried to the dark retreats of despotic incarceration. And these are termed "holy wars," providential interpositions to preserve the individuality and local interests of nations. And should some angel, in the human form, elevate himself to his natural position and proportions, and speak forth the fresh inspirations of liberty and universal freedom, he will be confronted by the united procession of ecclesiastical, sectarian and political powers, and be condemned either as a sentimental visionary, or else as the leader and embodiment of a diabolical conspiracy against the time-sanctified and sacred institutions of church and state. Although it is just and necessary to delineate and positively repudiate these human weaknesses and evils of despotism; nevertheless it is quite as essential to the cause of progress, that we should preserve generous and fraternal sentiments for those who are the agents and victims of such human vices and imperfections. Mankind's career is checkered and fearfully stained with sins of crimson hue, because the race has been, and is now, progressing from bad to better, from transgression to rectitude, from discord to a millennial harmonization of interests and attractions. There are always two parties in the world. One party is composed of nearly all the earth's inhabitants; the other of the very few intellects who have ascended the rugged sides and angular acclivities of human experience, and who, therefore, now stand upon the summit of the centuries, contemplating the deep valleys from which they have ascended, and the boundless territories of humanity below them!

The first party is mortgaged to conservatism; the second, to the ause of universal liberty, fraternity, unity, and progression. The former believe in supernaturalism, in providentially appointed prophets and messengers, and in especial and local inspiration. It is a party which supports and protects tyrannical institutions as ordinations of Jehovah. It crucifies the heralds of liberty and burns the man of living inspiration upon its altars of ignorance. Humanity's path is strewn with numberless thorns which wound only those who step, with a bold progressive tread, along the ascending way. This progressive path leads through many dark valleys, dismal solitudes, desert plains, and over innumerable mountains; and here and there are visible the disastrous consequences of long and bloody battles; and solitudes which compass many dungeons and tombs where ignorance has interred the friends of knowledge; the desert plains still support the gloomy pyramids of ancient despotism and mythology; and upon the summit of every mount over which the race has pursued its pilgrimage, are visible the huge cross, the bloody gibbet, the portentous gallows, upon which the thief and the Savior, the vicious man and the man of love, the assassin and the inspired reformer, have alike suffered the martyr's fate. The first, martyrs to the ignorance and inhumanity of man; the second, to human selfishness and systems of godless despotism!

The enslaving and pernicious influence of the partialistic doctrine of inspiration upon the human mind, is manifested in still another form of demonstration. It originates low and contracted conceptions of the Supreme Being and his system of universal government.

It gives the impression, and then maintains it in the most emphatic and presumptive manner, that God is local, partial, and particular in the manifestation of his sovereign purposes. It teaches that when the Lord selects, out of nine hundred millions of individuals, a few men as attorneys to write his will, he places them in a condition in relation to himself—which no reason can comprehend or philosophy explain—which renders them immaculate as to motives and invulnerable as to error and imperfection. This is the doctrine of the church. It enslaves the disciple, because it imprisons reason; and represses, with a giant power, the advancing tides of thought! The attorney's statements and averments must be received as truth without a question. Should any such especial revealments stand in open contradiction to any scientific discovery or phase of human experience, there is still no alternative, no choice permitted the disciple; because the doctrine of supernatural inspiration neither admits the remotest possibility of imperfection, nor the indulgence of any doubts as to the verity and eternal immutability of such disclosures. It confuses the natural harmony of creation and renders the illimitable universe a mere repository or cabinet of theological mysteries and superstitious phantasmagoria. By subverting, in the human mind, its instinctive perceptions of Nature's harmony; by removing God from the presence of the soul and shutting him away from all human accessibility in a court of heavenly splendor whose light, like an expiring taper, is flickering in the socket of an old theology; by beclouding and chilling the relations between man and man, and destroying all human faith in the immutable character of God and his government—I say, by doing these things, this orthodox or ecclesiastical doctrine of local inspiration proves itself to be the issue of a barbarian age, once rife with despotism and tyrannical institutions. And upon this ground, especially, am I impressed to regard this sectarian definition of "plenary inspiration" as trammeling, enslaving, and pernicious in its influence upon the mind of man.

Third: I come now to utter my impressions concerning the causes and principles of true inspiration. As I have already said, I do not employ the word as significant of any arbitrary or superficial inhaling of thoughts or truths proceeding from the Infinite fountain. On the contrary, the word comes to me ladened with a vastly higher and more elevating significance. The enlightened intellect will readily perceive that the individual can be truly and permanently benefited only by such inspirations and revelations as can naturally be breathed into and assimilated with the mental constitution. Any thing which merely passes into, through, and as rapidly out of, the mind, can not be of any lasting profit to the recipient. The flower is truly inspired by the light and warmth of the sun, because it possesses within itself the essential qualities and properties of beauty and development, and hence incorporates the descending elements of vitality in its own minute structures. It is not merely a vessel for the immediate reception and impartation of light and warmth; but it receives those elements, subjects them to a chemical analysis and distributes the various properties to the elaboration, development, and sustenance of its own particular individuality. And then, in accordance with the immutable principles of distributive justice and harmony, the flower breathes forth its precious odors with which it loads the passing breeze, and thus imparts pleasure and refreshment to many living beings.

Thus it is with man; every man, like every flower, is a recipient of this kind of inspiration—that is to say, the influx of thoughts, facts and principles, into the soul, which that particular mind may appropriate—first, to its own welfare and enlightenment, and then shed it abroad as the sun spreads its rays over the earth for the benefit and illumination of those who next require the pabulum.

Pure inspiration is confined to no particular person, age, or nation; it is as common and universal as the Spirit of God. Every thing that possesses life, no matter in what kingdom or stage of development, is to the same degree the recipient, exponent, prophet, and beneficiary of the universal spirit of the Supreme Being. Every thing that moves any where in the illimitable territory of Nature, sustains a relation more or less intimate to the spirit which animates the world. Every creature enjoys a living communion with the all-animating principle; and the relations which subsist between the little worm and the Creator of worlds, are just as intimate in principle as those enjoyed by man. Hence all things receive the Spirit of God, and bathe in it, and express it in the external, in exact proportion to their capacity and absolute requirements. The human soul is a far richer soil for the growth and nurture of heavenly sentiments, than Jerusalem or any ground which Jesus is said to have blessed and sanctified. Man's external organism is closely joined to the material world; but far more closely is his spiritual nature joined to that principle which enlivens and energizes the universal Whole. There is nothing between man and the bending heavens. He can bare his head beneath the dome of the living temple, and there is no obstruction intervening which can shut him from a contemplation of the gorgeous fabric. And so if he will but bare his spirit by removing pride, selfishness and sensuality, which circumscribe and entomb its fair proportions, he will find nothing existing between him and the enjoyment of that true inspiration of which I now speak.

All Scripture is given by inspiration—that is, all writing of whatever description accomplished by the human hand. For there are but four general sources of thought and knowledge, namely:—the life-springs of the soul; the suggestions of external nature; the well-springs of humanity; and the exhaustless fountains of the spiritual universe. Nothing, therefore, is absolutely self-existing or self-determining; because the illimitable empire of Nature is constructed and supported by a brotherhood of interlinking and commingling ties, sympathies, and reciprocal dependencies. The infinite cycle is composed of innumerable lesser cycles, as the infinite whole is composed of countless parts, which are the links in that Deific chain of celestial love and wisdom which encircles the lowest and highest, the parts and the whole; which constitute the magnificent temple of the Infinite Mind. It appears, therefore, as a matter of harmonious and reasonable necessity, in a universe of cause and effect, of principle and government, of progression and development, of sequence and consequence, that all inspiration must be derived from one or all of the four sources designated. Accordingly the contents of a popular serial magazine are just as much a product of a certain degree of inspiration as the contents of any other work in human language. A writer may walk in his garden and be attracted by the fragrance and beauty of a single flower. Several imperceptible, but no less decisive, changes may occur in his feelings, thoughts, and mental economy. An invisible communion is enjoyed by the mind and the flower. And on the morrow, if you will but examine the lyrical department of some daily publication, you may read the Scripture which is written by the inspiration of that tiny flower through the instrumentality of the human mind.

And let it be remembered that plenary inspiration and infallible knowledge belong to God alone. If any man should undertake to claim for any human publication its entire freedom from errors and imperfections, his claim is surely at the mercy of the school-boy whose reason can perform its appropriate functions. Again I affirm that God lives in the soul of every animated thing, and in the same proportion as his life-essence is immanent therein, so is that living object a receptacle of God's truth, an exponent of his goodness, a prophet of his love, and an expounder of his inspiration. Where God is, there is illumination. He has not withdrawn his spirit from nature, nor his germinating principles from the soul of man. The mind that will feel, may feel; so, likewise, he that would be inspired, will be, from one or all of the sources through which the Infinite communes with the finite. The spiritual worlds are but so many scales of music, extending from the remotest orb to Deity. And if man would learn of this celestial harmony, he must not stand away from it upon the barren desert of some mythological and superannuated faith; but he should walk forth and join the heavenly band, and strive to swell this symphony of the universal anthem of harmony, by becoming himself a harmonious note in the Divine scale. Again I say, God has not abandoned the "house not made with hands;" he has not left to perish any thing which he inspires with life and animation. He was not more in the world two thousand years ago than he is to-day. His will can not be expressed in one, two, nor yet in a million testaments; for what is man, or all the men that have ever breathed on this globe compared with the numberless myriads that people the Celestial Land which breaks upon us at the event of outer dissolution? Even the earth with all its possessions is as a grain of sand on the sea-shore when compared with the vastness, magnitude and numbers of other earths which have an equal claim upon the spirit and universal dispensations of Deity.

The religious mind may no longer examine the centuries past for the purpose of discovering the indications of the living God. Man may no longer yearn for a recurrence of the "good old days of yore." For God is more with us to-day, because we have progressed and approached nearer to him. The sun shines as brilliantly, the rainbow has as many tints, the earth is as much refreshed by rain, the streams murmur as musically away through the valleys and meadows, as in the days of Moses, Isaiah, or Jesus; the birds chirp as cheerfully now, the day is as effulgent, and night has lost none of the innumerable jewels, which shine through its curtains from the countless constellations, that deck the diadem of the upper firmaments. Let us, therefore, not turn back, but go onward with an honest and courageous heart. For as certain as this universe is warmed by Love and illuminated by Wisdom—yea, as certain as God is the unchangeable resident and proprietor of the magnificent edifice of the material creation whose bending dome is the spiritual universe—so certain are we, that every thing which decorates the habitation shall be forever devoted to the most wise and exalted purposes, and every human soul shall, forever, like an immortal taper, emit the divine light which the illuminating presence and omnipotence of the All-Perfect and Ever-Living God shall impart by the spontaneous breathings of his omnipotent spirit.

Fourth: In the first part of this discourse, it was remarked that true and exalted inspiration was enjoyed by that mind whose understanding was considerably unfolded and enlightened. I come now to briefly elucidate the mental state which is essential to the reception of inspiration from all the sources at the same time.

Let it be distinctly borne in mind that God is a God of principle, not of miracle; a God of reasonable, harmonious, and immutable character, not of fantastic displays, of design, or of supernaturalistic demonstrations of his presence among men. He can not, therefore, cause the bird to invent music, a Bonaparte to be a prince of righteousness, or a Nero to discourse harmony and philanthropic peace. Because every living thing is under the necessity of giving spontaneous utterance to that which moves within. The squirrel which can not sing gives utterance to the inspiration of its mind in its gyrations from limb to limb, and mound to mound; thus giving pantomimic expression to the indwelling songs which its tongue can not utter. So the bird sings without thinking as it breathes the common air. But Mozart, drawing his inspiration, first from the well-springs of his own mind, and then from the countless and ever varying sounds with which God has vocalized creation, writes out the Scripture of music for the world to read and reverberate. Thus the degree and quantity of inspiration enjoyed and expressed by the bird, the squirrel, and the man, are as distinct and manifest as the three receptacles are differing one from another. So different minds give rise to different degrees of inspiration. One is an inspired linguist, another an inspired poet, another a moralist, another a mathematician, and another is an inspired philosopher. While common people possess a multiplication table having only twelve figures to the side, the young inspired mathematician can not give scope to his genius without a multiplication table which is a yard square. So likewise, while the majority have a system of morals whose outer walls are so selfishly constructed as to encompass only the individual, the inspired moralist, who loves his fellow-men, breaks down the obstructing partition walls and gives birth to a moral system which is limited only by the remotest boundaries of humanity. The human mind is benefited permanently by inspiration when the reason-principle is illuminated; this constitutes true clairvoyance, and, also, the true spiritual condition. The latter state, as was described in the previous lecture, is enjoyed only by that soul whose social, intellectual, and moral faculties are attuned one to the other and all to the universal constitution of things. In addition to what has been already said on this head, the individual who would be alive to the universal inspirations of the Spirit of God, should ask himself these questions:

1st. Are my social faculties in a balanced condition? Do I sufficiently love my own personality? Do I obey the laws of nature in regard to food, exercise and slumber? Am I in any sense intemperate? Do I seek the society of the gay and superficial to the neglect of personal culture and important studies? Am I depriving myself of the true joys and inspirations of God by disobedience to the laws of my being in giving myself up to sensuality and merely physical gratifications?

2d. Are my intellectual faculties properly balanced? Do I yield myself sufficiently to reflection? Do I people my mind with objects, through the medium of perception, and then carefully analyze, compare, and devote them to good and benevolent purposes? Or do I permit my mind to be confused and distracted by the perpetual rushing in of external impressions through the medium of the senses? Or do I reflect too much upon a few things, and seclude myself from a wider and a higher field of observation? Have I a materialistic intellect which goes no deeper than the externals, the forms and the symbols of life and thought? Or, do I penetrate to the causes of things? Do I prove all things? Do I judge with an impartial judgment? Do I adhere to the administrations of reason? Do I regard reason as the light which lighteth every man that cometh into the world?

3d. Are my moral faculties properly balanced? Do I venerate justice as a principle? Are my aspirations after justice and equity confined to the ordinary and selfish circle of my own wants and requirements? Or, do I expand my reverence and application of justice to the circumference of all human rights and demands? Do I venerate any one system of morals and precepts as the true religion? Or, do I consider the truest and highest religion to be universal justice? What do I live for? Is it merely for personal interest and happiness? Or, do I love the neighbor and identify my interest, my justice, and my joy with the universal interests of mankind? Am I a desert which greedily drinks up the rain of heaven, and yields no flowers or vegetation? Or, am I a pure and healthy spring which slakes the thirst of the care-worn and wandering pilgrim, and then sends forth its numberless rivulets to augment the growth of healthy fruit and vines? What law do I revere? Is it the law of Moses? Or, the law of Love? What prayers do I utter? Are they the ceremonial orisons recommended by any priest, prelate, or religious chieftain? Or, is my prayer a desire unceasingly swelling my heart for human good and happiness? Do I love truth more than policy? Do I revere right more than might? Do I love Worth more than wealth or parentage? Or, am I a mere being of caprice and superficiality? When I prove all things, do I hold fast to that which is good, or that which is popular and expedient? Do I acknowledge that extraordinary individual privileges lay me under extraordinary individual obligations? Or, do I accept the privileges and acknowledge the obligations by the compulsions of law? Do I revere the God of Abraham, Isaac, and Jacob? Or, the Supreme Ruler of the universe?

He who would become the receptacle of true and high inspiration should propound to himself the foregoing questions, and give the world their appropriate answers, only through his life and conversation.

It is deemed proper to repeat here a conversation, on this subject, between a Spirit in the second sphere and a Mind on earth.

Mind. "Canst thou inform me how to obtain true light, and enjoy inspiration?"

Spirit. "Man is the manifestation of a central power—an original, indestructible development of an Incarnative Principle. What he feels most, is Genius. This is unfolded by the harmonious quickening of all the spiritual forces. This is a result of growth. The true Man grows up, like the tree in the primeval forest, luxuriant and strong—armed at all points, inhaling inspiration from all directions and breathing a corresponding influence abroad in turn."

M. "Where shall I seek for the elements of inspiration?"

S. "If any man will know of the doctrine, let him do the will of my Father. True Genius alone inspires. The good man images the fair features of the Divine Mind. This atonement or harmony of the human with the divine, places the interior genius at once into sympathy with the immortal tides of Truth; thence flows inspiration. In nature, genius subordinates all to its own force; but force itself is melted into fluid, flowing over and enkindling all—conforming all things to Beauty's Law."

M. "Are the elements in this world, or in the world of spirits?"

S. "The elements are every where, separate from no life, connected with all being. True harmony—i. e. the Genius of the spirit—is the vessel into which those omnipresent elements flow, taking the vessel's form, and becoming organized accordingly. A kindly and sympathizing influence must be thrown around individual minds, to induce the lofty aspiration upon which a full inspiration rests."

M. "How can this Influence be obtained?"

S. "By consociation. The individual must be placed in a society where true Genius presides and inspires. Channels of Wisdom must be opened. The appetites must be allayed, the passions chastened, the affections softened, the imagination expanded, reason vivified, the understanding enlarged; then the law of harmony changes the very elements of common life into inspiration. Every mind is able to aspire; and all have some light from the spiritual Orb which shines ever over the fields of being. Men shall be one with God. Behold, the rising sun! The Era is very near!"

Properly considered, the spiritual state is the complete development and harmonization of the individual. On some future occasion I will explain the physical, organic, and moral laws of man's being; and show, by aid of various illustrations, how his obedience to these laws will secure the happiness which he seeks, and the inspiration which the reasonable intellect devoutly yearns to enjoy. For the present, I leave this subject to your reflection, with the earnest prayer that your souls may be permanently enriched by a judicious application of the principles unfolded.

LECTURE XXIII.

THE PHILOSOPHY OF ORDINARY AND EXTRAORDINARY DREAMING.

Every one who understands any thing of physiology is fully aware that the Brain is the seat of all sensation and thought. It is the source of the strength and energy displayed in the vital and muscular systems, and is the chief agent of mental manifestation.

The mystery of dreaming is rendered more mysterious by the dark curtains of slumber, which invariably hang between the phenomena and our perceptions. These mystic surroundings must be rolled up before we can look in upon the more enchanting scenes of the mental Theater. I will, therefore, first present to your minds the philosophy of *sleep*.

Sleep is simply the counterpart of Action. Sleep and Action are the axes upon which the sphere of common life revolves. The most tranquil and happy period, which any one can remember to have experienced in this physical life, is midway between sleeping and waking—between rest and activity. How we love the twilight hour! How it induces the mind to go within, there to contemplate the many events which cluster upon the vines of memory! And more than this; the eye of the mind, thus turned in upon itself, looks far into its own history, and realizes something of that sublime nature which seeks involuntarily an eternal residence in the upper world.

The twilight hour—being the interlude between the states of action and rest—is the properest season for reverential meditation.

This is the time to disengage yourselves from the outer world of objects. The man of genius devotes this season to himself, and withdraws from outer things for the sake of contemplation. He turns his attention to half-remembered ideas and arranges them into a new order in his mind. The many images of creation stand in all their relative positions before his mind, and thus he looks at nature through his memory and inward consciousness. The mind is in its finest mood at the twilight hour, when the front brain is not surcharged with either blood or thought. But the case is quite different with the Brain, when the Sun sends down its rays to earth. The heat and light thereof render the cerebrum positive—fill it with blood, and prevent it, to a great extent, from exercising its powers of imagination. But when the Sun has passed away, then the front Brain is thrown partially into a negative state, thus permitting the higher faculties to play more unrestrainedly in the empire of thought.

The mind can not think as clear when the sun shines as in the twilight hour. Because that portion of the Brain, which controls all the agents of superior thought, is the chief ruler of all that takes place in the physical economy. It directs all muscular action, guides the body in the discharge of all its voluntary functions, and dispenses energy to all the various physical dependencies. Consequently, it is too much engrossed with the cares of the body to do much thinking; and besides this,—the Sun renders the Brain too positive for deep, clear, and pleasurable contemplation.

Hence it is, that, when the soft hour of twilight arrives, the man of genius glowingly conceives his best thoughts, arranges them with the greatest facility, and realizes the most happiness. When the heavens are tranquil and the vesper-star is seen above the clouds, when all the vast landscape glimmers on the sight, then the mind sees burning thoughts and words, so eagle-like, that it can not but be exalted and serene.

Few people reflect upon the operations of the inward spirit. And yet every one realizes a difference in his feelings—one class of sensations when the sun shines from the firmament, and another, when the dreamy folds of the approaching night close in upon the Brain and the senses. The twilight hour is the period for tranquillity and religious contemplations. Because the front brain is less positively charged with blood and nervous energy then; and the whole internal being is abandoned to a most luxurious exercise of its various affections and faculties.

But let us examine the state of sleep. What a fair counterfeit of death, is sleep! It is almost death. The Brain is not so fired with life. All the portions of the front brain are quieted, and the back brain, the cerebellum, is the guardian of the night. It keeps the blood flowing through the dependent organism; causes the heart, liver, lungs, &c., to perform their appropriate office; and thus maintains the connections between the body and the soul, whilst the larger or front brain, with all its numerous dependencies, is permitted to rest in undisturbed slumber. This is perfect sleep. Now what is the state of the soul in perfect sleep? I answer—it is folded within itself. The brain and body are wearied and weakened by the activities of the day; hence the mind draws its faculties together, as the sensitive plant folds its leaves against the human touch, and passes, quietly, into the more interior recesses of the mental structure. The mind, in perfect slumber, finds a retreat from all sensuous disturbances in the back portions of the brain,—the cerebellum is the dormitory of the soul. But the faculties of the mind are not altogether destitute of action; the soul can not be perfectly in a state of inertia—the laws of the mind are Association, Progression, and Development. Its happiness consists in its harmony; not in any description of inactivity or indolence. Let it, therefore, be distinctly understood that, when the mind is sleeping, it is not in a state of inanition, but in a greater degree of harmony, and in a state of more interior retirement, than is natural to the ordinary awakened condition of mind.

I now come to the phenomena of dreaming, which succeed the event of sleeping.

There are two kinds of dreams—one class emanate from the Earth-land; the other, from the Land of Spirits. First, let us examine the causes of those which proceed from external or terrestrial sources. The majority of dreams originate in the faculties of the soul during sleep. Some physical disturbance has disquieted the mind. Various diseases produce various dreams. But what is a dream? It is an indiscriminate play of the Will among the memories and affections of the mind. The difference between ordinary dreaming and *ordinary thinking*, consists simply in this: that while the mind is partially reposing, it does not separate the thing thought of from its occurrence; whilst, when the mind is wakeful, it clearly discriminates between the thought and its subsequent execution. Did you ever reflect on the remarkable fact, that the Wish to accomplish any thing in a dream is immediately followed by the impression that the thing desired is actually done? Much of the profundity of mystery attached to dreaming consists in the fact, that the Soul takes her wishes for granted, confounds thinking with acting, and blends past experiences with present memories and emotions. But ordinary dreams will be more or less rational according to the order and vividness with which the mind is accustomed to think and reason. We think and dream, strictly, in accordance with our experience and habit in combining ideas, and also according to the various dispositions of mind which are incidental to our common nature. By a kind of metempsychosis or transformation, the peculiar quality of foods and medicines is transferred to the brain during the period of repose. For instance, the mind can be impressed very powerfully by the *life* of meat. Some persons will dream of droves of cattle, simply by eating plentifully of beef-steak just previous to retiring. The psychological action of medicines and disease upon the mind, has been sufficiently elucidated in my lectures on man's psychological state. I will, therefore, pass on to amplify the proposition, that the mind manufactures the fabrics of its ordinary dreams—all of which can be easily explained upon physiological principles.

Much of the mystery of common dreaming disappears, when we consider the singular manner in which the mind blends thoughts with actions—and phantasm with serious realities. Past memories and present sensations are so ingeniously wrought into new scenes and characters, that the mind itself becomes amazed and confounded with the representation. Popular Theology is merely a species of dreamy superstition, endeavoring to explain mysteries according to preconceived opinions; just as, in our ordinary dreaming, we undertake to explain one decided absurdity by very dexterously supposing another. In dreaming, the mind accounts for many mysteries with such amazing complacency that the strangest combination fails to excite surprise. The prophetic powers of the human mind are sometimes excited during the periods of slumber, when the Soul can easily feel future events, by projecting its faculties along the line of coming probabilities. In this manner the prophets of the olden time gazed upon the general nature of future events. Such dreams the Prophet Daniel sometimes experienced, and such also he was frequently called upon to interpret. As a conclusion, then, of this branch of the subject, let us bear in mind that the phenomena of ordinary dreaming are traceable mainly to defective slumber, to impaired health, and to unresting thought; to the simultaneous and indiscriminate operation of the Will with the faculties of thought or reasoning. Such are, in short, the dreams of the Earth-Land—the mere play of the mental faculties under the influence of some disturbing cause,—connected with the world and body in which we at present reside.

I come now to consider the dreams which emanate from the World of Spirits.

I allude to no fancy of the mind—no scheme of the imagination; but to a sublimely beautiful truth. Dreams from the Spirit Land! What poetry can be more poetical than Truth? What more romantic than Reality? Who would willingly resist the flowing in of high sentiments; the influx of divine principles? We read in the New Testament how "the angel appeared unto Joseph in a dream."

Let us now consider the philosophy of this class of mental manifestations. I have said that, in perfect slumber, the front brain is closed up so far as the voluntary action of the mind is concerned; while the back brain keeps the body supplied with vital energy and the means of involuntary action. Now it is a curious fact that the mind is never made to dream a spiritual dream unless this perfect slumber exists. The voluntary powers of the mind must be all suspended, and the Will and faculties of thought must be in a state of complete quiescence, before there can be a free and full influx of contemplations from the Spirit Land. This perfect slumber is seldom enjoyed; it is true, therefore, that "angels' visits are few and far between." The earth-children eat too much, and too often—are injudicious in their occupations—are mentally too inharmonious—to permit that complete retirement of the mind from the cerebrum to the cerebellum, during the hours of slumber, which is indispensable to spiritual influx. If the front brain is at all positive, when the body is sleeping, then spiritual influences can not enter. The mind is an instrument which, when it is tuned and set to a high note on the spiritual scale of music, the angels can awaken it to the sweetest melody!

When a person is sleeping a perfect slumber, whether common or magnetic, he is nigh unto the state of death. The higher departments of the mind are not occupied by thoughts. The strong and splendid elements of holy feeling are quieted; gathering vigor for the future sphere. The entire cerebrum or Front Brain is now a tranquil domain; and there is no sentinel at the gate of the temple, but the vigilant cerebellum. Hence the spirit of man may be called into harmonious play by a judicious touching of the various faculties in the superior brain, as in Phreno-magnetism. Thus the mind is ready for a dream of a high order.

Now if a spirit should approach a person thus slumbering, and desire to impress a dream upon the sleeper's mind, it would psychologically act upon the various organs in the front brain—upon such organs, I mean, as would develop or elaborate the dream designed. Hence the mind would be called into play by the Will of the Spirit. The mind would unfold any dream which the Spirit might Will—just as, when the musical instrument is skillfully played upon, it emits the sounds in the performer's mind.

This species of dreaming is not clairvoyance,—though I have seen instances where the dreaming mind has been perfectly and correctly impressed with distant objects and scenery; the result of impressions received from the Will of the Spirit that controlled the elaboration of the dream.

Now and then, our guardian spirits come from a fairer and serener Home than ours. Those happy children of the Father, beautiful as the mind can imagine,—they come to inspire our souls with kindred thoughts and higher joys,—they come to make us better, wiser, and happier.

As the Goddess of music takes down her lute, touches its silver cords, and sets the summer melodies of nature to words; so an angel from the Spirit Land comes to us in our profoundest slumber, and gently awakens our highest faculties to the finest thought and serenest contemplation.

Much that is termed Poetry in the world, originates in the enchantments and mysterious beauties, which, as a general thing, are supposed to hang in most luxurious clusters upon the Tree of Ignorance and Superstition. The invisible and the unknown excite the imagination, and this faculty finds a peculiar enjoyment in contemplating their mysteries, in giving expression to the apocryphal realities, which make up the unseen landscape, beyond the curtain that conceals the contemplated regions from the human vision. There are but few bold, vigorous, independent minds that can bear the full rays of the Sun of Knowledge; because the majority of mankind depend upon their ignorance for many enjoyments, intellectual entertainments, and delights.

There are, as I know by experience, numerous things which to perfectly understand are productive of much mental uneasiness. For example, it gives my mind disquietude to know the precise day on which an individual will leave the material body for the upper sphere; or to know to a demonstration that a person will be severely diseased and accidentally injured. And yet, the real source of the disquietude is not in the knowledge of the future circumstance which is to occur, but in the derangement which such information produces among the common relations subsisting between man and man. If my mind should be distinctly impressed with the terrestrial fate of some particular individual, then my intellectual relations toward that person are directly changed; and similar alterations or derangements occur also between his friends and worldly surroundings. This would place me in a wrong position, and disquietude would issue, as a natural consequence, from the discordant arrangements thus developed.

Let me explain this position to your minds more distinctly. I say again, that some species of knowledge impart pain and not pleasure; and pain can result only from unsound and erroneous conditions. To possess the positive knowledge of the external death of a fellow-being is to disturb that harmony, (however superficial it may be,) which a universal ignorance of the future has established between all members of the human family. If that person be a tradesman, I, having a knowledge of the time of his decease, arrange my accounts with him accordingly. If he should ask me my reasons for this course, then comes the temptation to tell a decided falsehood in explaining my motives for acting in a certain manner toward him, or to utter my impressions truthfully concerning his demise. In either case the effect would be injurious. If I should express the truth, it would produce a general derangement in the relations subsisting between this man and his surrounding connections in the world. No amount of skepticism on his part could save him from the legitimate effects of such a statement. He would relax, unconsciously to himself, his interests in things about him, and do very much toward verifying the prophecy to the letter. On the other hand, if I should express a falsehood, or, in any manner, allow my mind to equivocate and finally to utter prevarications to him, then I am positively injuring myself, by doing wrong from right premises. The consciousness of this wrong doing would develop the mental disquietude of which I speak; or, the uneasiness would result from the derangement which the other course might create amid persons temporarily tranquil and harmonious. For these reasons, I uniformly prefer the "bliss of ignorance" to the discomfitures resulting from a knowledge of the class of facts described. And I am filled with gratitude for a knowledge of my own mental faculties and will-power, whereby I can repel the influx of such prophetic impressions as would not tranquilize, but unnecessarily disturb numberless minds.

Aside from the class of circumstances above alluded to, I deny that either true poetry or happiness depends upon our ignorance of unseen and hidden causes or future events. If our interest in a matter subsides in proportion as we form an acquaintance with its inward nature and sources, the defect is generally in ourselves. To a healthy, well-developed intellect, with which the common impulses are subordinated and attuned, the appreciation and enjoyment of the Beautiful are never lessened or chilled by a knowledge of its laws and hidden sources. Yet there are minds to whom knowledge is a bandit, robbing life, and many of its environments, of their most precious mysteries. Many sweet enchantments rest upon the huge mountains of Ignorance, which run between and divide the great Hemispheres of philosophy and religion. Hence many cling to the mysteries of existence as a source of semi-intellectual or imaginative enjoyment. There are moments when every one would seek the causes of things; but few are capable of maintaining a keen relish for those beauties and delicacies whose inward causes have been ascertained. But we may rest assured that if we are interiorly healthy, our admiration and reverence of the beautiful and superior will become the more intense and exalted as we draw aside the vail of time, and contemplate those things which have a position fixed in the constitution of nature.

In continuation of the subject and explanation of dreams, it is wisdom to assure you that these mental phenomena are controlled by established laws, which may be practically applied to the education and development of the mind. I have already explained to you, the causes and physiological conditions of Sleep. I have shown you that Sleep is occasioned by a retirement of the spiritual principle from the external surfaces and the cerebrum to the interior membranes and the cerebellum; thus closing, so to express it, the outer doors and windows of the temple, and withdrawing from the sounds and scenes of the external world to a more close communion with the infinite universe of life. It was shown, also, that perfect sleep never exists unless the entire superior brain had yielded up its guardianship, and functional power over the body, to the cerebellum. All possible connection of sense between the spirit and the objective world must be perfectly suspended before the state of complete slumber can exist. All the voluntary powers must be in a state of transitional suspension in perfect sleep; that is to say, they must be in a passive state, neither positively or negatively acting in the mental or physical economies. But I know of no condition which can properly be denominated an *absolute suspension* of consciousness; though I have investigated instances, where the patients, while fainting or in an apoplectic coma, had the mind actively engaged in earnestly dreaming about persons and circumstances in which they had been previously interested, and, on recovering, retained *no recollection* of any thing which had occurred during the period of the attack. This is the only evidence in any person's possession that there is a cessation of consciousness; which is no evidence of any thing, in fact, but simply a suspension of the *powers of external* memory. For it is a strange truth, that, when the mind relapses and passes retrogressionally into a similar state of fainting or apoplectic coma, the spirit takes up the thread of its previous interior experiences, and continues to weave together the thoughts, perceptions, and abstract reasonings which the soul enjoys when, to all external seeming, the body is dead and the mind annihilated! The mind has two memories; a memory of the body and of the external world, and a more interior scroll on the deepest recesses of whose folds are traced those reminiscences and experiences which the soul has obtained from the world of spirits.

The philosophy of dreaming is so familiarly allied to the philosophy of sleep, that one must be comprehended to a certain extent before the mind can fully understand the other. As I have already said, there are two sources of dreams; first, the sensations and recollections of experiences obtained in the external world about us: second, the emanations which proceed to us in our slumbers from the spiritual beings which inhabit the inner universe.

The significance of dreams necessarily depends upon their nature and derivation. There are numberless varieties of superficial or cerebral dreams; merely the half-remembered sensations and reminiscences of the past, wrought up, during imperfect slumber, into uncommon shapes and phantasms. Now I would not disrobe ordinary dreams of all their interest and enchantment if it were impossible to furnish a far more valuable substitute. But knowing the possibility of the latter, I proceed directly to affirm, and then to prove, that the common or generality of dreams among men have not the least foundation in the law of correspondence or significance, which alone should entitle such mental phenomena to our attention and solicitude.

Almost all persons dream, more or less frequently and distinctly, concerning things which disturbed the mind on the succeeding day. Such impressions are purely external and worthless. They originate from imperfect slumber; from discordant or abnormal physical conditions; which intemperance in habit is certain to develop and enliven. The spirit has not in such case retired from the front to the posterior brain,—consequently, the mind has not resigned up, to a state of transitional suspension, its voluntary powers; thinking still goes on; but the Will, having relaxed its appropriate control over the functions of the faculties of thought, allows the mind to elaborate such forms, scenes, occurrences, and thoughts as flow, for the time being, from the memories of the past and from present sensations.

But these mental phenomena to most persons are enigmatical. The general ignorance of their source drapes them in profound mystery. The New Churchman refers them to spiritual influx,—from a class of spirits whose position in the other life is characterized by the peculiar nature and influence of the dreams. The greater our ignorance of the physiological causes of these psychological operations, and the profounder our love of the kindling enchantments connected with superstitions and mystery, the fresher and more imposing will be our imaginary speculations. Some minds are always dreaming. They imagine and re-imagine; then they systematize and construct. Numerous instances could be adduced in illustration, from the very pinnacle of literary aristocracy and regal theology; but every man's experience is deemed sufficient.

Throughout this course of lectures on the philosophy of clairvoyance and inspiration, I have constantly held up the mirror of nature, that each person might see a full-length portrait of himself, physically, mentally, and theologically. The whole philosophy of mental impressions and of psychological action has been, in various words and ways, illustrated to your comprehension,—more especially, the phenomena of ordinary dreaming. Almost all our dreams proceed from the outer world. We are objective and subjective by turns; a perpetual vibration between the inner and the outer; between rest and action, reality and imagination. And—

> "Dark thoughts and deeds to darkened minds belong;
> He can not live right whose faith is wrong."

Common and disturbing dreams never emanate from the world of spirits. Even when the mind dreams prophetically of some accident or circumstance, or is warned to avoid danger,—which has been shown to be frequently the experience of some minds,—even then, the soul does almost invariably its own work by extending its sensiferous faculties toward the future; thus feeling reflected upon its crystal bosom, those events which the laws of cause and effect are certain to develop. The habit of consulting a "Dream book" to discover the significance of the evanescent nocturnal cogitations of an uncontrolled intellect, is a serious impediment to mental quiet and growth. If the body be well, and if all its habits are concordant with the laws of physiology and temperance, the mind will at night retire from the front brain to the cerebellum, and all the ordinary mental disturbances, termed dreams, will completely subside.

The spiritual department of this subject is invested with a sacred interest. There is something deep, lovely, and positive in that philosophy which demonstrates to the unilluminated mind, the possibility, laws, and practicability of angelic intercourse and manifestations.

The conditions, on which these phenomena occur, now become themes of high and sacred interest; for they refer to the best seasons of the soul. There is no matter more incontestably demonstrated, more introduced and recommended to human attention by so many impregnable evidences, than the communion of men with spiritual existences. On this occasion, in addition to what has been already said on the spiritual state of man, I am impressed to explain the law and manner of dreaming by influx from the world of spirits. By fully understanding this branch of psychology, you will be enabled to accurately discriminate between dreams which have an interior significance, and those that originate in a purely external cause; being without meaning, except as warning voices from the regions of physical discord and disease.

In perfect slumber, the Will,—which is simply the intellectual principle in voluntary action,—has yielded its power entirely to rest. Then the superior faculties of the mind retire into the posterior brain, and the cerebrum is resigned wholly to the state of repose. Not a thought flits across the frontal region. Memory of the external world, is clasped as a closed casket, and all is quiet in the interior. This state exists always when perfect sleep is enjoyed. At a moderate estimate it may be affirmed, that, in consideration of the wrong living and intemperance among men, no one experiences the perfect slumber except for exceedingly brief periods; but when it is enjoyed in all its fullness, when the soul is resigned to the Will of God through a recognition of nature's laws, the individual is then on the confines of the other life. True sleep is, in short, a temporary death of the body and a rest of the soul. This state is distinguished from the imperfect slumber by the absence of every species of ordinary dreaming. For dreaming is thinking; a phenomenon invariably developed by the operation of the intellectual and Will powers in the vortical recesses of the cerebrum.

The internal connection between the intellectual faculties and memory, is clearly exhibited in the dreams which occur in a poet's mind in his moments of reverie, whether by day or night, when his excited imagination is "soothed with a waking dream of houses, towers, trees, churches, and strange visages, expressed in the red cinders," or emblazoned on the kindling skies of the Eastern Hemisphere. But the voluntary powers of mind hold no intercourse with each other in moments of perfect slumber; they are quietly reposing in the interior dormitory, whilst the involuntary powers, which are deposited in the cerebellum, are busy in maintaining the performance of the vital functions, and in watching the doors of the tabernacle whose inhabitants have gone to rest.

In this condition, the soul is prepared for the reception of spiritual impressions. The influx is easy, because there are no obstructions in the superior brain. The higher vessels of the mind are open; the deep channels, which the rivers of thought have established in the mental sphere, are ready for the inflowing of fresher streams; and, thus, the soul unconsciously unbosoms herself to the angelic powers, which come in at the midnight hour and extend to her their sweetest salutations. Now, the reason why *every person* is not visited by the spiritual dwellers of other worlds, is owing principally, not to any obstructions in the form of creeds and dogmas in the mind, but to the non-occurrence or non-existence of that perfect slumber and mental harmony which are so entirely essential. Religious and theological reasons do not naturally come into the explanation; for the laws which govern this mental state are purely physiological and psychological; though we must not overlook the fact, that the truly religious mind is more likely to receive the ministrations of angels than the individual whose habits are sensual and intemperate. There was no incongruity in the abstinence from food, accompanied with meditation and desire, which the olden seers occasionally practiced; it prepared their minds for the admittance of a spiritual illumination. It is well known that Newton investigated the phenomena of light and color, only when he practiced the most perfect abstinence from every species of animal food; because he had philosophy enough to know that a full and excessive stomach is not compatible with deep, critical, consecutive analysis and thought. The same fact in psychology was known by Celsus, who said:—"Obesus venter non parit subtilem intellectum." In describing to you the temperance of habit which is required to obtain the spiritual ministrations of angels, I do not design to influence you to any *intemperance* in your abstinence, which is too frequently the case with unbalanced or impulsive minds. Temperance in all things is the only "straight and narrow way" that leads to the heaven of mental happiness.

When the soul is passive, when its various instrumentalities of thought are all resting quietly, then the spirit from the other life can draw nigh and awaken the faculties to a higher kind of exercise. Let it not be supposed, however, that the spirit *transmits* its own thoughts to the sleeper's mind, and thus develops the dream; on the contrary, as will be hereafter shown, the faculties of the slumbering spirit are gradually called into such action as will perfectly elaborate that dream which the guardian spirit may desire. It is a sweet moment when this species of influence may be enjoyed. The spiritual power steals over that portion of the front brain in which the proper faculty is located. When reached, the guardian gently brings its functions into action, and thus awakens in the sleeping mind a train of thought, or generates the materials for a truthful vision of some distant land.

In this place I will relate an instance, which came under my own interior observation. It was in the case of a lady whose death is described in the first Vol. of the Great Harmonia. It was several months previous to her departure from earth, when she was seated by the window in her parlor, gazing, with the expression of one lost in reverie, at the distant mountains. Although I had entered the room a few moments before, and had spoken a few words, yet she remained abstracted. On observing this, my earnest desire to perceive the action of her mind in that condition, enabled me to rapidly pass into the Spiritual State. By directing my internal perceptions toward her, I beheld a female guardian *spirit* standing immediately behind her chair, watching her mind. Being also in the spiritual state, I could distinctly see the mental operations. She had become bewildered by thinking upon a subject which could not be easily solved. The fatigue of brain, in consequence of the protracted mental effort, had induced, temporarily, the perfect slumber. The action of the intellectual and will powers were, for the time being, entirely suspended. At this point, I saw the guardian spirit pass her beautiful hand over the moral organs, and extend her fingers, in an earnest, positive manner, toward the left temple. The emanation from her hand was soft and penetrative—like the softest aura, and I beheld a thought *evolved* from the faculties in that locality. This thought passed, like a breath, into the upper portions of the brain, and was then joined by several others, which the guardian had caused to come forth from the different faculties.

Now, this was a dream, full of significance. It originated from a spiritual influence; not from any imperfect slumber or unsettled thoughts. The lady did not know, however, that she had a guardian spirit. Therefore, on awakening from the reverie, which she did a few moments after this spiritual impression had been made upon her, she exclaimed—"How beautiful and clear was that dream!" Before she uttered this, I had returned to my ordinary state, determined not to inform her what I saw in her case until she should express to me her thoughts. Hence I inquired: "Have you been dreaming?" She replied: "Yes, but I did n't lose myself more than five minutes, I think; and yet I dreamt out what I must do in regard to a certain matter which has been on my mind for the last two weeks." Said I: "Do you mean to follow dreams in matters of importance?" "O, no," said she; "but when I can lose myself in my chair for only five minutes, and awake with a better plan of proceedure than I have ever had before, I will certainly act upon it." I then related to her what I had seen, much to her surprise and gratification.

But let us come to the application. You will perceive, by the above illustration, that the mind can be psychologically acted upon by spiritual beings. Spirits may breathe their influence and sweet discourses upon the mind, without disturbing its repose or exciting the least suspicion that a divine power is acting so immediately upon it. And yet, when the human mind receives an impression from the spirit world, which takes the form of a clear and beautiful dream, there is no doubt but the true import of that impression will be recognized by the individual who obtains it. These impressions are never lost, when once imparted to, and distinctly developed in, the mind. The dreams which are generated by spiritual influences, may be distinguished from ordinary dreaming by an unerring rule—viz.: by the *clearness*, *beauty*, and *power* which invariably characterize the former; while the latter are generally obscure, disagreeable, and troublesome to the mind.

We must not, however, accustom our minds to depend too much upon the guardian spirit for direction and happiness. When we ascertain our duty and destiny, or obtain certain convictions concerning them, we should act in strict accordance with all the light we possess. Then it is,—when the individual has done, and is doing what he believes to be his duty,—that the higher influences rush into the soul. Yet it should be remembered, that these dreams can not be received from the spirit world, into the mind, unless the slumber be perfect and the state harmonious.

There is a philosophy of mental motion, which I desire you to understand. It is this: one mind can not think and feel in harmony with another mind, unless the motions of the two brains be precisely alike. Here is the foundation of all psychological phenomena. If a person thinks of a tree, for example, his thought is the result of the united action of the organs of "form," "size," "color," and "locality." If he thinks of a landscape, the same faculties are brought into requisition, combined with the contributions of thought from the organs of "Sublimity," "Ideality," and "Comparison." Now, should a spirit think of a landscape, and desire to impress a view of it upon the slumbering mind, the spirit would act upon and awaken the above faculties in such a way as nothing but the picture could be seen or thought of by the sleeper. Hence, when the spirit impresses the mind on earth with a dream, the component thoughts are not deposited in the subjected brain, but are developed therein by playing upon the right faculties in a right manner. Thus the mind of the sleeper is made to harmonize, in its internal motions, with the mental operations of the attending spirit. This is the way in which the common psychological phenomena are manifested. But it implies a contradiction of "Locke on the Understanding," whose theory was, that there are no "innate ideas," or inherent elements of thought. The truth is, that, even when man is made to dream a spiritual dream, full of interior meaning, there are no "ideas" imparted to the mind, but simply the faculties are played upon so skillfully, by the guardian spirit, that they can not but produce the desired impressions,—as when a competent performer touches the cords of the musical instrument, he compels it to give forth precisely that song which is agitating his own mind. He communicates to the instrument the motions of his mind; thus he makes it dream, (vocally, so to speak,) the actual perceptions of his intellect. He does not impart the music, for that is already existing and incorporated in the very constitution of the instrument; but he controls its motions and thus constrains it to express precisely such sounds as he may desire. So with spiritual dreaming: the slumbering mind,—whose intellectual and will-powers are all quiet,—is under the control of the guardian spirit; and the Spirit does not introduce thoughts into the mind, but touches the various faculties in such a manner as to cause them to develop the dream which is desired.

You will perceive, therefore, that the instrument of the mind—the Brain, must be perfectly passive in order to come under the immediate guidance of superior powers or beings,—like the harp, which entertains no will or wish contrary to the mind of the performer. By this, the law and method of spiritual intercourse, during sleep, may be easily comprehended; also, you can readily calculate the proximate number of spiritual dreams received and enjoyed by the people, by considering how many persons there probably are who enjoy the perfect slumber.

LECTURE XXIV.

THE SOURCES OF HUMAN HAPPINESS AND MISERY PHILOSOPHICALLY CONSIDERED.

Many persons have marveled at the mysterious providences of God. The many and various so-called dispensations of the controlling Power, among the earth's inhabitants, have long confounded the wise and delighted the foolish. The ways of God are supposed or asserted to be beyond the comprehension of men, and his wisdom unsearchable. "Canst thou by searching find out God? Canst thou find out the Almighty unto perfection?" His perfection "is as high as heaven: what canst thou do? Deeper than hell: what canst thou know?" Such were the meditations of the author of the book of Job in the Old Testament. This author displays the highest and rarest poetical talent in his drama of "Disease, the Devil, and Deity."

All physical disorders he refers to the mysterious dispensations of Providence; likewise, all his impatience, restlessness, and rebelliousness growing out of his afflictions. Every thing is referred directly to supernatural causes; and the doctrines of special providences have been chiefly derived from such theological poems as adorn the book of Job. According to this author, man must accord the ordinary circumstances and accidents of this existence to divine interpositions; such as hereditary diseases, famines, the common atmospheric phenomena of rain, and the correction or chastisement of men for unrighteous deeds. "Although," says the author, "affliction cometh not from the dust: neither doth trouble spring out of the ground; yet man is born unto trouble, as the sparks fly upward." Then follows the injurious effects of such a belief. The author does not conceive that he is experiencing the consequences of some infringement upon the physical or organic laws of nature; and that exemption from further affliction and disease depends wholly upon his return to nature's laws; but, by supposing the Lord to be the immediate cause of disease and punishment, he resolved to send upward to Jehovah his prayers; and thus appeals for further supernatural dispensations in the form of forgiveness and mercy: "I would seek unto God, and unto God would I commit my cause; who doeth great things and unsearchable; marvelous things without number; who giveth rain upon the earth, and sendeth water upon the fields." * * * "Behold, happy is the man whom God correcteth; for he maketh sure, and bindeth up: he woundeth, and his hands make whole; in famine, he shall redeem him from death; in war, from the power of the sword."

Considered in the light of an Epic Poem,—as an elevated fiction, designed to improve the morals and inspire a love for the supreme,—this book of the Old Testament is as valuable as any in the English language; but if it be received as the faithful relation of actual occurrences, it is one of the most formidable obstacles to the progress and well-being of mankind. It teaches the repulsive doctrine, that diseases and unhappiness flow from the will and dispensations of the Deity. It teaches man to be happy when he is sick and afflicted, because that such calamities are to be received as demonstrations of God's attention and regard for the individual. It teaches that, any description of organic disturbances may be removed by prayer and supplication; and also teaches the old Tartarean doctrine that, the Supreme Being is angry and vexed perpetually at the majority of mankind. Thus Job exclaims: "Oh, that my grief were thoroughly weighed, and my calamity laid in the balance together; it is now heavier than the sand of the sea; for, [here comes in the supernatural reason with the Tartarean doctrine,] the arrows of the Almighty are within me, the poison whereof drinketh up my spirit: the terrors of God do set themselves in array against me!" This is exceedingly sublime, terrible, tragical; it is no less erroneous, and fatal to human improvement. The author had neglected to obey the organic laws of his constitution, and was laboring under the penalty of his own transgressions; but he thinks his punishment is *especially* meted out to him, and believes that the Lord can be moved, by his mournful appeals, to mitigate the sufferings which he had brought, ignorantly, upon himself.

The consequences of a belief in such a doctrine have been openly manifested in the works of evangelical writers. The best of them expose the utmost ignorance of the nature and invariableness of the divine government. They all believe in "mysterious providences" —in "divine dispensations"—in supernatural "interposition of God" in the affairs of human beings. They betray the most fatal ignorance of the laws of mind, and the results thereof are transmitted to the poor and uneducated classes. Only twenty-one years ago a work was issued in Edinburgh, which contained doctrines of this general kind. For example: Mr. Erskine, a much beloved clergyman, in describing the condition of his wife's mind, says: "For a month or two the arrows of the Almighty were within her, and the terrors of the Lord did set themselves in array against her." Not apprehending the fact that natural causes always produce external effects, this clergyman called to his assistance, [not the laws and forces of nature,] but the neighboring clergymen to pray in her behalf! However, "she still continued to charge herself with the commission of 'the unpardonable sin,' and persisted in affirming herself to be a cast-away and abandoned of God." Now here is exhibited the pernicious tendency of the doctrine which is illustrated in the Epic Poem of Job! The clergyman supposed that the Lord had afflicted his wife for some wise end; whilst the actual source of her misfortune was located in the unbalanced state of her moral and intellectual faculties. If a religious mind is possessed of large Cautiousness and small Hope, the idea of a dark and fearful future, with apprehensions about the unpardonable sin, are not uncommon results. A brilliant intellect, which is constantly psychologized by Fear or Cautiousness, is just the mind to believe in the doctrine of hell, and to describe the "severe trials," the "sore afflictions," and "snares," which the everlastingly condemned are supposed to experience in the boundless regions of eternal misery. All Christian poets,—Milton, Bunyan, Pollok, &c.,—were mentally constructed upon this defective plan; which, if they had known less of the laws of Moses and more of the laws of nature, they could have altered to permit the admittance of a more harmonious faith.

Let us now examine the principles of the Divine government, as exhibited in the constitution of man: for it will be found that the true sources of happiness are hidden beneath the subject now presented to your consideration. By principles, I mean rules of action. In nature, every thing,—animate or inanimate, rational or irrational, —is governed by a class of rules or laws which are universal and invariable. It is now my impression to bring all previous definitions of nature's laws into a form or class, which has been adopted by three or four authors within the last half century. It seems that the principles which the Creator has instituted for the well-being and government of man, may be classified into laws:—Physical, Organic, and Moral. A brief definition of the relation of these moving principles to each other, is now deemed necessary.

I. The Physical laws are those principles which control the forms and general phenomena of the external world. They govern outer circumstances, and also, to considerable extent, the material organism of man. These physical laws are, in modern works on

Natural Philosophy, termed, combustion, decomposition, cohesion, and gravitation. These laws are fixed and invariable; operating with as much precision and potency in one department of creation as another.

II. The Organic laws relate to all physiological or functional forms of matter. They differ from the physical laws in this: they relate exclusively, in their sphere of manifest operations, to all organized matter,—such as possess forms, forces, and motions. They refer particularly to man, to the material department of his nature; and his physical health, harmony, and happiness depend, to a great degree, upon the uninterrupted operation of these Laws in his personality.

III. The Moral laws come into action exclusively upon the highest plane of Creation. They have strict reference to reasonable, intelligent, moral, or spiritual beings. They fix the sentiment of Justice in the soul; the inherent consciousness of Right and Wrong, —the feeling of having duties to discharge and moral obligations to observe. The moral law is active only in the human mind. It is paramount in importance to every other law; hence, it is implanted in the mental constitution of man, like the tree of knowledge in the fabled garden of Eden.

Now, inasmuch as man is constructed upon physical, organic, and moral principles, which are fixed and invariable; it follows, that his happiness depends upon his obedience to these laws; that, to disobey and disregard their positive requirements, is to be deformed and miserable. Obedience invariably brings with it its own reward; disobedience its appropriate punishment. Or, to speak strictly philosophical, every action is succeeded by its natural, legitimate consequences. The government of God, therefore, may be said to rest, so far as it relates to mankind, upon physical, organic, and moral laws; and that all rewards and punishments, all penalties and chastisements flow, not from any volition or special interposition of

Deity, but from the obedience or disobedience of these established laws by man. Hence, it is within man's power to be either happy or miserable. The means of happiness lie about and within him, to use which as his wisdom and nature demand; and the Deity never sends from heaven any rewards for good deeds, nor punishments for bad ones; because his laws are sufficiently perfect to punctually administer happiness or misery to the obedient or disobedient creature, and always in strict harmony with the extent of the fidelity to, or with the magnitude of the transgressions of, these universal and inexorable principles. This philosophy, as you probably perceive, is based upon nature; not upon the doctrines inculcated in the book of Job. According to this philosophy of the government and punishments of God, there is never any occasion for special or mysterious providences or divine dispensations. The laws of nature are adequate to all rewards and just punishments, as I will now proceed to illustrate.

Let me, in the first place, illustrate the operation of the Physical Law upon man.

The physical law relates, as I before said, to the material or external world; also to the corporeal organism of human beings. And it will be seen that this law can not be infringed upon without an appropriate and corresponding amount of punishment. If a man should throw himself from the top of a tree he would most certainly fall to the earth, and receive the legitimate consequences of his violation of the physical law. In obedience to this law, a stone thrown into the air will return to the earth. In obedience to this law, the moon, the sun, and stars revolve and travel through the bending skies without interfering with each other or the earth. In obedience to this law, the flowers unfold upward; the dews ascend to form rain, and the rain descends to moisten the earth. In accordance with this law, the whole universe is maintained in a state of eternal equilibrium. Now, a perfectly righteous man, so far as the organic and moral laws are concerned, is not exempt from the legitimate workings of this law. Should the angel Gabriel himself, in a *physical* body, walk over the Niagara Falls, he would experience a severe fall or loss of outer life; because, simply, he had violated the physical law which governs the equilibrium and relation of all things. Nor would it make any difference in the magnitude of the punishment had he *known* the consequences before experiencing them; neither would he suffer less if he had violated the law by accident; for the consequences which succeed the transgression of the physical law are visited alike upon man or animal, saint or sinner; because it does not refer to the moral law, hence, is never attended with moral punishments. A tree, stone, beast, or man, would be rewarded or punished in a similar manner, by obedience or disobedience of this physical principle.

Let me, in the second place, illustrate the operation of the Organic Law.

This law determines the relations between animate and inanimate bodies,—between those things which are, and those things which are not, in a state of functional organization. In obedience to this law, an organized body placed in a bed of burning coals would soon experience disorganization as a consequence of the violation. And every creature, whether animal or human, would receive precisely the same effect if preceded by a similar transgression. The fool and the philosopher would alike decompose in a perfectly heated furnace; so would each experience the legitimate consequences of taking an over-dose of cicuta or any other poison. Here you perceive the moral law does not come into action; for man and beast are alike treated under the operation of the physical and organic laws, always in proportion to the extent of the obedience or infringement. Again: if a man places himself in harmony with the organic laws, he is certain of corresponding happiness. But if he should place himself out of harmony with these laws, and become intemperate in his diet, exercise, and in the gratification of the lower propensities, he would experience pain and bodily disease; although, at the same time, he may be the most religious and philanthropic person in the world.

Let me, in the third place, illustrate to you the operation of the Moral Laws.

These laws refer particularly to the mind. They give birth to all ideas of duty—of right and wrong—of individual responsibility. A man is always punished *in proportion* as he infringes upon *his sense* of right; although this sense may be partially developed, or altogether, in some persons, educational. A wild animal, having no connection whatever with the moral law, may destroy a large number of human lives without experiencing the least disturbance of mind; but a man, having the law written upon his nature—"thou shalt not kill"—should he destroy an equal number of human beings, will certainly suffer internally to a degree proportionate to the extent of *his* convictions of right and wrong.

Those who do not know how to reason upon the principles of the Divine Government, are always in the dark as to the mysterious providences and dispensations of Deity. To such persons, the world is replete with the mysteries of godliness; and the ways of God to man are dark and unsearchable. They can not understand why,—admitting this philosophy of rewards and punishments to be correct,—why, the good and pious man is frequently afflicted with pains and bodily diseases, while the evil and blasphemous person is as frequently in the enjoyment of perfect health. The problem of the *success* of the bad man when the good man fails, is yet unsolved in many minds. But I perceive no mystery in this matter, because I have learned to discriminate between the physical, organic, and moral laws. There is none absolutely righteous. One man may set at defiance all the requirements of the *moral* law; but that same man may live perfectly consistent with the requirements of the physical and organic laws; and consequently, while he is deprived of internal peace and delight, he would enjoy all the legitimate results of his obedience to the lower laws of his being, in the form of physical health and organic vigor. Another man may disregard all the requirements of the physical and organic laws; may eat too much, too fast, too often, may exercise too little or too much, may be intemperate in various ways; but he is, notwithstanding, very honest, pious, and hospitable—obeys the ten commandments—does not "walk in his garden on the Sabbath, but reverently to, and from, meeting;" and yet, he is, perhaps, like the Poet Job, laboring under severe bodily afflictions. Disease has laid its ruthless hand upon him; he is deprived of many physical and intellectual comforts; and, were this person a clergyman, he would probably say: "the arrows of the Almighty are within me, the poison whereof drinketh up my spirit; the terrors of the Lord do set themselves in array against me." Now many people fail to perceive the equity of the administration of rewards and punishments in the case of these two individuals; hence argue the necessity of future retribution. But a little reflection will make this matter very plain. One man is diseased, because he is suffering the consequences of violating the physical and organic laws of his being; the other man is perfectly healthy, because, although he constantly violates the moral laws, he keeps the lower laws of his nature free from any description of infringement. So the moral man suffers from physical transgressions; and the physical man suffers from moral transgressions. There can not be any confusion in the operation of these laws; they operate, to a certain extent, independently of each other, and always with the most positive and perfect justice. A man is certain to reap whatever he sows. These laws "render unto every man according to his deeds" in the present state of existence. If he sows the grain in Hartford, he reaps the harvest in Hartford; not in New York or Boston. And if he "sows wild oats," he is certain never to get *wheat* in return! Thus it is, that justice is exercised toward every man in the general providence of God.

It is sometimes asked: "How can the man be punished in this life, who has committed every species of outrage; who has crimsoned the ocean waters with the blood of hundreds of good, pious, and virtuous men?" My response to this question is very plain. First, this man has transgressed the moral law; hence, if he be punished at all, he must of necessity receive a moral punishment. Second, his punishment must be in exact proportion to his inward *consciousness* or condemnation of wrong; the consequences of his moral transgressions will, in other words, be visited upon him according to his consciousness of the transgression.

You now ask: "Is this all the punishment so wicked a man receives?" In reply, I am impressed to re-affirm that, the Laws of Nature are so perfectly arranged, and are so positively certain in their operations, that no person can escape the legitimate consequences of his actions, be they good or evil. But some persons oppose what they term, "facts" to this theory, and say: "there are individuals who suffer more in committing a petit larceny than others do in murdering their fellow-beings. And again: some men suffer severely in committing the first murder, but the second crime is less thought of, and the third is committed with apparent pleasure."

True, here seems to be a difficult problem to solve by the foregoing philosophy; but it is merely a seeming difficulty. I think we should "judge not according to appearances, but with a righteous judgment." If you could see into the hidden nature of that wicked man, you would recognize the nature of his punishment—the consequences or penalties of his crimes, all distinctly written, not by an angel in the skies upon a book in the courts of heaven, *but by the angel of his heart, upon his moral constitution.* Let me further explain this proposition.

You will all acknowledge, I think, that the finest and most harmonious minds are capable of the highest and most heavenly enjoyment. The best ear catches the best sound; the soundest eye sees the most beautiful things; the healthiest body enjoys the most of material existence; and the keenest moral faculties receive the most perfect happiness. And you will also acknowledge the plain fact, that he who impairs his physical health not only suffers pain, but is also deprived of much physical happiness; so likewise, he who disturbs the harmony or blunts the sensibility of his moral system, not only experiences the immediate results of the shock, but also impairs his ability to enjoy the high happinesses of the inward spirit.

Suppose, for illustration, you place your finger in contact with the fire. According to the organic law, disorganization of the parts would ensue. The textures and nerves would lose their normal properties, and the infringement would be attended with intolerable pain. Now, if you should repeat this act frequently, the work of disorganization would be terminated, and insensibility of the parts would follow. You will perceive that the *pain* is the *smallest* portion of the punishment. You may now place the same finger in the fire with perfect impunity; without pain. But the maximum portion of the punishment consists in the *loss* of the finger; consists in your inability to use it pleasurably as you did previous to the transgression.

Suppose again: you violate the organic law by the immoderate use of spirituous liquors. At first your punishment consists in languor, headache, sickness, &c.; but by a frequent repetition of these organic transgressions, the same quantities of these liquors may be taken without producing *any* sensible effect. You continue the practice without suffering, as you first did; therefore, the question now arises: "how is this transgressor punished according to his deeds?" He is punished, I reply, *in the diminution of his enjoyments.* True, there is some enjoyment in the uncontrolled gratification of the animal propensities; but that enjoyment is the same as the brute experiences; it is low, beastial, and miserable! Thus he is punished in proportion to the magnitude of his offenses.

Suppose again: you turn a pirate. You are cruel, dishonest, and blasphemous. You set at defiance all the requisitions of the moral law; and, in the exercise of your powers, you destroy a fellow-being. In the "heat of the contest" you care nothing as to the act. But when a quiet hour arrives, the horrors of that deed look you boldly and accusingly in the face. Your sufferings are intense; but you blunt sensibility by alcohol, and soon forget the first murder in a second; this in a third; and so you become used to horrors and murders, and care very little about them. Now, the question is: "how is this man adequately punished for his manifold transgressions of the moral law!" I answer, he is punished by a moral loss; or by being positively *deprived* of those exquisite enjoyments which constitute the heavenly state. The proper development and exercise of the moral faculties and powers constitute the happiness of heaven. But the pirate is in a low and negative state; his enjoyments, at best, are but beastial; and he sustains the great calamity of an impaired or undeveloped moral nature.

But even this punishment would be easily sustained, were it not for the fact, that this life is but the commencement of an endlessly progressive existence! A man might "sear his conscience" by habitual crime—might indulge in the ungoverned gratification of his own animal inclinations—might reduce his condition to that of the brute; but the consequences of his transgressions do not cease with the act of transgressing! Here is the important point. Here we must continue to be philosophical. The consequences which follow the violation of the physical or organic laws generally cease with this life; but the superior law—the moral law—the "higher law,"—that which transcends all other laws—lives immortal in the human soul! If a man violates his moral sense before he sleeps, he will certainly feel the consequences thereof on the following morning. Nor does it make any difference within him, whether on the morning he awakens on earth or in the Spiritual World! He takes the record of his moral violations with him,—on his moral constitution; and, when he becomes fully awakened to his condition in the Spirit Land, he readily perceives and feels the legitimate consequences of his deeds, whether good or evil. He sees and feels that his punishment consists in the *small degree* of happiness which at the time he is only capable of enjoying. He sees and feels that he has neglected to develop and improve his moral and religious faculties; and that, in the same proportion, he is punished by being deprived of those high happinesses with which the morally just are constantly blessed! "The science of man's whole nature," says George Combe, "animal, moral, and intellectual, was never more required to guide him than at present, when he seems to wield a giant's power, but in the application of it to display the ignorant selfishness, willfulness, and absurdity of an overgrown child. History has not yielded half her fruits, and can not yield them until mankind shall possess a true theory of their own nature. Many persons believe that they discover evidence against the moral government of the world, in the success of individuals not greatly gifted with moral and intellectual qualities, in attaining to great wealth, rank, and social consideration, while men of far superior merit remain in obscurity and poverty. But the solution of this difficulty is to be found in the consideration, that success in society depends on the possession, in an ample degree, of the qualities which society needs and appreciates, and that these bear reference to the state in which society finds itself at the time when the observation is made. In the savage and barbarous conditions, bodily strength, courage, fortitude, and skill in war, lead a man to the highest honors; in a society like that of modern England, commercial or manufacturing industry may crown an individual with riches, and great talents of debate may carry him to the summit of political ambition. In proportion as society advances in moral and intellectual acquirements, it will make larger demands for similar qualities in its favorites. The reality of the moral government of the world appears from the degree of happiness which individuals and society enjoy in these different states. If unprincipled commercial and political adventurers were happy in proportion to their apparent success; or if nations were as prosperous under the dominion of reckless warriors as under that of benevolent and enlightened rulers; or if the individuals who compose a nation enjoyed as much serenity and joy of mind when they advanced the bold, selfish, and unprincipled to places of trust and power, as when they chose the upright, benevolent, and pious,—the dominion of a just Creator might well be doubted. But the facts are the reverse of these."

There are other points of thought, connected with this subject, to which I shall, on future occasions, direct your attention. But I now conclude this discourse, by urging you to the strictest obedience to all the laws of your being. For physical happiness, obey the physical laws; for organic happiness, obey the organic laws; for moral happiness, obey the moral laws; but, let it be remembered that, one set of these laws can not be violated without, to some certain extent, disturbing the peace of the general economy and life. The moral law holds a superiority over every other law; and this is the most important principle for every man to obey. In this lies the true sources of happiness, and that peace which the world can neither give nor take away.

LECTURE XXV.

A BRIEF EXPOSITION OF THE SATAN WHICH TEMPTED JESUS OF NAZARETH.

Occasionally it may be proper and useful to take a text and to preach a sermon. And yet there are evidently two evils flowing from this custom, so universally adopted throughout Christendom. One evil is that exhibited in the nature of the discourse which succeeds the text. A mind selects some passage from the Old or New Testament, writes it down at the beginning of the book, and then bends all its energies to elaborate a sermon which will conform strictly with the apprehended letter and spirit of the text. Now this is an evil. And yet the mind is favorably disciplined by the method. But the evil consists in the determination on the part of the clergyman, or any one who pursues this custom, to write just what the text implies, or nearly so, and let the sermon go for truth. Good maxims are very suggestive, and may be taken as mottoes to a discourse, but to frame a sermon from the mere suggestion of any passage is to allow the mind no opportunity to avail itself of fresher inspirations. Sermonizing upon texts has become a profession like every other trade. It requires, however, considerable native talent and mental energy to render such a profession successful and attractive. If a man designs to write his discourse with special reference to the letter of the text, then he requires no little genius in order to analyze and expand the ruling thought. His talent must be displayed in commentation. He must be very ready to criticise the meaning—must show considerable grace and ease in tracing words back to their Greek and Hebrew derivations—must know how to read the Latin text, and then he is safe in the community. The people like him—will hear him preach—and he is certain of an occupation. He is a pleasing expounder of texts, and makes the Bible read exactly to suit the views of his denomination.

Now this is wrong. It is positively injurious to the mind; it can not expand under the mechanical influence of such a profession. The doors and windows of the soul are shut to every thing but a denominational exposition of the text selected. The intuitional powers of the inward nature are thus weakened. The reasoning energies are circumscribed in their operation, and the whole internal being is compelled to draw its nourishment from the supposed spirit of the leading passage. Now, how much more wise would it be, and consequently beneficial, to search the stupendous temple of Nature for Truth, and, when the seeking mind arrives at a principle, by internal development, which some other mind has expressed in appropiate language, to accept that expression as evidence that the same principle of Truth had been seen and felt by another. In this method, the soul would find the means and paths of progress. Every thought would then have some real and valuable significance. But if a man makes a business of expounding texts, how can that man's mind develop? How can he know whether his text is true or not? How can he discriminate between true inspiration and the imaginations of religious leaders and chieftains? His soul has no individual development, and hence, he seldom gives utterance to sentiments, which, like cannon-balls, might serve to demolish the loftiest edifice of thought and error known to olden teachers.

Another evil growing out of sermonizing from texts, is exhibited in the injurious custom of writing a discourse of mere speculations, and then, in order to have the whole accepted as truth, seeking for passages or a passage of Scripture adapted to the general subject, as a kind of Divine Authority or indorsement of the whole. Now this practice is wrong, because it prevents the proper expansion of the mind. The speaker is never impressed to employ texts, either as suggestives to the understanding or as indorsements of any sentiments uttered, principally because of the sectarian and contracting influence which necessarily flows from the custom. But on this occasion I have a text presented to my mind. And yet Reason is admonished to preside at the investigation of its meanings; for, under Reason's inspection and jurisdiction, it may be converted into a principle of plain practical utility. If clergymen should allow reason, instead of the text, to be the *umpire* in the analyzation of any thought, the world would be more certain of two important things —less professional preaching, and more real Truth.

Your attention is now solicited to the following passages:—

MATTHEW, IV. 8, 9, 10.

"The devil taketh him (i. e. Jesus) up into an exceeding high mountain, and showeth him all the kingdoms of the world and the glory of them; and said—All these things will I give thee, if thou wilt fall down and worship me. Then Jesus said unto him—GET THEE HENCE, SATAN!"

First. Let us consider what this text does not mean.

Second. Then let us discover what it does mean.

Matthew is the alledged historian of these passages. But this is highly questionable; for this gospel is "according to Matthew," that is, perhaps, as it was supposed or remembered, by some other writer, as Matthew believed and related. Now no one will say that this account was written at the precise time the circumstance is supposed to have occurred. The great difficulties attending the art of writing in that early period, are sufficient to prove that no penman could have written the words as fast as they fell from the tongue. No; these passages are recorded in the past tense, and are a relation of what tradition had preserved from oblivion. But what do they not mean? They do not mean that Jesus was tempted by a prince of evil, in *propria persona*. This is the error of the historian, who, from his faith in tradition and in a mystical system of ethics, common among the ancient Essenes, unquestionably believed in an *evil invisible spirit*, that could, at will, become visible and take any form and assume any appearance whatever. A belief in a spirit of evil—in a real wicked personality—was, as it now is, a remnant of Persian and Chaldeanic mythology. There was no Bible when this circumstance of the "temptation" occurred. Christianity was then being born—the drama was being performed; and hence could not have been transferred word for word, incident for incident, to paper, because the alledged historians were themselves very prominent actors therein. Tradition, and tradition's memory, had to supply the materials for the formation of the New Testament. And among other things recorded as actual occurrences, is the incident under present consideration. But I have affirmed that it does not mean that Jesus was tempted by a satanic personage, though I perceive that the writer believed the latter. Therefore, let us now inquire into its real meaning.

It means simply, that Jesus listened occasionally to the whisperings of his passions. He was a man like other men about him; only more spiritually minded and philanthropic than they. His mind, nevertheless, was sometimes influenced by the subordinate elements of his nature. He has been magnified into a supernatural being, however; and it is therefore hard for the thus educated mind to think of him as being a Man among men. But Reason is now the master of this text, and hence we get at a true solution of the circumstance.

You all know how common a thing it was in those days, (and it is so even now in some countries,) to personify sentiments or principles. Faith, Hope, Charity, are all exhibited in the human type; and poets cause them to speak, and to breathe forth corresponding thoughts. And there are gods and goddesses of poetry, amusements, music, flowers, summer, and impersonations of all the seasons. This custom was adopted by Jesus. When he alluded to the temptations presented to him by the devil, he simply meant the *temptations of his loves* and lower or unspiritual passions. Satan is the name given to an accuser, one who calumniates another—a libertine—and to one who deceives! Any undisciplined passion of the soul may constitute this Satan. In the text it appears, that Jesus named the suggestions of his organ of acquisitiveness the temptations of Satan. When he listened to the insinuating whisperings of his acquisitiveness, he calls it being tempted by the devil. This language is altogether figurative.

It seems that Jesus was putting his own strength to the test. He was preparing himself for all emergencies. He tested his ability to withstand hunger by fasting for many days. But when he became skeptical concerning his power to work miracles, he called it being tempted by the devil. Thus his skepticism caused him to say to himself—"Command that these stones be made bread." But instantly his higher spirituality caused him to feel and say, in substance—"This is too material—man does not live by such bread alone, but by every word that proceedeth out of the mouth of Truth." Then, again, he became skeptical concerning the protecting presence of his guardian angels. He, therefore, proposed to throw himself down from the pinnacle of the temple, and test the fact, whether his guardian spirits would bear him up from a disastrous fall. But this test he directly considered too low and sensuous; hence he says—"Thou shalt not tempt the Lord thy God;" that is, it is wrong to test spirituality by such material demonstrations. So, also, his organ of acquisitiveness caused him to question himself concerning his power to withstand the temptations of wealth. This passion said—"Worship mammon, and I will give you the kingdoms of the world, and the glory of riches." This is all the satanic influence there was in the circumstance. How frequently the same devil tempts our countrymen to ascend the high mountains of Mexico, there to contemplate the supposed riches of California! Or, to climb the exceedingly high summits of commercial speculation; there to view the kingdoms of the world and the glory thereof! Alas! what empty glory! What self-destructive joy! Every man is sometimes tempted, as was Jesus, by the same class of faculties. Skepticism, sensuality, love of power, love of riches—these are the misdirected elements of the mind, which constitute all the Satan there is in the wide universe. These elements of the mind are intrinsically pure—they only require to be subjugated to the reason-principle. But how shall this be accomplished? I answer, mainly by a sound judgment and a strong and steady will—by the soul's omnipotence! When you are thus tempted—do as Jesus did—say to that passion's misdirection—"get thee hence, Satan"—be firm in willing this; and you may be assured that good angels will extend to you their aid, and render your life a continuous joy!

In this connection, I am moved to present you with the brief exposition of another passage of Scripture:—

LUKE, XII. 5.

"Fear Him which, after he hath killed, hath power to cast into Hell; yea, I say unto you, FEAR HIM!"

According to the letter of history, Jesus uttered this admonition. The life, teachings, and death of this personage are matters of history,—familiar to all the inhabitants of Christendom. He is esteemed by many as the only Son of God; by others as a very extraordinary member of humanity—a highly developed child of the universal Father. Those who do not regard him as the counterpart of Jehovah—invested with the disposition and power to save the world—consider him gifted far above any other man which ever lived before or since his time.

He is deified for his meekness, benevolence, and wisdom. The talents of educated priests have been employed for ages in exaggerating his personal idiosyncracies. His every attitude has been devoutly contemplated; and poetry hath stretched forth her hand and bathed his character in the glowing enchantments of mystery. The consequences of all this are living in popular faiths. Every creed has it Idol—every idol, an Altar—every altar, a Priest.

The human soul must love something—the indwelling religious sentiment must have some object or personage to reverence. But there are very few who can sufficiently separate themselves from the externals of life to reverence a Principle. Hence, the masses worship objects and personages,—they can not comprehend the celestial sublimity—the eternal beauty and holiness,—which characterize a Principle. The thought is too profound; the Truth is not enough physical. But to the spiritually or morally enlightened, all objects and personages are meaningless except as signs of thoughts and principles. St. Paul is not a being to worship, but a person who should forever stand in the garden of memory, as a sanctified representative of Zeal and Conscientiousness. Thus every man should live; but no one object or personage deserves the reverence due to Principle.

Yet the impressions of youth are strong. First convictions form for themselves deep channels in the mind, and flow therein with a peculiar determination; hence most people find it exceedingly difficult to turn their thoughts in new directions. I am pleased that the mind is so constituted, that early impressions make the deepest channels therein; because when mankind become wiser and better, they will then know what convictions should be given to their children. It is just as easy to learn a good habit as a bad one—just as easy to live in harmony with the established Laws of Nature as with the Laws of the United States. And when parents become more enlightened upon the subject of the human mind—how it is constituted and capable of receiving impressions which will endure—then we may expect better children; better men and women.

In the present state of religious education, the majority of people believe that the author of our text was more gifted with wisdom than any other being known to history. This idea has crept into the mind during our cradle hours. Our parents have taught us this conviction, even at the dining-table. Sunday-school books have illustrated it to our youthful minds, and we think early in life that we believe it firmly.

Now it is with no desire to injure your esteem for any good being, that I bring before you a new train of thought.

We are admonished most emphatically to Fear Him who has power to cast both soul and body into Hell. We are told not to fear him who can merely destroy the body—that is, not to fear man, but we must fear God! Wherefore? Because through fear we will be constrained to obedience.

It is not my impression to compare any scriptural texts on this subject; but mainly to present a few reflections on the Wisdom of the admonition. It may be said that the words were addressed not to us, but to those immediately surrounding the author of the saying. It is of no possible consequence who the text was originally addressed to; it is sufficient for us to know that it is received as the utterance of one who is supposed to have had the highest Wisdom—expressed by the only Son of God.

The human race has been unfolding, step by step, for countless centuries. It began at the lowest point of human development, and has ascended the ladder with a firm, progressive tread. It has passed through all the intermediate stages of growth—from savagism to barbarism, from barbarism to civilization. The human Tree has been growing a long period—it has put forth many thorns and unseemly branches—but now, that the fruit begins to appear, and promises ripeness and abundance, we may easily reconcile ourselves to the imperfections consequent upon its gigantic growth, and learn to comprehend the whole system aright.

In the savage and barbarian ages we find the Doctrine of Fear prevailing universally. Fear and cruelty are twin-born—the parent is, Ignorance!

The experience of the world is, that no being can be benefited or reformed permanently through the exercise of Fear. Fear is the parent of Hatred. If a slave serves his master through Fear, then that master is the object of hatred and detestation. War, murder, envy, malice—all, flow from a low state of mind; and fear is one of the most conspicuous manifestations thereof. Fear may compel obedience, but it can render no one wiser, holier, or happier. All tyrants rule their subjects through fear; but no subject can be truly loyal under its degrading and brutalizing influence. The passions may be checked in their wild impetuosity by Fear, but not educated and subdued. Fear can overthrow the Empire of Reason, can spread ruin and desolation throughout the soul's dominion, but no one is made better and nobler by its power. Fear is a child of Ignorance; it belongs to the barbarian ages, and to low states of mind.

And yet, friends, we are told to "fear him who hath power to cast into hell—yea, to Fear Him." But why shall we fear him; because, according to this doctrine, by fearing the power of the master we will obey his commands.

Go into any so-called evangelical church, and you will hear this doctrine preached in one form or another. The faculty of fear is strongly appealed to—the preacher admonishes you to "prepare to die—to flee from the wrath to come." The motives presented to you for being good and charitable are all low and degrading. You must repent to-day—prepare to die—and be a follower of Jesus. Wherefore? Is it because it is reasonable and happifying to be good and wise? Nay; no such exalted motive is presented to you. You are not to strive for goodness on the ground that it will benefit yourself and the universal community of man; but because he imagines God is angry with the wicked—because there is a hell—

because there is a devil—because it is the only way "to flee from the wrath to come." "Yea, I say unto you, Fear Him!" And what are the consequences of such preaching? I answer—the consequences are stamped upon the minds of the people. They become politicians. Every thing must be done from policy or expediency; almost nothing from Principle. The doctrine of fear prevents the natural development of the mind—the moral faculties are not strengthened and unfolded, but merely played upon by the skillful preacher. If you see a man doing good under the influence of fear—because he fears Him who hath power to destroy both soul and body in hell—then you behold a miserable slave to a low and degrading policy. He serves the master, because he fears the lash! This doctrine smothers all reverence for principle; and compels the mind to worship objects and persons.

Those who have been "converted," as it is termed, under the preaching of hell-terrors, are usually not in the least improved in the moral department of their nature. A *moral man* is a man of principle! He loves good, and Truth, and Wisdom, not because he is in *fear of going to hell* if he did not love them, but because these virtues are intrinsically lovely and beneficial. Why do not the disciples of fear steal from, and murder, their neighbors? Why do they refrain from the various vices? Are they good, because they love the Right? Because they love peace on earth and brotherly love among all men?—Because they reverence a Principle? Would that it were so! But the doctrine of fear could produce no such exalted manifestations of character among men.

On one occasion, a preacher of this barbarian doctrine addressed me thus: "Sir, I hold your system to be pernicious in the extreme. It would destroy all moral obligations—open the flood-gates of vice—and fill the world with crime and desolation.

"Why to tell the truth, sir, if I believed as you do—if I did not believe in a hell, in a devil, and in eternal retribution—I would go immediately into the pleasures of sin—would steal, murder, &c.—and leave all religion, and take care of my own gratifications."

I replied briefly, that I was sorry that he was not a man of Principle; possessing a better mental organization. He acted altogether from the sensation of fear. He did not murder, simply because he *feared* him who was capable of casting both soul and body into hell!

Can the human soul be improved under the preaching of such a doctrine? Surely, there is nothing of humanity in it—nothing of that celestial nobility which belongs to the upper spheres. And yet, friends, who was it that originally preached this doctrine? Does it sound like the Wisdom of God? Could it have been inculcated by an Only Son of Jehovah? You may believe that it was, but I do not. Nevertheless, I do believe that it was taught by Jesus of Nazareth; who at other times, and in better moods, said that every thing depended upon "Loving the Lord your God with all your might, mind, and strength, and the neighbor as yourself."

There is no possible compatibility between Love and Fear. The Principle of Love is the great lever of reformation. Fear is certain to subject and paralyze the soul, but Love draws the soul above. If I should serve God because I love him, then I am internally benefited and happy; but then, I can not, at the same time, obey the other commandment—"Yea, I say unto you, Fear Him"—for Love and Fear can not be practically and beneficially experienced toward any one being. Hence I am moved to conclude, that priests and poets have greatly exaggerated the Wisdom of the great moral Reformer; for there is nothing more clear, on the page of sacred history, than that, in several instances, Jesus played upon the faculty of fear in order to induce and secure obedience to divine laws.

But there is nothing more clear, on the other hand, than that he recommended the Principle of Love as the grand agent of reformation. It is likewise true that he sometimes identified himself with a Principle of Perfection; so much so, in fact, that most Christians forget the Principle in their reverence for the Individual. Now this is wrong. For in proportion as we become man-worshipers, we fail to embrace those eternal principles of moral reform which alone can benefit man and elevate the race.

Another scriptural passage was presented to my mind recently for a brief elucidation; which I now proceed to unfold before you:—

JOHN III. 3.

"Verily, verily, I say unto you, except a man be born again, he can not see the kingdom of God."

The popular idea of heaven is grounded in the lowest form of selfishness. It is based upon egotism and a narrow individuality of character. All the great efforts made, to attain the kingdom of heaven, originate in the sentiment of self-importance and consequence. Nothing can be more unhealthy to the moral system of the community than the common ideas of heaven and the government of God. There is nothing of humanity in the doctrine. It refers solely to individual welfare and happiness. A Son has an account open with his Father. The creature is doing a moral business with his Creator. Every man for himself. Each has a separate account. The debt and credit system is the mode of management. Every thought, word, deed, and action is noted down,—the good ones on the right, the evil ones on the left. And when the day of settlement arrives the account will be made out to that date, and all delinquents are forced to pay all dues promptly. But suppose the individual is unable to settle? Suppose he has not the sum demanded? What then? Why, according to the popular doctrines of the future, he will be served as the delinquent population of the State of Connecticut used to be—namely—cast into prison for debt!

The prisoner may have plenty of wealthy friends and relatives in heaven. They may have been just as sinful as he; but, no matter, they repented at the eleventh hour—complied with the terms—and had their drafts honored. They may feel somewhat disposed to assist the sufferer—may have a vestige of humanity left within them—may feel a slight emotion of sympathy; but they need not feel disturbed. All that is necessary for perfect peace is, to turn their faces toward the Heavenly King. Although his countenance is frowning heavily upon the condemned debtors, yet they see so much righteousness in the law of eternal imprisonment for debt, that they instantly forget all sympathy for the suffering myriads, and break forth in one common anthem to the Lamb of God that *taketh away* the sins of the world!

How do you like the picture? You may object to this English translation of one of the greatest works of the "old masters" in theology, but you can not but acknowledge the faithfulness of the copy. It may be a too *literal* interpretation for professional artists in the theological academy—it may not please those who make concordances and commentaries; to them it may lack warmth and breadth,—but it is, nevertheless, a very plain rendering of a doctrine which has been taught for centuries in a mystical nomenclature.

It is every man for himself. A system of eternal selfishness. The whole transaction is between the individual and his Maker. A man is not to expect heaven on earth. He is to do certain things to deserve heaven hereafter. This is the doctrine. Of course, the different sects have different paths marked out on their charts, leading to heaven. One goes by Faith; another by Works; another by uniting the two means; others go altogether upon the vicarious atonement; and others by the eternal ordination of the Deity—but it is an individual and selfish method after all. How degrading and enslaving is all this doctrine! How it contracts our hearts, and insults the reason which God has given to man! All this anxiety about the future is wrong. "Sufficient unto the day is the evil thereof." The truly religious soul knows nothing of a *future* hell or heaven. The present is the *whole* of existence. To the exalted mind, there is properly no past; no future! All is present—a gigantic and all-containing *now*—casting its lights and shadows on either side, making heres and theres, yesterdays and to-morrows.

The doctrine that we are getting ready to die—living here in pain and bearing crosses in order to exist in heaven hereafter—is a low and uncultivated idea of existence.

A man may offend his conscience by committing murder—and he may flee his country to escape detection and be at peace; but is he capable of fleeing from the disapprobation of the still small voice? Nay—the angel in his heart has been wounded—its tender nature has suffered deeply from the transgression; and the man may go to the ends of the earth to escape; yet that white-robed angel will look up into the eyes of the murderer and speak the words of condemnation, and so sweetly, and fraternally, too, that nothing can exceed the *fineness* of his punishment. There is nothing that can condemn evil, but goodness. The angel of the human heart looks mournfully upon the wrong deeds of the creature man. The still small voice is forever in the presence of the transgressor; and there is no escaping its noontide and midnight injunctions.

How many people there are who desire to keep on the safe side! They reason thus: we had better believe in a hell; for, if there be a hell, we will be more safe than they who deny its existence; while, on the other hand, if there really be no hell, we will be just as safe as those who do not believe the doctrine. But to the exalted mind, there can not be any future retribution or arbitrary punishment. The righteous government of God is evidently based upon the principles of cause and effect. The commission of crime and the consequences of crime are inseparably connected. They walk together. The results of actions can not be avoided. If a man sins he as *certainly* suffers,—not from any arbitrary infliction of punishment, but wholly from the natural consequences attending the peculiar nature of his sins. The creature man is afflicted immediately—"in the day thou eatest thereof thou shalt surely die." A man reaps just what he sows; and his hell and his heaven are not a matter of selfishness. Because—

A man can not sin and suffer *alone*; neither can he do right and be happy all within himself. Humanity is all one vast organization. When its heart beats the blood flows to the furthest extremities. One member can not suffer without the other members suffering with it. Unity and sympathy of the parts constitute the golden chain which binds the whole together. Therefore, there can be no absolute isolation; no happiness or misery in the parts, which the *whole* does not realize to some extent. The sighs of Emerald Isle are to-day living in bone and muscle. The ignorance of parents, is preserved—more conspicuously than the sculptor's thought in the chiseled marble—in the bodily and phrenological developments of their offspring. The long and unshapely limbs, the flattened nose, the protruding lips and retreating forehead of the child, are unmistakable tomb-stones! They indicate where the parents have *buried* their low and uncultivated thoughts! Society never inflicts a punishment upon an individual, which is not paid back with interest compounded. And every evil carries with itself the elements of decay—this inherent sickness renders evil a self-punishing process. Therefore individuals and societies are equally the causes and victims of sin. And there can be no isolated, individual, selfish, local and circumscribed misery; because the whole is inseparably joined as the elements of one body—a community of interests.

"Unless a man be born again he can not inherit the kingdom of heaven."

Nothing can be more true than this. But what is the kingdom of heaven? Is it a state beyond the tomb? Is it a realm far away in the mystic depths of infinitude?—A place where the Spirit of God prevails?

The kingdom of heaven is within you. It is neither here nor there; it is not left behind in the perfumed bowers and holy labyrinths of Eden, nor yet, in the far-reaching future; IT IS IN THE STATE OF THE SOUL. But what is the new birth? Is it any miraculous alteration of man's nature? Is it a transformation of the heart from wickedness to righteousness? I reply—

"We know that we have passed from death unto life, because we love the brethren." That is to say, we have the evidence of the new birth in ourselves in the fact that we love our brethren. But who are our brethren? Are they, those who believe as we believe—adopt our creed, our formularies, and hear our ministers preach? "If we love those who love us, what reward have we?" Are our brethren those who live in the same country with us?

"Ye are all brethren." "Of one blood made he all the nations, kindreds, and tongues" of the earth. Here is the philosophical answer to all our inquiries. The kingdom of heaven is a state of mind, and the new birth consists in *dying* to a low, contracted selfishness. We must not seek heaven for our own selfish purposes. The meanness of the motive defeats the object. Nor must we imagine that our heaven is altogether in the future state. It is within our souls. We must have it developed within us, or we can never find it. We must die to selfishness. We must live to make each other happy. We must enlarge our benevolence, and be willing not only to see mankind as they are, but to assist in augmenting the world's happiness. We must forget self on the lower plane of being, if we would be happy. "Blessed are the peacemakers, for they shall inherit the kingdom of heaven." That is, he who can carry about, in the unseen chambers of his heart, a disposition to make peace on earth and good will toward man, is already in a kingdom of peace.

But how is it with those who worship the popular methods of going to heaven? Do they love the brethren? Do they seek the welfare of humanity? Nay, nay,—each is selfishly going to obtain a mystical state of blessedness in the future life. Every one is very solicitous to secure the safety of *his own* soul—every one for himself—the multitude is immense, but he who gets on the top is esteemed the most fortunate man, though he may have trampled hundreds beneath his feet. Nothing can be more pernicious than this low, sordid, bigoted idea of heaven! Those who adopt this idea, generally pray for the welfare of their friends, and for the condemnation of their enemies. They pray that God will especially bless and protect "my father and mother, sister and brother, and nephew"—the remaining members of humanity are patronizingly recommended to his tender mercy. Such people generally select the inhabitants of their heaven. They would not go to heaven if murderers, robbers, and licentious men, are to go there; yet they very conscientiously believe that Moses, Joshua, Solomon, and David, will be numbered among the glorified.

Man must die to contracted egotism and be born again into the sphere of universal love. He who contracts the dimensions of his heaven to the few whom he may chance to love, is, indeed, the maker of a very small elysium. Just in proportion as a man limits the boundaries of heaven, does he keep himself from enlarged and high enjoyments. The wider the sphere, the greater are the sources of happiness. He who lives expressly to extract his happiness from rich viands, from the wine-cup, and from the fashionable sources, knows no more what true heaven is, than he who has invested all his living interests in a gaming-house. So, also, he who thinks he can be truly happy by confining all his attention merely to the righteous regulation of his household, and to the properest care of his own person, is sure to become the victim of disappointment. The soul must put its feelers forth into the realms of humanity.

The individual must live with *strict reference* to the welfare, progress, and happiness of the whole. He must not seek heaven for his own selfish happiness, nor desire hell for the gratification of his low dislikes and hatreds; because he, by so desiring, or by being able to thus desire, is certain to meet with a train of unbroken perplexities and disappointments. This is no theory. The law of cause and effect renders this philosophy inevitably true. There is no escaping it. Now what shall we do to be saved? To be saved from what? Why, from a life of discord and perplexity?—from sin and from its sad consequences? The answer is plain. Live not in the past, neither in the future; but in that unmeasurable infinitarium which constitutes the Present. We are just as much in eternity now—this very moment—as we ever will be. And there is no other infinitude than this Present time. The infinite and eternal NOW! is all we have to call our own! The past is nothing—the future is nothing! If we would be good, and temperate, and kind to ourselves and to our neighbors, and consequently happy,—this is the time! The religious soul is happy now. It is not prospective, it is absolute.

It is desirable to be rightly apprehended in these assertions. I mean to say, that your progress and future happiness depend wholly upon the use you make of the eternal Now. Therefore, our "way, truth, and life," are distinctly defined. We must be right in heart and head *to-day* in order to secure a happy to-morrow. Do what is right under the circumstances. Do your best! Be certain that your still small voice—the angel of your heart—approves of what you do. Those who live thus can say: "we know that we have passed from death unto life, because we love the brethren!"

LECTURE XXVI.

THE AUTHORITY OF THE HARMONIAL PHILOSOPHY.

There is a simplicity—a beauty—a majesty—a holiness—a celestial grandeur—an unchangeableness belonging to a Principle of Truth, which is seldom perceived by the earth's inhabitants. The soul thrills at the conception. The energies of Reason swell into a higher strength, and the affections kindle into a serener ecstacy, at the thought that, Truth is the source of all eternal realities—the origin of all that is high, divine, and infinite.

But let us inquire, what is Truth? According to my impressions, the Truth is something more than that which endures only for a time. Any thing which is temporary—fleeting and evanescent as the passing breeze—should not be dignified with the name of, nor receive the esteem which belongs properly to, Truth. Truth is the same yesterday, to-day, and forever. It is the same always and every where. Absolute Truth is immutable. He that teaches a doctrine which is absolutely true, does not proclaim a thing which is temporarily certain; but an everlasting substantialism which rests upon the immutable authority of God. But he who proclaims that which is destined to decay—to become obsolete and useless—does not reveal a Truth of God, but merely a circumstance in the constitution of things. He speaks of things merely; not of that immutable principle whereby those things are held together in harmonious concord.

When Isaac Newton saw the apple fall to the earth, he did not regard that circumstance as an eternal Truth, but simply as an illustration of some great natural principle. And when he probed the secrets of creation, and discovered what he termed the "Law of Gravitation," he forthwith drew a line of distinction between the falling of that single apple, and the principle whereby all apples fall and worlds revolve.

Moreover when Newton ascertained the existence of the Law of gravitation, and when he communicated his discovery to the world, he did not set forth a private and peculiar thing, based upon personal and historical evidence, but an absolute and immutable Truth, founded upon the authority of an eternal God. The Truth of the existence of the Law of gravitation did not rest upon the authority of Newton, not upon the falling of an apple, but upon the existence of God.

If we take this position in regard to Truth, we shall then find that there are not many Truths in the universe. I do not mean by this that there is consequently a great multitude of falsehoods; but that the "mystery of Godliness" is not so very mysterious, complicated, and incomprehensible as we have been taught to suppose. Newton did not invent the Law of gravitation, nor did he find it; for it was never lost. It was not his private personal property; for it was then, always had been, as it always will continue to be, the public and universal revelation of the spirit of God.

Nor was it a mystery, an evanescent fact, destined to vanish in the Revolutions of ages; for that principle which causes the apple to fall, not only, also, causes the earth to revolve, but likewise all the earths in the universe. Now, I ask, which deserves to be termed Truth—the falling of the apple, the revolution of this earth, the revolutions of all the planets, or that immutable and magnificent principle by which the immeasurable universe rolls through the realms of Infinitude? Methinks you answer—the principle is the Truth! Now, on this ground, you perceive that one Truth controls innumerable things. Thus we return to the proposition, that there are not many Truths, but numberless items in the boundless fields of Creation which no one mind, except God's, can at one embrace fully comprehend.

It is my desire that you clearly understand what I mean by the dignity of Truth. I mean that, that which is God's eternal Truth, is perfectly independent of any human being; while that which rests upon the private and personal authority of any individual, is not an absolute Truth, but a fact—a thing—or a circumstance, which, like the individual upon whom it rests, is destined to pass away.

My impression is to free your minds from superstition. He is free, indeed, whom the Truth makes free! But suppose you identify persons with principles, are you then in a state of freedom? If you believe in the Law of gravitation *because* Isaac Newton taught its existence, then your faith is based upon personal authority, and not upon the Truth—consequently, when Newton, as an authority, dies, your faith will be very likely to die at the same time.

The Bible is supposed, by many, to be God's eternal word. It is termed God's truth; but most believers fail to discriminate between the book itself and the Truths which it unquestionably contains. And others again, confuse the writers with the Truths they wrote—thus, making the divinity of the ten commandments to rest on Moses, the doctrine of immortality to rest on Jesus—while, if a doctrine is eternally true, it depends no more upon the existence of Moses or Jesus than the Law of gravitation depends upon the existence of Isaac Newton. God's Truth is absolute—it is binding yesterday, to day, and forever. But a doctrine which depends upon individual authority may be a total fabrication of the fancy; and, like the insect that flits away its brief moment of existence, the doctrine glides away into the shades of forgetfulness.

If the Bible is God's Truth, then the existence of the Book can not be essential. The duty we owe to ourselves—to our neighbor —to the God of the universe; these are matters of intuition. A man must feel the action of this Law, else he can not be the object of responsibility. And if he does feel it, there are no human authorities that can render this intuition more a Truth. He who consults his intuitive powers obtains a conviction of something like the existence of a God; he learns this Truth from the operations of his own mind; from the very nature of man; and the idea of his duty to himself and neighbor flows from the same source. Now, if these feelings depend upon the existence and teachings of Moses or Jesus—or, upon the indorsements and authority of any other personages or circumstances,—then we are not sure but that, when the authorities die, our feelings will expire with them. While, on the contrary, if the doctrine of love to man and love to God be an everlasting moral Truth, then it was just as true and binding before Moses and Jesus lived as it now is, or ever will be. If the doctrine of Love to the neighbor rests upon the personal authority of Jesus, then it was not binding before he taught it—consequently, if this position be assumed, it is certain that the Old Testament did not contain God's Truth; because, according to the Bible, what was true and binding six thousand years ago, is, to-day, untrue and useless. And, on the same principle of reasoning, what is true to-day, may, by to-morrow, become a falsehood; because whatever depends upon human authority to be believed, is like a foundation of sand, certain to separate and disappear.

Again, I say, my impression is to free your minds from the brutalizing influence of superstition.

You may think that you are not superstitious. If you are not, why do you shrink from an investigation into the history of the Bible and Christianity? If you should take a hammer, and, before the honest barbarian, commence the demolition of his sacred Idol, he would forthwith prostrate himself before you and implore you to leave his God untouched. His prayers and lamentations would almost rend the sympathetic heart. A benevolent man would cease the work of destruction, and set about the enlightenment of the untutored mind. But what would you say to that idolater? The answer is clear. You would say what your missionaries always say for you,—"Poor, benighted heathen! how we pity you in your lost condition. O, that the Lord would open your blinded hearts, and cause you to see the emptiness of your Idols, and the debasing influence of your idolatry." Thus the Christian prays for the heathen.

I know it surprises the barbarian exceedingly to tell him that he is an idolater—so it will surprise you when I tell you that I, this moment, stand in the midst of Idolaters! This is an Idolatrous Land. I feel myself here in the capacity of a missionary.

When it is my impression to show you how you idolize books and personages, you break forth in tones of wounded reverence, or excited indignation, and cry against the mind that would destroy your Idols only by appealing to your reason.

The heathen says—"If you take away my Idol, what shall I do?"

The Christian says—"If you take away my Bible, what shall I do?"

The heathen exclaims—"I am lost, if you take from me my blessed Chreechnar!"

The Christian exclaims—"I am lost, if you take from me the truth as it is in Jesus!"

The parallelism is perfect; only the Christian's idolatry is generated and conducted upon a higher scale—though the kind is perfectly identical. It is therefore demonstrated that you are still clinging to idols—to objects and personages. Consequently, you fail to obtain that firm and everlasting appreciation of the Nature of Truth which would exalt your minds far above man-worshiping, and all forms of superstition. When we believe that Christianity rests upon the private and personal authority of Jesus, then we place our faith at the mercy of the student of Geology and Astronomy. When we believe that Christianity stands upon the contents of the New Testament, then we expose our faith to the mercy of the unprejudiced student, who investigates in order to know what to believe; not to support some favorite dogma. It is my happiness to believe that all which is essentially true in Christianity, is no more dependent upon the authority of Jesus, or upon the New Testament, for its existence, than the Law of gravitation depends upon the authority of Newton, or the circulation of blood upon the personal testimony of Dr. Harvey.

If Christianity be true, then God has written it on the broad pages of Creation,—upon the human heart,—upon the crystal bosom of Nature's unchanging Laws. It then stands upon the highest and purest foundation—upon the Rock of everlasting ages; the eternally unfailing and immutable Truth! And how safe is such a foundation for all Christian doctrines to rest upon! for then if all the prophets, evangelists, and apostles were deluded enthusiasts; if the great moral Reformer, himself, was the victim of many errors; yet it is all the same—the Truth remains unshaken and unchanged. Suppose it should be proved that the Evangelists were deceived in a thousand things, or that the entire Bible originated with human beings; would the existence of God, the immortality of the soul, the Law of universal Love, our obligations to man and Deity, cease to be Truths?

Nay, nay. He who framed this vast universe, has written all the Truth there is in Christianity, or in any other system, imperishably upon the constitution of things. Nature is the only infallible authority. For the Bible is made of paper, pasteboard, and ink. It depends upon ten thousand contingencies. A slight variation of the tense would render past meanings future, and future past,—a misprint would alter the whole system of Christianity,—and we can never be perfectly certain that we have the language of

Jesus in any particular case; for historical Christianity—that is, the relation of what Jesus did and said—is not written according to his own expressed commands, but it is all written "according to Matthew, Mark, Luke, and John." Now the fact can not be disguised, that the Apostles were mistaken in several points—that there has been considerable discussion as to which books shall constitute the Sacred Canon;—does this seem like the handiwork of God? All the writings of Paul were rejected in the first compilation of the New Testament; in the second examination, they were received and voted to be inspired. But the herald of the (so-called) New Jerusalem church—Emanuel Swedenborg—again rejects all the writings of Paul, and pronounces them wholly uninspired. The Presbyterian, and other sects, think that Swedenborg had no right to decide upon what books shall constitute the Sacred Canon; but I think that Swedenborg had as much right as the Emperor Constantine and his favorite Bishops.

Again let us inquire, What is Truth?

This is the question of questions—the beginning, middle, and end of all inquiry! It springs up with the elements of life; flows with them through all the labyrinths of existence; and sends its glittering sprays infinitely more high than the most ambitious imagination can soar. This question transcends all thought, and spreads out beyond all conceptive magnitude; because it is the golden belt which girdles infinitude, the jeweled crown of the spiritual universe.

But how can a question of such magnitude receive an adequate answer? Can a question which the great moral Reformer, himself, could not, or did not answer, be answered by us? Indeed it would seem that an angel's mind could not reply to an interrogatory so transcendingly sublime and all-embracing; nevertheless, it appears to me to be stamped by Deity with a very simple and imperishable definition. But first let us examine the answers, which would emanate from different portions of the earth, to this question of such vital and universal interest.

Imagine yourselves traveling in the beautiful land of Persia. From its fair sky the sun gives off a soft golden light, the birds sing, the waters murmur, and Nature every where exhibits beauty and gladness. Your mind yields to meditation. You contemplate the world of objects about you, the religious feeling is awakened; you think of your own creed, the belief that has been taught to you, and unconsciously you ask yourself, aloud,—"What is Truth?"

You are overheard by a fire-worshiper standing near, and he answers you—"the Zenda Vesta!" This book is his Holy Bible. It contains all Truth. It is Truth. It tells him to worship the brightest object in Nature, he therefore falls upon his knees and adores the shining sun. The Sun is his God, or rather it is the place where he imagines his God resides in light; and this faithful disciple of his creed, of the belief taught to him, urges you to worship the Truth. But you doubt his religion; regard his Bible as the fabrication of some impostor; and leave the Persian to his idolatry.

You journey on, and every where Nature still prompts the question—"What is Truth?" The Brahmin, the Chinese, and the Turk, they severally refer you to their Bibles, to their objects of worship, to the founders of their religious creeds and institutions.

But you doubt them all. And finally you come to Christendom; perhaps to Hartford. Here, in this civilized land, you feel confident that your question may be satisfactorily answered.

You meet one in the street and ask—"Can you inform me 'What is Truth' in matters of religion?" "Yes," he replies, "willingly; you will find it explained in John Calvin's Commentaries upon the Sacred Scriptures." But a Baptist neighbor overhearing the conversation, remarks—"Yes, you may find much Truth in the theological writings of John Calvin; but, my friend, allow me to remind you of a certain passage of Scripture which says—'He that believeth and is baptized shall be saved, and he that believeth not shall be d——d,' &c.; now this passage John Calvin misinterprets; Baptism is not a mere sprinkling, it consists in total immersion."

But a member of a very liberal sect, listening to the discussion, remarks—"It seems that you are too much sectarian in your views. One calls himself a 'Baptist,' another a 'Calvinist;' but, as I find all sects to have some truth and much error, I take only the Bible as my standard. I hold that to be the plenum of Truth; although I see many things in it which my limited understanding will not permit me to fully analyze and comprehend. Notwithstanding this, I recommend you to seek for Truth only in those inspired pages; pray for light, and read sincerely."

This is the way of the world. The question—"What is Truth" —is answered every where according to the educational convictions of the individual. The fire-worshiper is just as honest as the Turk; the latter as the Christian. Hence, in order to get any thing like a reasonable reply to this question, we must disrobe our minds of all preconceived opinions, and ask the deepest intuitions of our nature. Remember, friends, we may consult testimony to get at historical matters; perception for external things; reflection for logical matters; but if we would be enlightened upon religious or moral subjects, let us interrogate—Intuition!

But some think this source altogether too feeble and uncertain. They suspect themselves—lose confidence in their own ability to get at Truth. They dare not trust the nature which the Deity gave them. For the doctrine of innate depravity has gone abroad —the whisperings of the soul are regarded as the ascending sparks of wickedness—and the children of earth dare not obey the invitation, "Come, let us reason together."

And yet, I am impressed to affirm, that the deepest source of

Truth is Intuition. By the deepest source, I mean the highest power in man's profession. But what is intuition? I answer, it is the innate power of feeling a Truth—the flower of Wisdom—the conclusion of all Reason—the genius of the soul. I venture to say, that you all can, if you will but open you minds to the full penetration of thought, feel what truth is. Forget your sectarian thoughts, and you can easily see, what is Truth? Try it.

First, to begin, Does it not seem to you that Truth is always simple? Does it not always seem to you that error is always complicated? If these things do not at first appear to you truthful, just think of all the inventions in the world of science and art. The best invention is always the most simple—so much so, that common minds wonder that they had not thought of it before. The Truth is easy and simple as the growth of flowers; while error is forever dark, complicated, and mysterious.

Now it is my impression, that Truth is not susceptible of any possible limitation. It is not the thing of an occasion. It is not Truth yesterday, probable to-day, and possible to-morrow. For it must be every where and at all times the same, unchanging and progressing Principle. You can not confine it within the covers of any written volume—it depends upon no man's word to deserve attention or credit. For Truth is God-made. If a man speaks the truth, he speaks God's Truth—he but vocalizes the most celestial life-song known to Deity.

Now if this definition of Truth be correct, then people generally have erred greatly in the use of proper language. For example, we say that it is a Truth that yesterday was cold; but this may be true only in certain localities. For at other points of the compass it may have been warm—showing no universal principle. Therefore, it would be far more proper to term all occasional or local occurrences, FACTS; and those things TRUTHS, which have a broad, unchangeable and universal application. In other words, let us assign to Truth a position far above individual minds and local circumstances—superior to every thing, but God.

If this definition be adopted, then our aspirations after Truth will transcend all men, all books, all creeds, all institutions. If we adopt this view, then we will arise nobly superior to all forms of sectarianism and pursue the golden pathway, which leads the pilgrim eternally upward to the City of the Living God.

I have said that the question "What is Truth?"—admits of a very simple definition. Let me state the proposition, and see how it will suit your Intuitions.

Truth is the universal relationship of things as they are; error, is the interpretation of things as they are not.

God has unfolded things just as they are; therefore, he is the author of the relationship of things; therefore, He is the Truth. Now it matters not how much or how little I know of this universal relationship of things; for, if I understand only the first particle of the relation of any thing, so far I have infallible Truth. If I comprehend the first principle which binds a piece of iron ore together, then I know something of Truth—and no human authority can make it more true, though a wiser man may conduct me to more Truth, in the same, or in other and higher, departments of Creation.

Now the question arises—how shall we know when we have the Truth? I answer—divest your minds of all local prejudices in favor of this or that sect, of this or that authority—and listen, like a child, to the subdued whisperings of the soul which God has given you. There is nothing more true, than that no man can enter into the kingdom of Truth and happiness, unless he becomes simple-minded, and as a little child. By simple-mindedness I do not mean weakness or imbecility. Far from it. I mean an honest, guileless, uncalculating, truth-loving state—a state which, in the past and present conditions of human society, is about as frequently developed as a Christ is born. No wonder the great mass of the world regard a naturally developed and harmonious individual as a divine curiosity—as a God-sent messenger; for a good and truth-loving soul is no more likely to be born of ignorant parents, or of parents educated in the past and present methods of society, than good cloth is likely to be manufactured by bad machinery, or music to flow from defective instruments.

By willing strongly to see and feel Truth, irrespective of any creed, men, books, or systems, you are certain to get it; or, at least, you will get all you can possibly employ to any advantage. If you seek any thing wonderful or mysterious, then you do not seek the Truth; for Truth is so exceedingly simple that most people pass it by unnoticed. There are myriads of mysteries, but that is not owing to the Truth, but wholly to our ignorance of their nature and relationship. The great standard, it seems to me, is simply this—Facts are things; Truths are Principles. Things exist; when they are rightly related one to the other, the *relation* is based upon, and is, the Truth. From this relation the music of harmony issues perpetually. Discord issues from error; the relation is wrong. Friends, see well to this doctrine in all the departments of your existence—and now is the time to think, to feel, and to do right! For, by putting off this state till to-morrow, you defraud yourself of immediate happiness and do a similar injury to the neighbor.

It is no part of my plan, friends, to impair your faith in Truth; I desire, only, to arouse you to a higher appreciation of it. Do not think, with the "poor, benighted heathen," that the Truth is always dependent upon your Idols for its existence; that when your Idols are demolished, your faith dies with them. But let your understandings expand, and thus obtain reasons for the inward hope. Reject the miracle as the foundation of your faith, and take the principle. For marvels confound and stultify the intellect; but Principles are certain to dignify and expand the whole nature of man.

I come now to the application.

This discourse is upon "the Authority of the Harmonial Philosophy," but it was deemed wisdom to premise thus much in order to bring the whole subject comprehensively before your minds.

I thank God that I am permitted to raise my voice against the deification of individuals—against every species of idolatry and superstition. For I stand before the world in a peculiar position; mainly in a misinterpreted position; and I am thankful, very thankful, that I, at least, can do my part toward accomplishing a correction. I do not think that I stand in any danger of being deified; for I have too much faith in the reasonableness of this age; but I am regarded, by some minds, as the *founder* of the Harmonial Philosophy; and this idea is what I now desire to correct.

The authority of the Harmonial Philosophy, is Truth; it is not based upon the Revelations of "Davis," but upon the Revelations of Nature. All Truth may be found in Nature, and in the nature of man, because God lives in Nature; therefore, when we study Nature we study God; therefore, too, in proportion as we comprehend Nature, in the same proportion we comprehend God. The terms Revelation and Development are synonymous. Hence when we examine the Developments of Nature, we examine the Revelations of Nature; and when, with the good Paul, we contemplate the sidereal heavens and behold that all stars are glorious, only differing in glory, one having more glory (or divinity) than another, then we behold the "Divine Revelations of Nature." There are persons who have tried to cast ridicule upon the term—"Nature's Divine Revelations;" which ridicule could only proceed from a low-minded idolater, or an atheist; for if it be believed that God is the source of all life and sensation—the cause of all creation and development—then the tree, and the bird, the flower, and the distant star, are unlike the unfoldings of a Divine Principle! And when we study these chapters in Nature, then we are studying "Nature's (or God's) Divine Revelations."

Moses, Paul, Fourier, Swedenborg, and other individuals, may have been sufficiently enlightened to read and interpret many of Nature's (or God's) truths; but it is the truthfulness of what they reveal,—and not the revelators, themselves,—that constitutes the authority by which those Revelations should be tested and regarded.

One man may be a Poet; another a Philosopher; another a Governor; another a Moralist;—that is to say, one may be a Christ, another a Shakespeare, another a Newton, and another a Plato,—but it is not the individual, it is the well-ascertained truthfulness of what they write, that constitutes the true object of affection and reverence.

All books and all men might be swept from the earth at once without in the least impairing aught which is eternally true; yea, the Temple of the Universe might be reduced to an impalpable powder, but Truth would yet stand unmoved and unchanged!

LECTURE XXVII.

CONCERNING THE USES AND THE ABUSES OF THE SABBATH IN THIS COUNTRY.

On this occasion, the origin of the institution of the Sabbath, so-called, will not be considered. For at best, such a consideration could be but a matter of historical interest to the ethnologist and antiquarian, being not at all essential to a proper estimate of the Day as a period of freedom and universal rest.

But I will simply remark that the Sabbath, as you probably all know, is supposed by theologians to have originated with the Deity. It is asserted, and in all possible seriousness too, that, after the fatigues consequent upon the exertion of creating the heavens and the earth, and all that in them is, the Lord rested upon the "Seventh Day," and hallowed it. Hence, we are told, admonished, and commanded to regard this Day, above every other, in honor to the greatest, completest, highest event that ever occurred in the history of the Creation.

In consequence of this mythologic faith, the world is replete with many and various superstitions upon the subject of the Sabbath. All true mental philosophers know, that superstitions always produce two effects upon the human mind—both of which are discordant and injurious: either they impel the mind to do this or that religious act from a sensation of fear, or, the opposite extreme is developed, and the individual becomes skeptical and disregards many things which might be exceedingly happifying and morally beneficial.

One of the evils growing legitimately out of the present view of the Sabbath, is, that of compelling many persons to keep the Day, not as a day of freedom and for the purposes of moral culture, but wholly from a fear of offending Jehovah. And this fear invariably injures the moral dignity of the mind.

God is represented as continuing the Laws of the universe without variableness throughout the week; but on Sunday, it is said, he will perform some of the most wonderful miracles in order to properly punish the transgressor of the Mosaic Law. He is said to overturn boats on water, strike barns with lightning, and subvert various natural Laws, in order to punish the Sabbath-breaker. If this doctrine be fully believed by the people, I can not understand why our State Legislatures interfere with the more certain methods of God's government!

The popular Sunday is generally considered too holy a day for the discussion of social, scientific, and secular matters. The sciences of physiology, the subject of Temperance, the Slavery question,—these topics are considered rather too worldly for Sabbath-day discussion, especially by the gentlemen of the gown. Hence it is, that most people adhere very strictly to devotional principles.

But there are persons who break over the restraining rules of the Sabbath, and unfortunately devote the day to riot and unhealthy amusements. This is all wrong; but it is mainly chargeable upon the superstitions, commonly attached to the day; for, owing to these erroneous notions, it is observed either very sanctimoniously through fear, or disregarded altogether; and both extremes are vicious and baneful.

Persons with certain constitutions and occupations will, (because they can easily,) submit to the restraints imposed upon them on the Sabbath; while other and differently constituted persons, with different occupations, will reject these restraints (because severe and not adapted to their needs,) and plunge headlong into the careless indulgence of their sensual desires. This is owing, I repeat, mainly to the way in which the Sabbath is regarded.

That the Sabbath is the most holy institution which man ever developed, except the "Golden Rule," is clear to a demonstration; and, on the other hand, that the past and popular methods of regulating and observing it are very imperfect, and opposed to the physical and social happiness of man, are facts no less conspicuous and certain.

If there be any Truth in this wide universe, that Truth may be found in Nature. If there be any thing which man can not subvert—which he can not alter and change to suit his follies and caprices,—that thing is Nature! And if we can be perfectly certain of any thing, we are certain that Nature is the unfolding of that Principle, called God. But no man can be as certain that any book is the production of Deity. If men have misconceived the true import of Nature, and have suffered from their ignorance of her laws,—the fault is their own, not Nature's or God's. But experience educates the mind. And besides this, as an explanation of this ignorance among men, we should remember, that, it is the eternal tendency of Nature, that every thing should grow from imperfection to perfection—from inferior to superior; and mankind involuntarily obey the inexorable operations of this progressive Law.

We are perfectly certain that the Divine Principle controls the operations of Nature. And we are admonished to be "perfect even as our Father in heaven is perfect."

But how shall we discover what constitutes his perfection? Shall we take the opinions and dogmatic speculations of religious chieftains; or, shall we see and understand for ourselves? Shall we consult Moses and Paul; or, shall we learn to read the innumerable chapters of the great, unalterable volume—the boundless creation—whose imperishable leaves lie spread out in every direction before us?

It is a self-evident proposition, I think, that Man is the most perfect and important Part of creation. His personality is constructed upon certain physiological and anatomical principles; which principles are pre-eminently more worthy of consideration and reverence than any known human institution; like the Sabbath. This I feel to be sound reasoning. Now, let me ask—can any day be truly righteous which must be observed at the risk of violating the common Laws of man's being? It is a notorious fact, that the popular laws respecting the regulation of the Sabbath, are no more adapted to man's physical health and social happiness than the government of Russia.

Six days of each week are devoted to the various kinds of manual labor and mammon. Masters drive their slaves into excessive industry. Capitalists speculate on the productions of the laborer. And every body is justified in practicing many things during the week, which things, on Sunday, are preached against as crimes and offenses. Owing, also, to the popular superstitions respecting Sunday, every laborer is obliged to work more on week-days than is consistent with the laws of health; and then, when the Sabbath arrives, the reaction is so great in the opposite direction, that most people are wholly disqualified for the enjoyment of those moral instructions meted out to them from the pulpit and from other sources.

As society is at present regulated, the laboring part of the community perform too much manual labor during the six days, and then are urged to hear and learn too much on the Sabbath. Consequently, the majority of all communities absolutely dread, in one sense, the advent of the day; while only the few are at all organized and situated in a manner which renders the day to them a welcome and profitable season.

The sanctimoniousness and ceremoniousness of many good but bigoted conservatives on the Sabbath—the prison-like rigidity of their methods and requirements—constitute a powerful reason why many persons (young men especially,) disregard the observance of the day to a considerable extent, and go off antagonistically into various kinds and degrees of vice.

Now, according to the impressions which I receive concerning the constitution of Nature and man, there should be a more interesting and profitable use made of the Sabbath. The reasonable mind sees distinctly that all days are equally holy and worthy of the highest appropriation. This, evidently, was the opinion of St. Paul. The doctrine which permits the people to be wicked six days of each week, and then devotes the seventh day to rest and repentance, is a low and sickly superstition.

If it be right, according to the Nature of man, to walk the fields, to sing a national song, to read secular works, or to dance, on Saturday; then, if there be any consistency in the character and moral government of God, the same identical exercises are right on Sunday, or on any other day, named in the Calendar.

The word Sabbath means REST, but the Blue Laws of Connecticut, made a labor of Rest. They were named in accordance with the Mosaic Creed. They compelled a person to sit still from sun-rise to sun-set on the Sabbath, which is hard work. These Laws say—"No person shall run on a Sabbath day, nor walk in his garden, nor elsewhere, but reverently to and from meeting." These Laws were framed not on the doctrine that God dwells not in temples made with hands, and that the earth is full of his glory. The wide expanse of heaven, the earth covered with verdure, the lofty forest, the waving corn, the magnificent roll of mighty rivers, the murmuring melody of the cheerful brooks—are scenes which inspire the mind with religion, gratitude, and delight.

We are told, I repeat, to "become perfect even as our Father in heaven is perfect." But how, I ask, can we be like God unless we examine and imitate his works and ways, as exhibited in Nature and in Man? When we contemplate the works of God—when we see flowers grow, planets revolve, and tides flow, just as rigorously on Sunday as upon any other day—then we see the way in which the highest authority regards the different days of the week, Sundays not excepted. The laws of anatomy and physiology are never suspended—the human body and mind are never without physical and mental needs on Sunday—hence man is admonished by these unalterable laws, which God has written in characters of fire upon his constitution, to observe and obey them as much on the Sabbath as upon every other day. The works of Nature are the works of God. And I am moved to venerate His Laws, not the Laws of Moses; to imitate His ways, not the ways of any religious chieftain. I feel impressed to do on Sunday precisely what I should on Monday, if it is necessary; that is to say, any thing which is good enough to be accomplished on Monday, is, likewise, good enough for the Sabbath. Therefore, I would have people live on every week-day as righteously as they should on Sunday; and on the Sabbath as upon every other day; thus, converting this whole existence into a perpetual Sabbath—or holiday.

The sanctimonious profession among the clergy, is, that Sunday is a day set apart for moral instructions and especial holiness. But I tell you an undeniable Truth, when I say, it is the harvest-day of the Priesthood! The Sabbath is a day on which they sell their merchandise, and, generally speaking, "to the highest bidder." A tolerably good criticism on the "Lord's Prayer," or an elucidation of "the Sermon on the Mount," is sold to the congregation, on Sunday, for a price varying from five to fifty dollars! Indeed, I speak but the truth when I say, that Sunday is the day on which many good shepherds shear their sheep! It is, to tell the truth, the great shearing season throughout Christendom; and the people love to have it so, forsooth, because it "pays well" in all business transactions during the week. In the six days "thou shalt do all thou hast to do." The people labor incessantly through the week.

Deacons, church-members, and other sinners, are all busily and fashionably engaged in gathering their harvest of dollars; but, on Sunday, the Priesthood have their turn! Your duty is to gather wool all the week as best you can; but on Sunday it is also your duty to have some of it neatly, and rather pleasantly, sheared off! Now this is all the more sinful, because it is done under the cloak of Piety.

Religion is designed to exalt human nature; it is calculated to make the understanding and the conscience free; to inspire the mind with a generous hope; consequently it can not legislate restrictions, nor impose servile obligations, upon any true mind, because it is a sublime spirit of liberty and love—breathing universal toleration and free principles. Such are the teachings of Protestantism. In the light of true religion, a man is free to do right; not to do wrong. He must watch and obey the law of Harmony; this is his inherited and absolute right; this is freedom of Conscience. Sabbatical legislation, therefore, with a view of politically regulating and governing individual conscience, is no more consistent with true religion than usurpation is reconcilable with republican principles.

Only think of the absurdity,—Three sermons in one day, given to the people to digest during the succeeding week. Now the truth is, that nothing can be more indigestible than nine-tenths of the sermons preached! But suppose, for the "sake of argument," that all the sermons were digestible; then, according to the nature of the human mind, one-third of the number would perfectly subserve all the purposes of education and moral holiness.

My friends, there is a vast difference between going to church to see, or to be seen; or, because it is fashionable; because it makes you respectable; because it augments your business interests; because you need the physical exercise and mental diversion—I say, there is a vast difference between going to church for these motives, and going expressly for the purposes of instruction. If you should go for educational purposes, exclusively—then, if there be any truth in the Laws which God has written upon man's constitution, it is positively certain that one, good, truthful, well-written, sixty-minutes' discourse is all that you can fully appropriate to the development of your nature!

I do not feel impressed to tell you, on this occasion, what reformation should be made respecting the observance of this day. "I have many things to say unto you, but ye can not bear them now."

A religious enthusiast would make the Sabbath the very hot-bed of superstition; while a fanatical reformer would destroy the institution altogether!

It is no impression of mine to do either. On the contrary, it is my interiorly obtained conviction, that the Sabbath should be, like every other day, devoted to perfectly good uses. It should be a Day of Rest for Man and beast—truly a day of rest! For Man, it should be a day of scientific and religious culture—a Day of Freedom—of perfect freedom; not of universal bondage to slavish superstitions.

MISCELLANEOUS ARTICLES.

WHAT SHOULD CONSTITUTE THE STANDARD OF JUDGMENT UPON RELIGIOUS SUBJECTS?

It is unnecessary to affirm this question to be one of great magnitude and vital importance. It concerns every thinking, reasonable mind. It not only addresses itself to the understanding, but also to the affections. It does not *begin* and *end* with the present; but it originated with man and extends and ramifies far and wide throughout the innumerable realms of the eternal future.

Every thing must be measured—its height and depth, its length and breadth, must be discovered and determined. But before any thing can be measured, we must first obtain a true standard of measurement—an eternal and unchangeable principle of judgment—a rule or a law whereby the truthfulness of any subject may be ascertained and its exact magnitude determined.

The foot measure, constituted of twelve inches, has determined the extent of territories, the dimensions of our earth, the magnitude of distant planets, and the greatness of many constellations! And the pound weight, constituted of ounces, is capable of deciding the density of an orb; but before any thing could be measured and weighed, it was first necessary to ascertain and determine a fixed standard of judgment. This proposition is a simple, self-evident fact. Now there is an important principle embosomed in this proposition, which demands attention. It is this: the human mind first discovers continents, and then ascertains their dimensions—the earth is first inhabited by man, and then he weighs and measures it by the standards of judgment which have been erected. Every thing is thus open to man's investigations; and all truth, though divine as Deity and aged as the Universe, is left for man to discover, to unfold, to comprehend, and to apply to the wants and necessities of his being.

Every truth is unchangeable; but its discovery and application are ends which man must himself accomplish. Astronomy was a magnificent science before man existed; yet it would have remained as nothing had not man contemplated the stars, and, with his Reason, investigated and discovered their stupendous magnitudes and sublime phenomena. So with every science, every philosophy, every theology. Man first discovers and then decides the magnitude of its truthfulness and the utility of its application.

What standards has man erected upon religious subjects? For, if there be standards of judgment upon these subjects, it is positively certain that man has originated them in the different stages of his development from savagism to civilization. The further we advance in civilization and enlightenment, the more truthful man's theology and religion become. While, on the other hand, the deeper we descend into man's history the more mythological is his theology and the more arbitrary and ceremonial become his religion. We will now briefly examine man's Authority upon religious subjects in the various stages of human developments.

In the Savage Age, when men like the distant hills were wild and uncultivated, there existed no *authority* so imperative and absolute as Desire and Fear. The impulse, the inclination, the desire to do any thing whatsoever constitute the rule of action. The Cannibal desires to pursue, kill, and eat a human being. He, therefore, does it; for it is to him as if the unseen powers had commanded the deed. A blind, undeveloped, unrefined instinct and impulse actuate the savage mind, as hunger causes the wild beast to destroy the victims beneath its power. Fear is a powerful ingredient of Authority in the Savage Age! Let but the thunders speak, and the savage mind is dismayed with unspeakable terror. The lightnings indicate the presence of some angry Deity—the howling storms are but the mutterings of an unseen monarch, threatening vengeance. Anarchy, confusion, dismay, walk like phantom-giants through the mind of the savage, and Fear becomes his master. But let the sun shine out in its glory, bathing the distant scenery with its golden light, and the savage will forget his ceremonial offerings to unknown Gods and will plunge, regardless of consequences, into the commission of the most atrocious crimes. Desire and Fear are the only *religious authorities of the savage.* But let us take another step in human development; and we will perceive quite a different standard of judgment upon religious subjects.

In the Barbarian Age, I discover a distinct modification of Desire and Fear—the authorities become Strength and Mystery. Chieftains are now chosen; and physical strength is worshiped. The most powerful and colossal man is the greatest object of adoration. The Barbarian is fully persuaded that the invisible powers select the mighty and fearless chieftains as earthly agents. A Samson is a Deity. The Idol of the Juggernaut is the impersonation of the barbarian God. And the Will of a Chieftain is Law! There is no monarch so powerful and so worshiped as the Hero of the desert tribes. At his command, the savage starts, the barbarian obeys, and the mother casts her child in the Ganges.

But Mystery plays an active part in the arbitrary government of the superstitious barbarian. The tempest, the thunders, the lightnings, the mournful melody of the forest winds, the sublime throbbings of the deep sea,—these are awful *mysteries* to uncultivated minds. Hence they have a God of the tempest—a God of the storm—a God of the sea. The stars are portals opening upon some Buena Vista. The sun is the chariot of some glorified chieftain. And the barbarian is naturally influenced by soothsaying, by sorcery, by enchantment, by a great mystery, by any thing which spreads a strange vapor over the feelings, and stimulates the imagination to the conception of grotesque and fantastic wonders. "The mysteries of Godliness" swell the uncultivated mind with amazement and adoration. The elephant is worshiped for its strength; and its sagacity is deified for its mystery. The early tribes of Arabia believed the elephant to be either the impersonation of some adventurous nobleman of the skies; or else, the form which some invisible magician, or genius, in his wrath, compelled a chieftain to assume by way of revenge and punishment. But let us take another step in human progress. Succeeding the savage and barbarian ages of authority, is the Patriarchal era.

In the Patriarchal Age, the standard of religious judgment is constituted of Position and Title. Strength and mystery are now converted into form and order. Strength has assumed the dignity of position; mystery has resolved itself into title. The barbarian chieftain becomes a Priest, and stands between the people and their unknown Gods. If the "wandering Jew" desires his wants and prayers and gratitude conveyed on high, he must find an attorney —an intercessor and an interpreter—he must go to Moses or to Aaron. All sacred covenants are confined to the chieftain or the patriarch. If the pilgrim would speak with God, he must seek a Priest—one who can enter into the subterranean interiors of the pyramids—or, a Moses who can converse with the Lord upon the distant mount; for Position is the highest authority in religious subjects known to the dweller of the patriarchal age. And Title, also, exerts a powerful influence upon the undeveloped mind. Call a man 'Monarch,' or 'King,' or 'Ruler,' or 'Prophet,' or 'Pope,' or 'Priest,' or 'Bishop'—and you have invested him with a power, an imaginary influence, which the uneducated mind can neither understand or resist. Hence, the people consent to be taught, and controlled, and governed by some ambitious, and, perhaps, pious man, whom they soon deify and worship. Your patriotism must be confined within the dominion of the 'Monarch.' Your aspirations after political freedom must not expand beyond the territory of the 'King.' Your legislation must not conflict with the Laws of the 'Ruler.' Your yearnings after the events of the future must be kept within the scope of the 'Prophet's' vision. And your thoughts and conceptions of religion—of immortality—of God, must not widen beyond the dogmatic theology of the 'Priest,' the 'Pope,' or the 'Bishop.' This is a conspicuous feature of the patriarchal age. Catholicism indicates this stage of religious progression.

I have not now time to delineate and amplify the peculiarities and theological restrictions of the patriarchal stage of human progress; and, therefore, pass on to the brief contemplation of the age of Civilism, which is the present.

The Authority in this age is composed of Doctrine and Wealth. Order is still unfolding out of chaos; the darkness of previous ages is fast dispersing; and the mounts of truth begin to break upon the human mind with a startling grandeur! Position resolves itself into Doctrine—Title is lost in Wealth. Men are less revered; but Doctrine is the standard of religious authority. It is not *who* preaches, but *what* is preached. The people engage a clergyman and tell him what form of doctrine they require him to disclose. Priests, Popes, and Bishops are now more at the disposal of the multitude. People do not any longer believe all truth and religious instruction to be exclusively possessed by theological teachers. The enlightened mind no longer believes all inspiration to be confined to the prophet, nor to the pope, nor to the church, nor to the clergy; but the belief now is, that the "word of God"—that all inspiration—that all sacred and religious truth, is to be found *only* between the first Chapter of Genesis and the last sentence of Revelation. Verily, all the desires and fears of the savage—all the strength and mysteries of the barbarian—all the positions and titles of patriarchalism—have ultimated themselves in the Doctrine and Wealth of this, our Age!

But there is a still higher standard of judgment—an Authority which we can all aspire to be, and yet it will forever be in advance of us!

I desire your attention to the Age which has dawned in the souls of a few of us, but which is destined to be the borial crown of all nations. This is Republicanism! In this Age, there is no Authority but NATURE AND REASON! Nature the great exponent of God; and Reason, the great exponent of Nature,—these are the supreme Authority upon all things which pertain to man and his Maker. Surely, this is self-evident. Even now, reason is employed to read the Bible, to interpret its sentences, to amplify texts into sermons, to deliver those discourses—to manage all things, in fact, in Church and State; because a person, who is not blessed with a full share of intelligence, is never intrusted with any important office in either institution.

Nature is the Universe; it stretches out far and wide as the only sure and unchangeable manifestation of God. It is a Revelation of his character, his designs, his laws, his wisdom, and his love. I do not mean by nature what Christians mean by that term when they say that "Nature harmonizes with Revelation."

They mean the stones, and trees, and flowers, and, now and then, they venture to elevate their thoughts to the stars; this is a low and materialistic view of Nature!

In the "Republican Age," which is to come, the estimation of Nature is nothing less than the infinite universe, with all its material and spiritual possessions!

And Reason is forever to be regarded as superior to nature,

because it is the power of the soul whereby man reads the vast revelations of Nature and *communes* with the Living Mind.

This, then, is my reply to the question under consideration—Nature and Reason constitute *the only true standard upon religious subjects.* With this standard before us, we may advance forever and ever, and never reach further or higher than it extends; for the *Great Mind of the Universe* is the author of all truth, and all truth will be found to be subordinate to the immeasurable standard by which it shall be forever determined!

THE CONSTITUTION OF THE HARMONIAL BROTHERHOOD.

FROM the Interior—from the world of spirits—I am impressed to present for your consideration some thoughts and resolutions concerning our present and future organization.

A natural and firm foundation—something approximating to the harmonious structure of the kingdom of Heaven—must be first established ere we can proceed to a declaration of our sentiments, and to a practical application of our glorious principles to our mutual education, and to the re-construction of modern society. We profess to be the faithful followers of Nature and of Nature's God! Therefore, to be consistent and truthful, we should divest ourselves and our organization or constitution, of every error and artificial form which deface the moral and social world about us.

In the first place, let us be truthful to Nature, and, therefore, to Nature's God.

Hitherto you have organized your society upon the superficial methods of the undeveloped world. It is my impression that you have trammeled your movements and your personal development, by a false and unnatural constitution. You profess, or rather you all desire, to be moved by the spontaneous and immutable principles of Nature; and yet you have an arbitrary election of officers.

Let me direct your attention, for a few moments, to the revealments and processes of Nature. She conducts her stupendous operations according to *groups*, *series*, and *degrees*. Every class of minerals has a single system of development. It has a *type* and a *head* of formation. The flowers arrange themselves according to specific gradations of refinement. So with animals, and so with man. So it is in the planetary systems. You will find neither President, Secretary, nor Treasurer in our Solar System. The sun does not have any record made of its doings, other than the legitimate impression which it daily makes upon the orbs which roll beneath its power! The tides ebb and flow according to principle! The violet gives forth its native fragrance without a Secretary to record the quantity of its delicious emanations. And the rivulet gives out its low, murmuring music without any artificial organization.

And look at Man, as existing in the order of Nature. His organization has no President, Secretary, and Treasurer. He has but *one head*, *one heart*, *one conscience!* Now I am impressed from the spiritual world to consider man as the best and highest type of organization in being—it is the best for societies or nations, because it is the order of the universe. He has but one Brain—a sensorium; but this is wisely provided with senses and other means of holding fraternal commerce with the external world. This is the true form of an organization.

I have not now time to trace the intrinsic beauty and harmony of man's physical and spiritual organism; but I proceed, presently, to apply the principles of his constitution to the formation of an Universal Harmonial Brotherhood. As I have already remarked, our object is, or it should be, the development of the kingdom of

Heaven on earth! But let me assure you, brethren, that a President, a Secretary, and a Treasurer, will never pertain to an object so exalted and so divine. In an undeveloped condition, we must have officers corresponding to these, but let us quickly learn to gravitate to our respective positions, without all the form and ceremony of voting.

Let us now proceed to our new and educational organization. Let the human form—the organization in which God has expressed his image—be our inward and external model.

In the first place, the human body has a head, or a *brain.* This brain supplies the dependent system with the energizing principles of motion, life, sensation, and intelligence.

In the second place, this brain, and the entire system through it, are supplied with appropriate *senses* which serve to connect the whole internal organism with the external world; and the whole organism is also supplied with appropriate agents, or instrumentalities of locomotion or progress.

In the third place, the conventional names of the superior senses, as you all know, are, the *Eye*, the *Ear*, the *Tongue*; the physical instrumentalities of progress are the *Hands* and the *Feet.* Now let us consider ourselves as ONE HUMAN BODY—a Natural Church. Of this, a faithful disciple of Truth hath said, "The body is not one member, but many. If the foot shall say, 'Because I am not the hand, I am not of the body,' is it, therefore, not of the body?" * * * "If the whole body were an eye, where were the hearing? If the whole were hearing, where were the smelling?" * * * "And if they were all one member, where were the body? But now are there many members, yet but one body. And the eye can not say unto the hand, 'I have no need of thee': nor again the head to the feet, 'I have no need of you.'" * * * "There should be no schism in the body; but the members should have the same care one for another. And whether one member suffer, all the members suffer with it: or one member be honored, all the members rejoice with it." All this is the plainest philosophy of truth. Now let us apply it to ourselves. Let us remember that we are, as an organization, but just born—just emancipated from the confinements of superstition and error.

Let us draw a sponge over the past; let us abolish our previous organization; let us date our existence from this hour; let us call ourselves "The Harmonial Brotherhood."

Now to be natural, and therefore truthful, let us have a "*Brain*," to supply us with the physiological or functional principles of Love, Wisdom, Harmony, and Progression.

Again: To be perfectly natural, let us have an "Eye," an "Ear," and a "Tongue;" let these senses be called *Mentors*, because they naturally occupy the position of counselors, advisers, and peace-makers.

Again: To be natural, let us have "two hands," and "two feet." Let the two hands be called *Executors*, because they naturally perform the office assigned to them by the brain and the senses. And let the two feet be called *Promoters*, because they subserve the high and lofty purposes of progress and development.

Let us now proceed to state our Constitution, and to define the duties of our officers.

THE HARMONIAL BROTHERHOOD,

ORGANIZED MAY 4TH, 1851,

HARTFORD, CONN.,

Whose Motto is "Universal Liberty, Fraternity, and Unity."

This Brotherhood shall have one Brain, three Senses, two Hands, and two Feet.

Resolved, That the "Brain" shall be called the *Sensorium*, whose legitimate duty shall consist in imparting the principles of motion, life, sensation, and intelligence to the dependent organism—that is, to inculcate, in his speech and life, the principles of truth, harmony, and reformation,—to provide the Brotherhood with the proper means and instrumentalities of education.

Resolved, That the "Eye" be called *First Mentor*, whose legitimate duty it shall be to call the attention and actions of the Brotherhood to order—to open the meetings, and to *see* that order and harmony be preserved at all times and every where throughout the dependent organism.

Resolved, That the "Ear" be called *Second Mentor*, whose legitimate duty it shall be to *hear* all questions, suggestions, or propositions, and to present the same to the Brotherhood through the Sensorium. Also to hear, and to seek out the cause of, and remove all dissatisfactions, dissensions, disturbances, and misunderstandings which may occur within the youthful, and, as yet, undisciplined organization. His duty is to be a peace-maker—to encourage every man to be a *law* unto himself.

Resolved, That the "Tongue" be called *Third Mentor*, whose legitimate duty it shall be to receive all donations of money or furniture, to keep the accounts, and to briefly report, on the opening of the first week-day meeting of each month, the nature and amount of the general and current expenses of the Brotherhood; and the amount and nature of the various donations, and how by him appropriated to the purchasing, paying for, &c., of such articles as are required.

Resolved, That the "Hands" be called *Executors*, whose legitimate duty shall consist in executing the decisions of the Brotherhood with regard to any external or physical movements which may at any future period or season be deemed wisdom;—more especially with regard to tendering the sympathies and assistance of the Harmonial Brotherhood to those among them who are sick, in trouble or distress; and to extend the same to all human society, without regard to sect, complexion, or country.

Resolved, That the "Feet" be called *Promoters*, whose legitimate duty shall consist in advancing the decisions of the Brotherhood with regard to its public festivals, feasts, amusements, lectures, reforms, and to the practical application or manifestation of its principles:—more especially to assist in perfecting the decisions and efforts of the Brotherhood with regard to its ultimate organization of *labor*, *capital*, and *talent* upon the reciprocal principles of universal distributive justice, as set forth in its Declaration of Independence.

Furthermore *Resolved*, That the Second Mentor, whose duty refers especially to pecuniary affairs, shall never openly ask the Brotherhood, during any one of its sessions, to assist in discharging its contingent or other expenses. All pecuniary assistance must come unsolicited and spontaneous, during our sessions, or whenever bestowed, or not at all. It is the duty of every member to privately and unostentatiously interest himself or herself in this, as in other things which pertain to our association; but *we will assemble in the distant groves—we will take pews under the spreading boughs of some old lofty oak*, rather than attach any pecuniary embarrassment or odium to the Harmonial Brotherhood. Resolved, therefore, that it is the duty of the Second Mentor of the Brotherhood to keep order among the members with regard to these pecuniary considerations.

Resolved, That hereafter—except in case of an emergency or inharmony, as defined in the provision below, there shall be no stated period for the arbitrary election of officers, either by vote or ballot; because when the little particle of matter in the stalk or body of a plant has become sufficiently refined to ascend to the exalted position of the fruit, then that particle naturally and spontaneously advances to its appropriate sphere. This is a law of Nature, and we are resolved that it shall also constitute our law. Therefore,

Resolved, That whenever any member of this Brotherhood shall have arrived at a degree of worldly liberty and moral harmony, which will qualify him or her to take the responsible position of the Sensorium, or First Mentor, or Second Mentor, or Third Mentor, or Executor, or Promoter, then the incumbent sensorial, mentorial, or subordinate officer, shall optionally vacate his or her position, which shall in such a case be filled by the thus morally qualified member. Providing, however, that in case this spontaneous gravitation of members to officership shall be deemed wrong—the evidence of which shall alone consist in a palpable and unnecessary succession of failures on the part of the officer or officers to discharge his or their respective duty or duties, then the Second Mentor shall present the proposition for a change to the Sensorium, and the latter shall present it to the Brotherhood, which should, in such an emergency, (that ought never to occur,) decide the election of another officer, or officers, by ballot. And, furthermore, it is provided, until the members of this Harmonial Body shall have learned to justly and naturally estimate their respective physical powers, outer circumstances, and moral qualifications to properly occupy the positions to which they should individually aspire, the ballot shall be the method of determining the desires and preferences of the Brotherhood with regard to those who shall be their efficient and peace-making officers.

Resolved, That the Harmonial Brotherhood shall embrace both sexes, male and female; each alike to be considered capable of voting, and eligible for office.

Resolved, That the members proper of the Harmonial Brotherhood shall consist of those individuals who have signed their names to the sentiments set forth in the Declaration of Independence, and that the officers shall be chosen from among them: nevertheless, resolved, that always yielding ourselves to be governed by the principles of harmonial truth, we will consider and fraternally esteem all men and women who are seeking to know the Truth, and who associate with us in this exalted pursuit (whether perfectly friendly or not to our Declaration and Constitution) as brothers and sisters, and as capable of voting for officers. And finally,

Resolved, That we will all aspire to be Sensoriums, and Mentors, and Executors and Promoters, in our "daily walk and conversation;" and that we will strive to be kind, and forgiving, and generous to all men. And that we will consider him who does his best, however little that may be, as conspicuously distinguished from him who does nothing, toward establishing among mankind the Harmonial Brotherhood, by which we mean the kingdom of Heaven on earth.

THE CONVERSATIONAL.

It is with pleasure I make the announcement, that my mind has been, for the past four weeks, pervaded with the interior impression that we should adopt measures whereby to cultivate and improve the rising generation. To better define our movement, I have submitted to you, a *Declaration of Independence*—an instrument declaring our independence of all those things in Modern Theology, Modern Education, and Modern Society, which tend, in any manner whatsoever, to arrest or disarrange the progression and happiness of Mankind. It is hardly necessary to repeat, that our objects are, the harmonization of individuals and the harmonization of society. In order to accomplish these ends, we should declare ourselves independent, and maintain our independence, of every thing which stands as a manifest barrier, between us and those objects. This constitutes the grand design of our declaration.

My present thoughts, however, are concerning our duty to the rising generations.

It is undeniable, that our children are taught, in the Sunday-schools, to believe in the most soul-revolting doctrines. They are educated to consider themselves "totally depraved," and as being under the "curse" of the living God. They are taught to regard themselves as sinners by nature, and as incapable of being good and heaven-worthy, independent of the Bible and the Church. They are taught to believe in a God of Love, who, at the same time, encourages Hate; and in a God of Heaven, who, at the same time, permits the everlasting duration of Hell. Our children are also taught, as we have been, to suspect every impulse or inclination, and to repudiate every attempt to reason upon religious matters, as the caprices and promptings of some imaginary demon. Thus, our youth become contaminated by the existing methods of religious education; and when they advance in years, and become men and women, they either become bigots and sectarians, or else skeptics and misanthropes. A sadness and gloom are consequently thrown over our minds; and we deprive ourselves and our children of two-thirds of that enjoyment and progressive happiness which are the inalienable rights of mankind. Now I propose, therefore, to establish a Conversational—that is, a meeting of our youth in this room, (say every Sunday morning between the hours of ten and twelve) for the purpose of Mutual Conference and Instruction.

This meeting shall be totally divested of all the melancholy horrors which appertain to the Sunday-schools of our churches, and which the most of us remember as the incubi of our childhood. Nay, not so! but we will teach our youth to revere the imperial laws of conscience; we will teach them that there is one true God, whose attributes are Love, Will and Wisdom; we will teach them the great principles of cause and effect; we will teach them that heaven consists in a condition, or a series of conditions; that Reason is the prime minister of the soul; that all war, and slavery, and tyranny, and despotism, and discord, and error, and transgression, are wrong and productive of unhappiness; and we will teach them to repudiate every thing (every where) which militates against the free discharge of our respective duties; that whatever trade, or profession, or law, or theology, or church, or priesthood, which restrains us in obeying our highest intuitions, is wrong and unworthy of our support. We will teach them to believe in and exercise universal love, and justice, and forgiveness, and every conceivable phase of righteousness. In a word,—we will teach them the morality of Nature; make them good men and women; and true harmonizers of society.

My impressions are, that "The Conversational" should be conducted in accordance with the principles of affinity or sympathetic association. That is to say, the meeting should give off or emit a cheerful emanation of brotherly love and good will to all men, which each child will feel and assist to propagate. Our instructions may be imparted by questions and replies. The children may ask such questions as they may desire; and the teachers should furnish what they conceive to be the proper answers. The teachers should be catechised by the pupils; and, *vice versa*, as wisdom may suggest. I am impressed to begin with the foundation principles of Harmonial truth, and progress, in regular order, to the sublimest revelations of Nature. It is our duty to throw around the young men of our city, the great sphere of these principles. Let us draw them into our "conversational." Let us make of them both students and teachers. Let us draw them away from their hiding-places—draw them from their intoxicating beverages; from their card-tables; from their vitiating habits—and convert them into moral reformers! Yea, into Philosophers, and champions of a universal Reformation.

And, friends, let it be remembered that our "conversational" should be attended by children of all sects and complexions whose respective ages may range any where between two years and a century! Because, except men become "as little children" they can not enter into the kingdom of Harmony. Or, in other words, we all should become students and teachers, willing to be taught and capable of teaching.

We will also have singing. We will have our children chant the anthem of Love, and Wisdom, and Use, and Justice, and Power, and Beauty, and Aspiration, and Harmony. Yea, we will put a "new song" into their mouths. We will echo the music of the spheres! We will teach our children to press forward—to progress —to aspire continually, and thus to "pray without ceasing." And more—we will do for our youth what the church has neither the disposition nor the power to do—namely—we will make them Happy.

Brethren, I have now given you my interior impressions upon the subject of beginning at the very foundations of existing errors and institutions, with the undisguised design of dethroning superstition, and despotism, and ignorance, and of building up a New Superstructure of peace and harmony. These impressions I do not recommend to you as infallible; but simply as worthy of your consideration and decision. You will be doing right, I think, to make this matter a subject for immediate action.